Sesame Street

T0355195

Sesame Street

A Transnational History

HELLE STRANDGAARD JENSEN

OXFORD
UNIVERSITY PRESS

OXFORD
UNIVERSITY PRESS

Oxford University Press is a department of the University of Oxford. It furthers
the University's objective of excellence in research, scholarship, and education
by publishing worldwide. Oxford is a registered trade mark of Oxford University
Press in the UK and certain other countries.

Published in the United States of America by Oxford University Press
198 Madison Avenue, New York, NY 10016, United States of America.

© Oxford University Press 2023

All rights reserved. No part of this publication may be reproduced, stored in
a retrieval system, or transmitted, in any form or by any means, without the
prior permission in writing of Oxford University Press, or as expressly permitted
by law, by license, or under terms agreed with the appropriate reproduction
rights organization. Inquiries concerning reproduction outside the scope of the
above should be sent to the Rights Department, Oxford University Press, at the
address above.

You must not circulate this work in any other form
and you must impose this same condition on any acquirer.

Library of Congress Cataloging-in-Publication Data
Names: Strandgaard Jensen, Helle, author.
Title: Sesame Street : a transnational history / Helle Strandgaard Jensen
Description: New York, NY : Oxford University Press, [2023] |
Includes bibliographical references and index.
Identifiers: LCCN 2022060512 (print) | LCCN 2022060513 (ebook) |
ISBN 9780197554166 (paperback) | ISBN 9780197554159 (hardback) |
ISBN 9780197554180 (epub)
Subjects: LCSH: Sesame Street (Television program) | Sesame Workshop. |
Children's television programs—History and criticism. |
Television adaptations—History and criticism. | Branding (Marketing)
Classification: LCC PN1992.77.S43 S77 2023 (print) | LCC PN1992.77.S43 (ebook) |
DDC 791.45/72—dc23/eng/20230124
LC record available at https://lccn.loc.gov/2022060512
LC ebook record available at https://lccn.loc.gov/2022060513

DOI: 10.1093/oso/9780197554159.001.0001

Paperback printed by Marquis Book Printing, Canada
Hardback printed by Bridgeport National Bindery, Inc., United States of America

For Magnus & Jonathan

Contents

Preface

This book began with two frogs. More than two decades ago, I discovered that a well-known puppet frog on Danish children's television, Kaj, was inspired by the American Kermit the Frog. On a trip to New York in the early 1970s, a Danish television producer had seen *Sesame Street* and fallen in love with Jim Henson's iconic Muppet. The idea to copy Kermit, albeit in a more cheeky, moody, and jazzy version, clearly indicated a fascination with the show's entertaining puppets. However, digging a bit into the story revealed a much more ambivalent relationship with American media culture at the time, and with *Sesame Street* too, not only in Denmark but in all of Western Europe.

From my participation in children's television festivals and public debates on children's media consumption, I know that the mixed fascination and fear of American influence on children's media culture is still very much alive today. This interest seems obvious as American productions still hold a dominant position in the market. More surprisingly, perhaps, recent years in the United States have seen a curious interest in Danish children's television. When the Danish public service broadcaster has aired sex-ed programs with naked adults in full view, preschool television with mock Satanism, and a drama series for children ages three to seven with a man with a really long penis, these programs were covered in the United States.[1] My interest in how specific productions, particularly those of foreign origin, become accepted or rejected because of diverging views of children and media is the reason I wrote this book.

Since my first discovery of the link between Kermit and Kaj, I have written and researched a range of non–*Sesame Street*–related topics. Living abroad for many years, and especially the experience of bringing up a child in first Italy, then England, and lastly Denmark, has, however, kept my interest in diverging cultures of childhood, early education, and children's media strong and alive. The idea that *Sesame Street* was a perfect prism for a thorough and fun investigation of cultural transfer and demarcation—why some products succeed abroad and others do not—has never left me. In 2014 I was lucky to get two large grants from the Independent Research Foundation in Denmark and the Marie Curie Actions 7th Framework to support my research on the transnational history of *Sesame Street* and the wider questions of cultural transfer in which it is embedded. It is largely thanks to them that it became possible to visit the eleven different archives in seven different countries from which I needed material for this book.

The more I dug into the history of *Sesame Street*, the more certain I was that my book would not be aligned with the official narrative told by the show's founders and producers in their many publications. Neither would it concur with what the many online fan pages, fan wikis, and celebratory, popular histories tell about the show's beginnings in the States and abroad. It is not easy to confront well-established historical narratives when these are thoroughly intertwined with something near a global childhood nostalgia, as in the case of *Sesame Street*. Does anyone deliberately set out to challenge the histories told by the good people who produced a show that is part of wonderful childhood memories? I don't know. But I did not. My inner beast is a Labrador. However, during the long time it has taken to write this book it has become clear to me that my analysis does not support traditional *Sesame Street* histories on many accounts. So, when I read the scathing response of the president of Sesame Workshop (formerly Children's Television Workshop) to Harvard professor Jill Lepore after she had written a somewhat critical essay about the show's history in the *New Yorker* in 2020, I reached to my mental shelves for something comforting.[2] What I found was the memory of a chat with my brilliant developmental editor, who has helped me from proposal to finished book, Laura Portwood-Stacer. At some point early in the process when I aired my concerns, Laura plainly said, "I love *Sesame Street*, but that does not mean that I can't enjoy a critical read." I have found solace in my memory of that chat while writing this book, and I hope others will feel the same way as Laura (and I), because I know my book contains a substantial number of critical observations about the Children's Television Workshop in the 1970s at home and abroad.

While writing the book, I talked and corresponded with several people who were around when *Sesame Street* was initiated in the United States and first aired in Europe. Though I have not used this information directly in the book, it has helped me when looking for confirmation on how to undertake the study of my overwhelmingly large amount of material. These people include Lloyd Morrisett, Norton Wright, and Lewis Bernstein (all former employees of the Sesame Workshop), Lasse Sarri and Ingrid Edström (former employees at Sveriges Television), David Attenborough (former employee at

British Broadcasting Corporation), Paola de Benedetti (former employee at Radiotelevisione Italiana), and via the Prix Jeunesse's Kirsten Schneid, Ursula von Zallinger (former Prix Jeunesse employee) and Mogens Vemmer (former employee at the Danish Broadcasting Corporation). I am thankful they took the time to reply to my questions about events that happened more than fifty years ago.

Historians are nothing without archivists and librarians. Archival institutions and their kind, helpful, brilliant staff have been essential to this project. I would like to thank the staff that has made it possible for me to use collections held at the following institutions: the Special Collections at Hornbake Library, University of Maryland (in particular Michael Henry); the Rare Book and Manuscript Library, Columbia University; the internal archive at Norsk rikskringkasting; the National Archives in Norway; Dokumentarkivet at Sveriges Radio; the Danish National Archives; the archive at Norddeutsche Rundfunk; Rai Teche, Rome; the BBC Written Archives Centre; the Prix Jeunesse Foundation; and Staatsarchiv Hamburg.

The many visits to archives would not have been possible if my husband had not gone with me and taken care of our young son while I was browsing through old documents and watching 1970s television. In the middle of this project, such trips suddenly stopped being possible, not because of the pandemic (that came later!) but because my son frequently needed to go to the hospital. I would not have been able to finish this book had it not been for the amazing help and care he has received from the Pediatric Pulmonary and Allergology Service at Aarhus University Hospital. I would like to thank all the department's staff; they are the true superheroes of this world.

Some people helped me get this project started even before I began writing the book. I would like to thank Christa Lykke Christensen, Jeanette Steemers, Ingeborg Lunde Vestad, Laura Lee Downs, Philip Nel, Karin Lesnik-Oberstein, Kati Lustyik, everyone at the Department of Childhood Studies at Rutgers, and the members of the Entangle Media Histories (EMHIS) network, who all commented on the project in its early stages, individually and at seminars. Later, my colleagues in the Department of History and Classical Studies at Aarhus University provided great comments on an early draft of my book proposal's sample chapter. My colleagues' and students' interest in my project has been important in keeping me going. I was grateful for chats with fellow *Sesame Street* scholars Kathryn Ostrofsky and Abby Whitaker that helped me challenge my analyses. Other people helped me by giving comments on individual chapters, for which I am immensely grateful. These include Sherman Dorn; my writing and academic book club friends Rebekah Willett, Natalie Coulter, and Maureen Mauk; my lovely friends and fellow children's media history scholars Sophie Heywood and Meredith Bak; David Buckingham, who always helps me think harder and do better; and Gary Cross who has gone above and beyond when he, during the tough times of the pandemic, little by little took on the combined role of writing coach and devil's advocate. When I started panicking about illustrations, hiring Beth Corzo-Duchardt to help out was the one thing that ensured that they were not dropped completely. Thanks also to the peer reviewers for their comments on my proposal, which were important in shaping the finished product. Finally, without Oxford University Press, and especially my editor Norman Hirschy, there would have been no book. I cannot thank Norm enough for believing in my book and all the rest of the team, including Zara Cannon-Mohammed (project editor), Caroline McDonnell (cover design), Dharuman Bheeman (production manager), Henry Wilkinson (marketing manager), and Bob Land (copy editor) for being very patient with me and my many questions.

I would not have made it through writing this book without the support of my husband and my son who, when I am most caught up in my work, remind me that there are so many wonderful things that have nothing to do with academia. Watching television, playing video games, and reading with them is the fun that keeps me going. This is why this book is dedicated to them.

Introduction

Culture-Free TV?

Sesame Street "contains universally acceptable material, much of it already tested on audiences outside the United States, and is as nearly 'culture free' as TV can be."[1] This was the claim of the executive producer of international productions at Children's Television Workshop, Lutrelle Horne, in 1977, just before the launch of the Italian version of the show. A strong belief in the show's worldwide adaptability ran through much of the material from the Workshop—the production company behind the iconic program—in the 1970s. In fact, Horne had been quoted saying the exact same thing when launching the French and Swedish versions in 1974 and 1976, respectively.

The belief that children around the world could learn from *Sesame Street* was rooted in the Workshop's intertwined views of education, television, and childhood. Building on the universalist claims of all children's similar paths to learning inherent in cognitive psychology, the Workshop neglected fundamental cultural differences in education and views of childhood. Focusing on school-type skills that were easy to recognize as part of formal education such as numbers and letters and mixing them with appealing elements from American pop culture, the Workshop saw its program to be of universal value and appeal, believing it would benefit any preschooler, no matter their nationality, racial background, gender, or social class. The show's creators expected that *Sesame Street* would be welcomed with open arms everywhere. However, when the Workshop tried to export *Sesame Street* and its later iterations, it met both skepticism and direct hostility from foreign television producers. What the Workshop considered "universal," foreign broadcasters saw as ethnocentric and compromised with commercialism, unfit to serve the roles they wanted television to play in young children's lives. It was a cultural clash of international proportions that lay bare divergent approaches to childhood, preschool education, and the role of television in children's lives.

Sesame Street. Helle Strandgaard Jensen, Oxford University Press. © Oxford University Press 2023.
DOI: 10.1093/oso/9780197554159.003.0001

At first, *Sesame Street* won positive international recognition. The combination of Jim Henson's likable Muppets, the show's high production value, and an enormous effort to sell *Sesame Street* globally quickly made it the talk of the global community of children's television producers. Already in 1968, more than a year before the show first aired in the United States in 1969, the Workshop's president, Joan Ganz Cooney, had made its big ambitions known via an article in the leading international journal for producers and researchers of children's television at the time.[2] Later, at international festivals such as the Prix Jeunesse in Munich in 1970, the show not only won one of the two prizes for preschool television but also made a huge impression on more than two hundred participants who came from thirty countries located in five continents. The same year the original English-language version was sold by the Workshop's UK distribution agents to twenty-three countries and territories around the world.[3] In 1972, the number of places where some version of the show aired doubled with the premiere of the Spanish-language version for Latin America.

Despite the show's rapid international recognition and booming sales, the Workshop soon discovered a range of obstacles. These crept up, especially in Western Europe, where broadcasters—in contrast to, for instance, Latin America—had a long tradition of producing television for children. The Workshop saw the affluent European market as particularly lucrative but failed to anticipate how the differences between the preschool programs already on offer in this area and *Sesame Street* might cause resistance toward the program. Unlike what the Workshop's president, Joan Ganz Cooney, told an Australian journalist that for "good or ill the whole world is being Americanized and paced by '*Laugh-In*' and other US shows," television in the rest of the world was not like that in the United States.[4]

In the United States, children watched an average of fifty-four hours of television per week, according to one Nielsen survey in 1968.[5] In some European countries, this was more than the entire schedule for adults and children combined. On average, European broadcasters would air less than ten hours of television per week for children and youths under eighteen.[6] Even if there is no doubt that children in Europe also watched shows that did not have them as their target audience, and the high US Nielsen numbers are hard to verify, the discrepancy between the amount of scheduled content on offer alone shows a vast difference between the two television markets. Another big difference was that American children's television was made for a highly commercialized broadcasting landscape. As we shall see, this was an important fact in the making of *Sesame Street*, even if the show tried to be an alternative to commercial offerings. European children's television was on the contrary planned with a public service mindset. This difference meant that while entertaining cartoon shows and live-action dramas (e.g., Westerns) were the norms in the United States, in a European context where public service broadcasters controlled most channels, such shows were special-occasion treats in an otherwise diverse schedule with a focus on balance between information, education, and entertainment.[7] Furthermore, diverging views held by the Workshop and European broadcasters on childhood and education meant that they saw television's role in children's lives very differently, making the sale of *Sesame Street* harder than first expected. Eventually, the differences also led to grave misunderstandings, bitter rivalries, and even threats of lawsuits.

European broadcasters found that the show expressed a particular American mode of preschool education and television production. To them, *Sesame Street* was not at all "culture free." Thus, even if children's television producers in Europe were impressed with elements of *Sesame Street* as a program, especially the Muppets, the show's overarching philosophy, its mode of production, and its business model presented significant obstacles. This meant that a substantial pushback followed the Workshop's early sales campaigns. In 1971, the head of the children's department in the British Broadcasting Corporation (BBC) warned the British press corps and members of the European Broadcasting Union against *Sesame Street*, concerned about its authoritarian tendencies as it, according to her, focused on teaching facts and right answers. The Danish Broadcasting Corporation never bought *Sesame Street*, and its Norwegian equivalent did not become interested in the program until the late 1980s. It took six years to convince Swedish Television to buy a few segments, and this only happened at the end of a failed pan-Scandinavian attempt to co-produce a Nordic version of the show followed by a lot of pressure on the Swedes from the Workshop. In their efforts to make TV a "spokesperson" for child liberation and empowerment, the Scandinavians found the idea of using television for formal educational purposes backward and counterproductive.[8] In Italy, Radiotelevisione Italiana only bought *Sesame Street* after the Workshop launched a year-long campaign to counter Italian accusations that the Workshop's overseas business model was too dependent on aggressive merchandising sales. The producers at the oldest network in West Germany, who had been positive from the start and found very attractive the idea of creating something entertaining and educational, also needed further convincing. The same was the case in France, where the national broadcaster remained reluctant even though the Workshop had had two of its most industrious sales agents placed in Paris since 1970.

To mollify its critics and get in on the affluent Western European market, the Workshop had to make *Sesame Street* available in a variety of ways to outcompete existing and emerging local offerings. Only after these adaptations were some European broadcasting corporations convinced to buy *Sesame Street* in some shape or form. Hence, it was only after substantial rethinking of *Sesame Street*'s aims and business model that the program ended up on many broadcasting schedules by the end of the 1970s. Along the way, this rethinking and constant negotiation with potential international buyers created and shaped the Workshop's business and corporate brand that paved the way for *Sesame Street* and its global spin-offs we know today.

While telling the revealing history of attempts to sell *Sesame Street* around the world, this book illustrates a broader point about the contested nature of children's media consumption. Debates about children's media are often brushed aside as inconsequential "moral panics" or labeled as unimportant because they are "just" about children. However, this book shows how discussions about whether to buy *Sesame Street* and how to adapt it to local needs were important arenas where stakeholders asserted cultural and social preferences regarding education and morals, as well as conflicting visions for ideal childhoods.[9] As the cultural clashes around *Sesame Street* in the 1970s demonstrate, concerns about childhood ideals and how media consumption would influence young viewers were extensions of ongoing debates about society's future and reflected broader societal and cultural tensions. Similarly, debates about childhood and children's media today are central to cultural and identity politics, and so, by historicizing these issues in relation to *Sesame Street*, this book provides a reflective backdrop for contemporary discussions on the role of media in children's lives.

To readers who already know something about the early years of *Sesame Street* and the Children's Television Workshop that produced it, exploring its history in the context of sales and business models might seem an odd and maybe even provocative choice. The dominant narratives of the show's early days focus almost exclusively on the Workshop's good intentions as a progressive, nonprofit company that tried to revolutionize the United States' grim, commercially driven children's television market for the better.[10]

A substantial part of the Workshop's history has been dominated by people deeply invested in its ideas and business.[11] The Workshop itself and independent researchers have nevertheless left out of their accounts the considerable part of the Workshop's story that dealt with financing, merchandise, strict brand protection, sales strategies, and the need to make revenue from international sales. There are understandable reasons for this; the program's history in the United States looks different from a domestic point of view. The nature of the US media system has meant that the Workshop from the beginning was not financially viable and needed a strong, positive story to market it to potential funders: the educational, anticommercial, and non-profit values of *Sesame Street* offered an appealing alternative in a highly commercialized, entertainment-focused media landscape. However, the Workshop's constant need to sell its product on an international market in order to raise revenue obliged it to act as a commercial predator abroad. This had lasting consequences for foreign broadcasters who had to fight hard against its smooth sales machinery and well-connected backers if they wanted to keep local ideas and ideals alive. Looking at the history of the show and the Workshop from outside the United States, the *Sesame Street* story begins to lose some of its glory.[12]

With its transnational approach situated within a broad context of childhood and television history, this book offers a new perspective on *Sesame Street*'s early history and the organization behind it. It investigates how the successful transfers and rejections were rooted in essential differences in views of television's role in children's lives, different ideas of education, as well as differences in the commercial American television culture and its public service–oriented European counterparts.[13] Using the cultural differences that the attempted transfer of *Sesame Street* reveals, I explore the relationships between media production and views of childhood and education. In doing so, this book makes a still broader contribution to the transatlantic history of American cultural expansion of the 1970s and the resistance it met.[14]

Exploring the early years of *Sesame Street* in a transnational context not only uncovers how the program was understood and received abroad, the comparison and contrast with preschool production elsewhere also provide new insights into its domestic history.[15] The parts of the Workshop that dealt with international sales and marketing collaborated closely with other staff. When sales of the show abroad, for instance, required reconceptualizing what educational content was, and how much time a child had to watch

Sesame Street to learn from it, this also impacted the Workshop's own understanding of the show.

Analyzing the development of *Sesame Street* before and after its US premiere in 1969 in an international context demonstrates how the Workshop drew on, contributed, and responded to international trends in television for young children. Looking at the Workshop's organization in an international setting shows how its business model depended on international sales not only of broadcast products (TV programs, videocassettes) but also so-called nonbroadcast merchandise—mostly books, audio recordings (e.g., long-playing records, cassette tapes), toys, and games. This business model of supplementing media sales with product licensing is very common today. In children's media, the attempts to make more profit from a program in this way are often tied to ideas of maximizing viewers' educational gains (with *Sesame Street* as a longstanding golden standard). Historicizing the intertwined development of commercialization and specific views of education and childhood, this book demonstrates that this trajectory was not inevitable or unavoidable for (global) children's media production. Rather, this development has often been a result of specific ideals and practical arrangements that deliberately, by choice or necessity, challenged competing ideas about the role of television in children's lives.

Sesame Street as Transnational History within a Global Framework

The focus of this book's transnational history of *Sesame Street* is Western Europe. Still, the region is situated throughout within a global context. Scandinavia, Italy, West Germany, France, and Britain were, together with Latin America, particular targets of the Workshop from the outset. Targeting affluent Europe, the Workshop followed the patterns of American market culture in the decades after the Second World War. International market strategies by US companies forged worldwide hegemony by ensuring success in the homeland territories of the old empires that had long ruled the hierarchies of social and cultural distinction.[16] During the Cold War era, Western Europe was the ultimate gateway to a lasting global breakthrough for almost any American product. The same was the case for the Workshop. For *Sesame Street* to be the new standard of preschool television around the world, broadcasters in Western Europe were the ones that had the cultural and financial means to support, or tank, its ambitions to make a lasting income from sales on a global scale. Analyzing the Workshop's early operations in Europe and how they related to its global sales strategies is therefore a way to understand how it first crafted and later consolidated its position as a major factor on the world market for preschool television.

In the book, I sometimes speak about *Sesame Street*'s history in a particular foreign national context, such as British or West German, sometimes of its Western European history, or about its transnational and global history. I consider these geographical and cultural scales, going from the local to the global, because I am interested in exploring *Sesame Street*'s success, growth, and limitations as combined aspects of the Workshop's early operations on a global scale. This means that the history told in this book addresses the multitude of aspects of cultural transfer, negotiation, and resistance that impacted *Sesame Street*'s international success.

In many academic fields that focus on cultural changes, there have for several decades been a heightened focus on studying historical transformations as an outcome of processes that exist beyond the nation-state. Researchers often focus on the specific materiality of cultural transfer by studying the movements of objects and persons within a particular chronological and spatial context.[17] What often unites these analytical approaches across disciplines is their rejection of the nation-state as the natural starting point for their analysis, as well as an interest in understanding cultural transformation processes as the outcome of multidirectional relationships—for instance, not simply something moving from one country influencing another. In my analysis of why the Workshop was successful in making *Sesame Street* known in most of the world within a few years, but also why and how it met considerable resistance during this period, I have drawn on these new analytical approaches.[18] Specifically, I have turned to the field of new global history to show how local ideas of preschool television from the Workshop in the United States came into international circulation and, in turn, provided a crucial context for the many local negotiations over *Sesame Street*.[19] New global history emphasizes mobility and exchange, processes that transcend borders and boundaries, and places these within a global context. It adds a new dimension to transnational history by emphasizing how global structures impact specific cases of transformation. Though most of the book focuses on smaller, regional scales like Western Europe and Scandinavia, or one country like Britain and West Germany, the analytical lens of global history has offered me a way of approaching how transformations happening in these spaces interact with changes in the wider region or even globally. One discovery this led to was, for instance, how the Workshop's setup of its first co-production relationship located in Mexico heavily impacted the co-production setup in West Germany as it tried to streamline relationships with broadcasters globally based on its experiences with the format produced in Spanish for Latin America.

As a historian interested in transnational phenomena, I have been lucky to have had the advantage of a rich body of archival source material from the 1960s and 1970s from many of the parties involved in the exchange between the Workshop and Western Europe. Choosing *Sesame Street* to be the center of my investigation of cultural transfer and resistance has offered a wonderful opportunity to write a multiscale transnational history because sources allow the tracing of networks of ideas, people, and money from one context to another. I have, for instance, been able to follow the development of the West German adaptation of *Sesame Street*, *Sesamstraße*, all the way from an encounter at a television festival in Munich, to a meeting in the Workshop's offices in New York over a reused copy of the production setup in Mexico, and finally to a discussion between local educators and the Workshop of whether antiauthoritarian behavior and children's uses of slang should be acceptable in the German program.

Unlike archives of many other private media companies, the Children's Television Workshop handed over documents from its earliest decades to a public archive, the Special Collections at Hornbake Library, University of Maryland. While most of these documents are about the Workshop's domestic affairs, many also relate to their international business in the 1960s and 1970s. These include incoming and outgoing correspondence *with* foreign broadcasters, but also internal correspondence *about* foreign broadcasters, making it possible to get an intimate insight into the Workshop's strategies regarding sales, promotion, and knowledge exchange. The same kinds of documents are available in parts of the Carnegie Corporation of New York's archives in the Columbia University library that hold records related to the financing and early days of the Workshop. Here, among other things, I discovered, how work on preschool programs in the United Kingdom had influenced the development of *Sesame Street*.

A rich collection of external and internal material has also been preserved from some of the broadcasters to which the Workshop tried to sell *Sesame Street*, including Danish, Norwegian, and Swedish organizations as well as the British Broadcasting Corporation (BBC) and German Norddeutscher

Rundfunk (NDR). For the Scandinavians, much correspondence was available regarding the failed attempt to co-produce a Nordic version of *Sesame Street*. This documentation allowed for a detailed study of cultural demarcation through such sources as minutes from heated multicountry phone calls, much-reworked drafts of letters to the Workshop, and papers prepared for meetings with its representatives. During my research for the book, it became clear that the situation regarding the preservation of archival material and the collaboration between the Workshop and broadcasters in France and Italy was very different from that of West Germany, Britain, and Scandinavia. The national public service broadcaster in Italy does not have an archive of unpublished writings that researchers can access. In France the attempt to create a domestic co-production was initially handled by sales agents whom the Workshop had hired to survey the entire European market, meaning that most documents ended up in the Workshop's archives. As such, the French and Italian co-production attempts came to play only a minor role in this volume because I had access essentially to only the perspectives of these broadcasters through the sources preserved in the Workshop's archive. Lastly, the small but important archive of the Prix Jeunesse Foundation in Munich provided crucial information about the Workshop's strategy on European and global levels. The foundation was, and still is, an important transfer hub for children's television because of its activities, which in the 1970s included a biannual festival attended by a global audience, biannual seminars, and a research center that conducted globally comparative research projects on children's television and published an important journal for academics and television producers.

Taken together, the material from eleven archives in seven countries allowed me to compare and contrast the Workshop's efforts in selling and co-producing preschool television in Western Europe in the 1970s. The vast amount of printed material that has been preserved both from the Workshop and foreign broadcasters has permitted me to write the transnational history of *Sesame Street* from multiple perspectives and see it as part of a larger history of fundamental changes in conceptualizations of preschool education, childhood, and television broadcasting in Europe and the United States in the late 1960s and 1970s.

The fortunate situation regarding the written material is completely reversed when it comes to audiovisual sources. Old episodes of *Sesame Street* are relatively easy to come by as they are published on DVDs, and some are on YouTube; a selection of old seasons have been made available on HBO

Max (albeit only in the States), and the documentation is generous in audio-visual historical accounts. However, the European counterparts are another story. Some shows were broadcast live and not recorded because long-term interest in them was deemed minimal. Much of the programming that was recorded was not kept because tapes were expensive and therefore reused; children's television was particularly vulnerable to this practice because of its low status in the cultural hierarchy. As a result, I have been able to see only a few episodes and clips from European preschool shows in the late 1960s and early 1970s. My descriptions of such programs mostly rest on the abundant written accounts of their content.

Sesame Street as a History of Education, Childhood, and Television Markets

Sesame Street's claim to fame was its status as a show that could educate children while also entertaining them. Nevertheless, contrary to what its executives might have claimed, it was a very particular kind of education that Sesame Street promoted. It was formal education: it was directed by a curriculum geared to teach simple school-type skills and facts as well as simple lessons about "appropriate" social behavior. The educational focus was born out of the Workshop's wish to address what it saw as educational shortcomings in American preschool culture as well as particular social challenges in the United States linked to economic and racial inequalities. Its ideals were connected to the Kennedy-Johnson era's liberal ideas of bringing poor Americans, especially poor Black Americans, out of poverty by providing equality of opportunity. Similarly, the Workshop wished to create an educational show that would help all American children do better in school, an idea rooted in its founders' narrow take on the relationship between psychology and education. Their belief in universal paths to learning led them to assume that they provided culturally neutral programming.

The assumptions of cultural neutrality and preschool children's universal needs for the same kind of educational stimulus shaped the Workshop's argument for Sesame Street as a program applicable worldwide. Its assumption that the needs of all US preschoolers—or its concept of them—applied worldwide, ignored the specific social and moral factors upon which the identification of such needs rested.[20] The Workshop's understanding was that all preschoolers needed the same kind of basic skills, such as numeracy and literacy, delivered in the same way, no matter their cultural background and other perceived needs for different kinds of social and moral education. In this way, the Workshop's ideas of preschoolers' universal needs suffered from the same misconceptions of universality inherent in US-led liberal internationalism, making the Workshop ignorant of the fact that the rest of the world did not face the same problems as the United States and therefore did not need the same solution.[21]

The Workshop took for granted that its educational goals could be realized on children's television. Presumably unlike the mere entertainment or amusement that local broadcasters offered on children's TV, *Sesame Street* was "educational." This claim of superiority was used to sell the show abroad, just as producers of "educational" toys had used this label to assert preeminence over their competitors' (noneducational) playthings for more than a century.[22] Preschool education was a highly contested but booming area across Western societies in the decades following the end of World War II. Governments were increasingly concerned with creating a larger educated workforce as well as providing a higher level of welfare across socioeconomic divisions. New theories of the plasticity of intelligence meant increasing confidence in what could be done to support children's early development.[23] In this light, education in its many different forms was seen as a way to fix societal problems related to social and economic inequality, but also get a head start in international economic competition and, in some parts of Europe, prevent the rise of new authoritarian regimes.

Establishing its pedagogical credentials gave the Workshop access to the preschool education market internationally. Even more, it offered new ideas about how television could foster preschool education via an elaborate production design, the key to the Workshop's initial success. However, the Workshop's stress on pedagogy was insufficient to win that market without revisions. Throughout the book, I investigate what "education" meant to the Workshop in different settings and how the Workshop used that definition to advance its programs in foreign markets. In doing so, I show how *Sesame Street* affected international ideas about and production of preschool television. I analyze in depth how local producers responded to *Sesame Street* while seeking to fulfill what they saw as the social and emotional needs of children that the American show neglected. As a result, this book also offers a range of counternarratives to the Workshop's impression about what was appropriate in children's television.

Sesame Street was not the first television program based on pedagogical ideas on how best to stimulate children who did not yet attend school. Broadcasters had offered programs for young children since the 1950s, but these had not been based on explicit pedagogical or educational ideals. However, in 1964, the BBC introduced the idea of using television for semistructured educational purposes directed at preschoolers with its *Play School*, which was soon exported to other countries. *Play School* was an alternative to what the BBC saw as the fantasy amusement most broadcasters offered to young children. However, rather than focusing on a fixed set of basic skills such as *Sesame Street*, it was loosely aimed at fostering creativity as well as social and cultural education and therefore centered on things that would be parts of the child's everyday life, such as animals, games, arts and crafts, the weather, feelings, family, and objects in the home or on the street. *Sesame Street* was built on a different educational philosophy. It introduced the idea of using television for systematic education, emphasizing the idea that children's television could (and should) be used for teaching skills before children started school. The clash of pedagogical and educational norms for preschoolers meant that even if European television producers, such as the BBC, embraced the Workshop's idea of making television educational for preschoolers, they were skeptical of *Sesame Street*'s educational goals and the teaching methods it employed.

While both European preschool programs and *Sesame Street* rode a similar wave of interest in preschool education and acknowledged that television played an important role in their lives, the differences in their views of childhood at the end of the 1960s affected the transfer of *Sesame Street*. Though there were discrepancies in how European broadcasters viewed the child-adult relationship, as some subscribed to a more utopian version of progressive education than others, progressive pedagogy compelled them to consider children's interests in a more rounded way than the Workshop did.[24] Moreover, at the end of the 1960s, especially in Western Europe, the 1968 youth rebellion and students' revolt challenged established social and cultural hierarchies, including that between children and adults.[25] In countries like Scandinavia, France, and Britain, progressive education had roots in movements from the first half of the twentieth century that also existed in the United States.[26] However, the expansion of the welfare states in Europe meant that there was more institutional room for resonance and systematic integration of somewhat progressive approaches when social upheaval in the 1960s pushed for equality and a break with established cultural and social hierarchies. Building on broader educational reforms, the counterculture's challenge of existing norms and hierarchies extended to a reassessment of what children were and what childhood should be, raising questions about the role of television in children's enculturation. Media producers, artists, psychologists, teachers, educationalists, sociologists, public intellectuals, and many others wanted to help define the right kind of television for children because they all believed that media consumption was formative in children's lives and thus also impacted society in the long run.[27]

Those European television producers who were influenced by the late '60s counterculture wanted to use children's media products to empower children and change society, whereas their critics from the establishment wanted children's media content that helped children fit into traditional social norms. In the area of education, the cultural disruption and challenge of established cultural ideals meant a forceful rearticulation of previous decades' more marginalized objections toward traditional, stringent educational methods and aims.[28] This included a strong opposition against the kind of drill routines and factual learning such as those emphasized in the educational approaches that informed the making of *Sesame Street*. Despite its liberal image (breaking with conventional commercial children's programming and having a diverse cast), *Sesame Street* mainly sided with the establishment when it cast its child viewers in the role of future pupils, making them ready for school by teaching them factual information and good behavior. The central idea of the young child as a future pupil is also why Joan Ganz Cooney believed that traditional workers in the field of preschool education had been "laboring under several misconceptions" when they had not devoted their attention to properly preparing children for school.[29]

European broadcasters' status as public service institutions gave them room to explore the needs and interests of children in relation to society without necessarily considering school or family as mediators. They could, for instance, choose to draw on the findings of sociologists who surveyed children's culture or simply ask children themselves what interested them or what kinds of programs they wanted.[30] This included the possibility of addressing their child audience as a social group with its own needs and wants, which did not necessarily align with those of adults or the educational system. These broadcasters often saw a focus on formal, academic education in television as a hindrance to serving children's interests rather than as an essential step in growing up. Thus, while *Sesame Street* might have fascinated European broadcasters, the fundamental ideas behind the show, what the

Workshop liked to call its "philosophy," at times appeared traditional and old-fashioned.

It was not only diverging attitudes toward education and childhood that made the Workshop's sales of *Sesame Street* difficult. The financial and political makeup of the television markets also posed a challenge. The broadcasting landscapes, rules, regulations, and technical infrastructures around the world were very different. Some television markets were as commercial as that of the United States, but most were not.[31] Public service television was usually funded by national budgets or license fees in Europe, making their "production ecology" (the sum of factors from policy regulation to institutional organization and personal networks that influence the production of television) much different.[32] In Europe, most countries had one or two national networks that produced and aired all content, and households could often choose only between one or two channels that broadcasted for a limited amount of hours during the later afternoon and evening. Only a few countries allowed advertising and sponsorships, and even if they did, this was highly regulated. Content, production, and scheduling also followed strict rules to limit the influence of commercial and populist tendencies, and one means to do this included quotas on the import of foreign programs.[33] The fear of television's negative influence was often tied to American commercial television and film culture, especially with regard to the impact of American media on the impressionable minds of children and young people. This dated back to European postwar debates about American comic books and their antidemocratic, violent superhero culture, and broader debates about the capitalist exploitation of young minds and hearts.[34]

The limited competition and the assured funding of European public service broadcasting meant it could afford to produce experimental, local, and short-term programs. Children's departments did not put as much focus on individual programs as the Workshop did with *Sesame Street*. As the Workshop's only program in the first years, *Sesame Street* had to encompass all its ambitions for preschool television and carry the entire organization. Furthermore, because audience numbers became an important way to measure success in the commercial US market, and this was decided also to be a success criterion for *Sesame Street*, it had to have high viewer numbers and be recognizable as a brand in the public to prove its success to funders. In contrast, European preschool programs were viewed as part of a wider schedule, and the number of viewers for a specific program was of minor importance. As European broadcasters controlled what was aired within their network's schedule and produced much of it themselves, a broadcaster's children's department could decide to make one program focus on education, another on entertainment, and it could make different programs focus on different educational, informational, or entertaining aspects. It was a "schedule approach" where individual programs for preschoolers were viewed in relation to other offers for the same and adjoining age groups.[35] Departmental policies guiding the content of the schedule were broad and general; the same was true for ideas guiding individual productions. This meant a lot of freedom in day-to-day production and made Europeans reluctant to make long-term commitments to fixed, expensive concepts like *Sesame Street* that would put lots of constraints on their schedule and room to make new programs.

An added challenge of selling *Sesame Street* was that international sales of the program had to bring home enough revenue to help keep the production of the US version afloat. This meant that the Workshop's mode of operation abroad came to liken the commercial institutions it had denounced at home. Abroad, the show needed to outcompete local broadcasters' programs because they often only had one channel and made few productions for preschoolers. The Workshop, therefore, had to consider how its often aggressive international sales strategies impacted not only its international reputation but also its domestic brand value when it acted as a commercial predator on the world market. It also needed to calculate how partnerships with other broadcasters and merchandise sellers could add to or damage its standing in the eyes of the international broadcasting community. Because the Workshop domestically and internationally wanted to brand itself as an alternative to commercial broadcasters and content producers like Disney, but still needed to build a stable income from sales, it had to find new ways of branding and selling *Sesame Street*.

The Chapters, the Argument

The Workshop's early domestic history set the stage for its international transfer and is the focus of chapter 1. The Workshop's history has been written and retold many times, especially by the Workshop itself and its affiliates. Often the focus has been how the Workshop's production model and *Sesame Street* stood out in a US context.[36] However, when written with the purpose of explaining the premise for the international sales strategies, as is central to this book, the choice of focus for the content and the design of the production must be shifted. Because of my ambition to write a transnational history within a global framework, the chapter is focused on presenting particular aspects of the American context needed to understand the Workshop's activities on a global market. My intention of understanding the European reception and resistance in depth means that I have emphasized factors in the development of *Sesame Street* that made the show different from European premises for producing preschool television, especially views of childhood, education, and the political economy of television production. There are overlaps in the existing historiography's emphasis on the show's roots in educational deficiencies and so-called cognitive psychology, but rather than seeing the show as an alternative to an entertainment-focused television industry, I focus on the ideas of childhood and the role of television on which the program was based. Looking also at the financial premise for the Workshop's activities leads me to offer a perspective that puts its somewhat overstated legacy as an alternative to the commercial market in the United States in a new light as I uncover how its financial basis in the States ironically fueled its aggressive, highly capitalistic behavior on the international market.

In chapter 2, I show how the Workshop created a global demand for *Sesame Street* and the strategies it employed to sell the show worldwide during 1970 and 1971. Choosing a focus that locates the Workshop's marketing strategy in Europe within its global sales plan, I show how its dealings in both these markets, the European and the global, were tightly linked. I focus on its use of events and sales agents to raise interest in the show, what the limits were of these strategies, and how Workshop staff made them work. I combine a historical investigation of the processes that created global demands with insights from television studies to emphasize the multitude of sales and branding strategies that the Workshop pursued in creating demand for *Sesame Street*. Its staff was extremely good at establishing personal networks to promote sales, but also skilled in knowing which people it might avoid, such as foreign research groups that employed other methods than itself and therefore had the power to challenge its entire brand. The chapter also shows how *Sesame Street* gained brand recognition when the Workshop's London-based sales agents offered the first season of *Sesame Street* for very little cost. It introduces the Paris-based sales agents who surveyed the lucrative, affluent Western European market for the Workshop. In the analysis of the use of sales agents, we get to see how the Workshop's anxiety about coming across as cultural imperialists was challenged by the agents' assignment to get European broadcasters interested in the show. Lastly, the chapter shows how and why the generic *Sesame Street* spin-off concept, Open Sesame, was developed from local experiences in France.

Chapters 3, 4, and 5 deal with efforts to sell and adapt *Sesame Street* to audiences in Britain, West Germany, and Scandinavia, respectively, and demonstrate why the Workshop succeeded and failed in these markets. Broadcasters in the three European countries were all devoted to a public service model, they all practiced some variant of "child-centered" progressive education that influenced their productions for young children, and the cultural upheaval of the late 1960s affected children's media culture to different extents in all three cases. The local combination of these trends was, however, different in each country, impacting how successful the Workshop was in selling *Sesame Street* in the three instances. Different ways of governing and producing children's television, as well as local variations in ideas of education and childhood, resulted in different understandings of the role of television in children's lives. All of this affected the Workshop's local success and failure in selling *Sesame Street*. From a global history perspective, this analysis allows me to compare all three regions in their response to the assumptions that the Workshop brought from the United States (chapter 1) and its global marketing and sales strategy (chapter 2). Each of chapters 3, 4, and 5, in this analytical setup, represents a different version of success and failure and something in-between, when it comes to the cultural influence and resistance of *Sesame Street* at the time when the show became a global phenomenon.

The Conclusion is a critical discussion of *Sesame Street*'s legacy. Here, I juxtapose findings from the book as well as more contemporary research on Sesame Workshop's international endeavors with literature from the Workshop itself. Comparing the differences in these two strands of literature and the diverging organizational histories they present, I explore how the Workshop's use of a particularly narrow version of its international activities continues to affect its ability to reflect critically on its international practices. I link its persistence in maintaining an idea of a universal view on children's needs to broader criticism of how the ignorance of US-led international liberalism works to maintain the power of an elitist US worldview.

My ambition is for readers to come away from reading this book understanding the transnational history of *Sesame Street* on two levels: first, as a historical case that is fascinating in and of itself. The transnational history of how *Sesame Street* was actively marketed and sold abroad demonstrates how similarities and differences in production cultures, as well as in views of childhood and education, impacted the program's international success. Second, I hope the book also contributes to a broader understanding of children's media culture historically and today. The story of the Workshop's successes and failures in selling *Sesame Street* abroad can be a starting point for discussions of how children's media are impacted by a wide range of views of childhood and education, as well as by its global marketing. Ideas of what kinds of media children should consume are never "culture free" but a product of the time, space, and circumstances under which they were conceived, altered, and negotiated. Definitions of children's needs and wants are a result of struggles over definitions of children and media in the abstract but also within specific media productions. The ideals that are ultimately favored depend on the wider (geo)political, social, and cultural structures at play within societies at large. Hopefully, the transnational history of *Sesame Street* can be a reflective backdrop for considerations of these important factors that all affect children's media and discussions about them.

1

Domestic Origins

The Workshop's Business Model

On April 5, 1972, educational researcher Richard Polsky interviewed Joan Ganz Cooney, the executive director of the Children's Television Workshop.[1] Polsky graduated a year later from Columbia University with a PhD thesis about the foundational years of the Workshop. The interview with Cooney was one of eight he conducted with people involved in its beginnings to generate data for his work. Unlike much of the rest of the overwhelming amount of work on the early years of the Workshop, the interviews and Polsky's PhD dug deep into the financial and political conditions for the Workshop's setup.

It was an odd feeling going through Polsky's interviews in the reading room of the special collections library at Columbia University forty-four years after they had taken place. At first, I had not been particularly interested in them. Polsky had, after all, been an employee at the Workshop, so I assumed I would get the same from his interviews as when reading papers authored by the Workshop's top people, many of whom have helped produce flattering accounts of their own work. However, as I read Polsky's interviews, I was genuinely surprised. He had asked some of the same questions I would have asked these people, and even his follow-up questions were occasionally spot on.

One of the reasons I was so happy about Polsky's research interest was that it helped me to see the Workshop's history from a new perspective. He researched the decisions that led to the production of *Sesame Street* not as a moral project with fixed goals, but as a result of economic opportunities, political maneuvering, and a particular interest in a rather narrow range of educational and psychological theories. This contextual approach did not portray the formation of the Workshop as simply "the right thing to do," as it often was by its top people, much of the US press, and in later popular histories. Instead, Polsky's work helped me see *Sesame Street* as an outcome of a particular view of television's role in young children's lives driven by an adherence to a particular take on psychology; moreover, it was rooted in the

Sesame Street. Helle Strandgaard Jensen, Oxford University Press. © Oxford University Press 2023.
DOI: 10.1093/oso/9780197554159.003.0002

techniques and ideas of the audience's engagement taken from commercial broadcasting (despite the Workshop's aspirations to be an alternative to just that). These choices, together with broader ideas of television, education, and equality of opportunity as defined within President Johnson's Great Society shaped *Sesame Street* in the United States. The show's American premises heavily influenced the Workshop's approach to the international market and therefore need to be understood to comprehend the transnational history of *Sesame Street*.

In the 1972 interview, Cooney told Polsky how she disliked when television producers branched out into something beyond their area of expertise because that to her was "real amateursville."[2] The distaste for anything amateurish or people trying to move out of their comfort zone might sound odd, as *Sesame Street* and the Workshop itself were styled as an experiment combining education and entertainment for preschoolers. But, in fact, it was a highly controlled experiment where many people involved had expertise in the area where they operated (research, production, marketing) and vast resources at their disposal. It was how these areas were brought together mixing different kinds of expertise that made it an experiment—not the individual methods used. The founders' established positions within their areas of expertise and the expectations of success that came with it determined the output not only of *Sesame Street* as a television program but also the Workshop's conduct as a company.

Sesame Street is known in popular memory for being an alternative to entertainment programs compromised by commercial aims, a bloom in the "wasteland," as the chairman of the Federal Communications Commission had characterized the US television market in 1961.[3] The program was indeed an alternative in the United States due to its explicit focus on teaching a fixed set of school-type skills, extensive in-house research, the diverse cast of actors that aligned it with the courses of the civil rights movement, and the fact that it aired not one of the three big commercial networks but on public television (first the National Educational Television network and later on the new network, Public Broadcasting Service (PBS)).[4] On top of that, the show's speedy pace, the deviation from a whites-only cast of stock characters, and its urban setting made *Sesame Street* different from commercial preschool TV offerings in the United States like *Howdy Dowdy* (1947–1960) and *Captain Kangaroo* (1955–1984).

However, it was a limited experiment. There was no exploration of new educational content. Teaching numbers and letters using drill routines that favored rote learning was not a break from the rigidities of traditional approaches to education.[5] Neither was the idea of teaching children "appropriate" social behavior. With the decision to draw on well-established psychological theories of child development and cognition there was little room for alternative ideas about children's needs and wants. Except for having a more diverse cast than what was usual for children's television, there was little questioning of existing social and cultural norms in relation to childhood and education. This made the ideals behind the Workshop's production quite different from what was happening in parts of Europe at the same time *Sesame Street* first aired. Influenced by, among other things, the youth rebellion's challenge of established cultural and educational ideals, European fora such as the European Broadcasting Union's subcommittee for children and young people started advocating for television to play an emancipatory role in children's lives.[6] These new ideas for children's broadcasting entertained by some of the European broadcasters would clash with what in comparison looked like an essentially conservative approach to education and the child-adult relationship on *Sesame Street*.

It was not only in relation to education that the Workshop chose to draw on traditional ideals and methods. It was also taking on the well-known commercial logic of American broadcasting, including the idea of viewer numbers equaling success and viewer satisfaction. The show's long-term survival and impact depended on its ability to be a real competitor to the commercial shows and therefore needed to demonstrate ratings success by its own standards. The method of presenting to it funders was that, besides being educationally effective, it was also an attractive alternative to existing programs thanks to a promise of high viewer numbers within its target group. Again, this was a very different conceptualization of viewer needs and television's role in the lives of children than the idea of public service engrained in European public service broadcasting. In Europe, viewers' needs were traditionally determined from a wide set of parameters rooted in dominant cultural politics rather than metric assessments of the popularity of specific shows. This could result in high-brow paternalistic ideals, but it could also allow for rapid-paced innovation, as in the area of children's television of the late 1960s. The different makeup of the European television landscape meant that besides the Workshop's traditional ideas of education and childhood, its reliance on established benchmarks in commercial television would also prompt resistance toward *Sesame Street*.

Though there was criticism of the Workshop and *Sesame Street* in the early years, later histories, especially those with a domestic focus, have neglected these "conservative" characteristics while emphasizing its "progressive" aspects.[7] This has meant ignoring how its overall philosophy and production design confined and even reduced the impact of progressive goals because they drew on particular views of childhood from within psychology, a focus on equality of opportunity through formal education, and standards of commercial television. The conservative goals somewhat limited the possibilities for being an alternative to commercial entertainment television and traditional educational ideas.[8] The way its different elements—for example, training basic school-type skills versus furthering racial equality— were presented by the Workshop in its funding applications, production, and research or press relations greatly impacted its domestic success. But the weighing of different elements also affected the transfer of *Sesame Street* to Europe and the rest of the world because the Workshop treated its positions, which were presumably appropriate to the American context, as applicable everywhere. The result was that because of its need to adhere to the boundaries set by dominant liberal ideas in the United States in the mid-1960s to gain wide public support, the Workshop came to subscribe to a set of goals that would seriously hamper its efforts to reach beyond an American point of view when operating abroad.

To understand the complexities involved in the development of the Workshop and *Sesame Street* that later impacted the transnational history of the program, this chapter analyzes their origins in a US setting. In particular, I touch on aspects of the show and the production company that helped shape the international transfer. These elements include the show's research design, the financing of *Sesame Street*, the Workshop's business model, as well as its place in the US media culture. For the benefit of readers who might not be familiar with *Sesame Street*, this chapter also briefly introduces the show's basic content elements.

In the Beginning, There Was Cognitive Psychology

To understand the ideas behind *Sesame Street* as an educational television show we must begin our story with Lloyd Morrisett. When the idea for *Sesame Street* first originated in 1966, Morrisett was executive vice president at the Carnegie Corporation. He had a PhD from Harvard in experimental, cognitive psychology and was interested in the possibility of using television for educational purposes. He shared this interest with a friend, Joan Ganz Cooney, who worked as a TV producer for an educational broadcasting channel in New York and had a bachelor's degree in education from the University of Arizona. The importance of Morrisett's background in psychology and the Carnegie Corporation's general interest in funding cognitive science and joining psychology research to social policy cannot be understated.[9] The philanthropic fund set up to support educational programs across the United States had in the 1960s taken an interest in early education as a possibility to reduce poverty and inequality of opportunity.[10] As the first funder of the study that led to the establishment of the Children's Television Workshop, the Carnegie Corporation's approach to childhood and education was critical for the Workshop's view of how television could be of use to children: Morrisett insisted that television should be explored primarily as a means to enhance children's basic educational skills.[11] This conception of the uses of children's television was not a given, inevitable, or universal; it was a very deliberate choice. Morrisett also influenced the choice of researchers who were recruited to the Workshop, which were to a great extent psychologists like himself. As a result, models from cognitive psychology about "appropriate" intellectual development happening according to a child's age—rather than, for instance, planning education in relation to their social background or interests—became central to the project.

The view of childhood as something that happens in universally applicable "ages and stages" is a fundamental component in most branches of psychology that deal with child development.[12] Building mainly on cognitive psychology in their understanding of children meant that the Workshop saw children as on their way to *becoming* someone more fully, and the way to develop them was through stimulation of the mind—a mind that was, in principle, assumed to work rationally and intellectually in the same way regardless of any external circumstances.[13] In this model, the rational-thinking adult was always the end goal, and a child's progress could be measured in terms of how far it was from this ideal. A concrete example of this understanding was illustrated in a speech by *Sesame Street*'s executive producer, David Connell, saying that "the average child from a poor background begins school as much as a year and a half behind his middle-class counterpart."[14] This linear, one-directional view of child development determined how the Workshop saw its role in providing all children with optimal opportunities to climb up the developmental ladder: using television to teach them a certain set of skills and facts, the Workshop would help them grow up the right way by preparing them for society's well-established educational and social norms. Though the plans for *Sesame Street* also included social education, the Workshop foregrounded intellectual growth. It believed that doing well in the educational system would be all children's ticket to a better life, no matter their background. An added emotional benefit of the focus on school-type skills, the Workshop believed, was the pride children would feel when they experience adult recognition of their knowledge of numbers, letters, and other basic concepts commonly associated with educational gains.[15] In this way, the Workshop encouraged children to navigate toward adults' opinions in general, and the established educational system in particular.

This view of television's role as an educator of basic skills and facts and the view of childhood it relied on were often the reasons why the concept of *Sesame Street* would later meet pushback in Europe. Here, a sociological and philosophical view of the child as already *being* someone was foregrounded, as later chapters show. This child-centered perspective, which was dominant in European children's television in the late 1960s, already existed in the interwar period's progressive movements, and even before. However, the zeitgeist of the youth rebellion and its influence on children's media culture pushed children's broadcasting to become more child-centered, treating the child more as a person in their own right, some even subscribing to utopian progressivism and questioning the role of children as default subjects to the educational system and the family.[16] The United States also had a progressive, child-centered movement in the 1940s.[17] However, it did not manifest in the mainstream areas of education in the decades after the Second World War.[18] The Workshop was part of a strong movement in American education from the 1950s and early 1960s that emphasized skills learned in a clear progression with fixed goals defined by experts and furthering of educational results by enhanced testing and reinforcement.[19] These fundamental differences in views of childhood and education affected how the role of television was seen on both sides of the Atlantic, and it is therefore essential to take a closer look at how psychology and definitions of education played a fundamental role in the Workshop's philosophy and the production model on which *Sesame Street* was based.

Encouraged by Morrisett, the Carnegie Corporation sponsored a study of how television could be used to educate children. Cooney carried out this study during the late autumn and winter of 1966, and later iterations were produced in 1967. As we shall see, it was clear all along that the answer to the study's question as to "the potential uses of television in preschool education" was to be rooted in how cognitive psychologists understood educational challenges and their solutions.[20] In the study, Cooney's premise was that young children in the United States, particularly the underprivileged, received insufficient intellectual stimulation to prepare them for school, both in existing television offerings and existing models for preschool education. Building on findings from developmental psychologist Jean Piaget and the educational psychologist Benjamin Bloom, she argued that the stimulation of not only the underprivileged but all children in their early years, before the age of four, could affect their IQ by 2.5 percent per year. For her, this loss was at stake when the proper education of preschoolers did not take place. She therefore also saw traditional preschool programs as misguided in their intense focus on emotional and social skills. In her opinion, children's so-called cognitive skills—which in the Workshop's narrow framework became the recognition of numbers and letters, visual discrimination, reasoning, and classification—could and should be stimulated from a much earlier age than American educators generally believed. Moreover, Cooney believed that strengthening preschool education by teaching goals set by experts and testing their efficacy would improve American society by enhancing the education of privileged as well as underprivileged children. This aligned well with broader US educational policies in the late 1950s and 1960s that were rooted in criticism of modern teaching, which was seen to have introduced inefficient and misguided educational methods and the freedoms given to inadequate teachers.[21]

In 1960s America education was commonly seen as a means to improve wider social problems, including those related to racial inequality and civil rights, as it was believed to create equality of opportunity.[22] In the context of the Cold War and the race for ideological world dominance, federal educational policy pinned its hope on evidence-based scientific data to create specific effects and efficiency in the educational system in order to form citizens who could outcompete the Russians. The preferred way to optimize the educational system was a "hard," data-driven approach aimed at improving education in practice based on empirical material: testing and adjusting input (learning goals) and output (educational achievement), rather than applying abstract theoretical ideas about what education was or should be ideally. It was more about finding solutions than understanding problems.[23] Information on practice in the form of empirical data should not be based on teachers' experiences but, psychologists argued, be collected and processed

Figure 1.1 Joan Ganz Cooney, 1970. *Keystone Press / Alamy Stock Photo.*

by researchers trained in statistical methods to find the best educational solutions.[24] It was experts who should define the educational goals and the methods for testing whether these were reached; teachers, who were increasingly distrusted as competent educators, should merely execute the educational system the experts devise.[25] This made way for a decontextualized view of education, stressing the framework of fixed teaching goals, methods, and matching testing as a universal idea that could be applied equally everywhere, regardless of the circumstances. This universal conceptualization of education meant that it could be positioned as a system that fixed society's social problems because it avoided addressing wider structural inequalities that could not be solved through the idealized equality-of-opportunity model.

The idea of cognitive psychology as the scientific solution that could revolutionize education became a core idea in the Workshop's philosophy and program production. It thereby placed itself squarely within a then-current American trend of individualizing social problems by treating them as psychological.[26] As education was also understood as a tool for individual achievement and upward mobility, the responsibility for a positive life trajectory was placed on the individual and—while future citizens were growing up—that child's home environment. Broader questions of what caused

greater social and economic equality, such as racism and unrestrained capitalism, were often ignored both in discussions of education in general and
within the Workshop. In the Workshop, Black children and later also children belonging to other minorities were an implicit focus. Still, questions of
racism or racial bias were seldom addressed directly in its discussions because education was not seen as a social and cultural construction but a universal system. Children were almost only talked about in two categories in
the Workshop: privileged and underprivileged. This might have been an opportunity to bring up economic inequality in relation to children's unequal
access to education and prerequisites for learning, but this simply did not
figure as a pertinent problem.

Cooney's study argued that middle-class and disadvantaged preschool
children alike did not receive enough intellectual stimuli, but saw it as a particular problem for children from underprivileged homes.[27] The report thus
acknowledged that some children did less well in the educational system.
Still, it only probed for an explanation in the area of preschool education, and
only as this area was conceptualized by psychologists who defined barriers to
learning as individual, not structural.

The interview data for Cooney's study were drawn almost solely from
cognitive psychologists.[28] Her views were closely aligned with the Carnegie
Corporation's perspective, which also gave her a list of people they suggested
from whom she should seek counsel. She highlighted the research by
Carl Bereiter and Siegfried Engelmann, who, even if not explicitly labeled
behaviorists, argued in a not dissimilar fashion that drill routines, simple
instructions, and rapid repetitions most efficiently met underprivileged
children's need for formal education.[29] Cooney closely referenced their book
Teaching Disadvantaged Children in the Preschool in her proposal both as
inspiration for teaching methods and content for a preschool show.[30] This
meant emphasizing bite-size, factual learning that would be taught by significant repetition. These ideas heavily influenced *Sesame Street*'s design
and ideas of effective and efficient learning: teaching basic skills that children could learn by heart and that were easily recognizable in a common-
sense understanding of what it was "useful" to know in a school setting. The
Workshop's approach also resembled a traditional, common-sense idea of
teaching, rote learning, where the pupil is believed to learn by repeating what
the teacher tells them. Bereiter and Engelmann's views of efficient teaching
matched well with Cooney's fondness of Martin Deutsch's studies that linked
problems with educational progress to deprived home environments.[31] The

link she created between deprived home environments as the cause of under-privileged children's educational progress (Deutsch) and the solution being to train children in basic school-type skills (Bereiter and Engelmann) made her conclude that if television could teach basic skills preparing children for school, it could likely play a positive role in their lives, particularly in those of underprivileged youth.

Cooney would later state that her report was inspired by "educators and psychologists [who] were beginning to believe that the achievement gap between disadvantaged and middle-class children could be narrowed by injecting intellectual stimulation into the early years of the disadvantaged."[32] However, she did not explain how a mass medium like television when pro-viding the same program to privileged and underprivileged children would be able to do something in particular for one group and not the other.[33] The underprivileged children Cooney referred to in her study were mainly chil-dren from minority groups, primarily Black children living in inner-city areas.[34] Concerns over the link between poverty, racism, and the educa-tional achievement gap that existed between these children and their (white) middle-class peers had been the attention of the Johnson administration's Head Start program launched in 1965. In Head Start, as later in the Workshop, the gap between poor (Black) and middle-class (white) children was not seen as caused by racial inferiority, as it had been earlier.[35] However, society-level explanations such as structural racism were not central to the wider picture. Instead, solutions that focused on the individual's action such as doing better in the educational system, were perceived as a possibility to close the achievement gap and, in doing so, a critical tool to achieve equal opportunity in the United States. The Johnson administration did take some steps to change the educational system's racial and socio-economic biases. Still, the focus was on raising the preschool academic skills of the disadvan-taged as a means of equalizing educational opportunity, not the "root causes" of social inequality like racism.[36] In effect, this approach obliged children to adapt to the existing educational system with all its biases.[37] This explains why Sesame Street's way of addressing the achievement gap has been called a "deficit model," as it tried to make up for one group's perceived deficit, rather than critically exploring why this deficit occurred and why it was seen as a deficit in the first place.

In the Workshop's deficit model, the individual children and their home environment were seen as missing vital skills and access to them—and there-fore having a deficit to overcome. A centrally placed Workshop employee,

Robert Davidson, said in his interview with Polsky that the show's curriculum had to be "consciously compensatory for underprivileged children." Davidson assumed these children were not getting enough cognitive stimulation at home because parents "may not speak to them very much, certainly not in an educational way."[38] *Sesame Street* was thus a conservative solution to an educational problem: it assumed the achievement gap could be fixed by teaching underprivileged children more of the same things they would be taught in school, and in a way that had a traditional focus on drills and repetition. Helping underprivileged children score higher on quantitative measures of academic achievement superseded the potential for a more progressive goal: critically addressing social inequality. This neglect of underlying structural problems that influenced children's lives became an issue in the transfer of the show, especially to West Germany and Scandinavia, where producers of children's television partly embraced the medium as a means that could make children challenge oppressive social norms.

Cooney's study of 1966 made clear that she did not want television to be just another classroom, even if it would draw on traditional educational methods and outcomes. As a television producer, she was interested in the medium's format and how it could be used to teach in new, more entertaining ways than traditional educational television.[39] From her own world of television production, she knew something that fit perfectly with Bereiter and Engelmann's ideas of how to influence children: commercials.[40] In her study, Cooney noted how children learn from commercials. She understood that advertisements affected behavior and provided mental stimuli in ways that were not dissimilar from Bereiter and Engelmann's behavioristic-inspired drills and rapid, routine approach. Educational use of drills resembled advertising in the way they emphasized learning through repetition of bite-size pieces of information trying to affect consumer or student behavior through a constant barrage of the same message. It meant *Sesame Street* became a highly instructional show.[41] The ideas of using commercial techniques to teach, fostering a narrow set of skills traditionally associated with the educational system, and using a psychometric focus to ensure efficient teaching and effective testing became cornerstones in *Sesame Street*'s educational approach.

Two things in the 1966 study were not linked to the idea of cognitive stimulation of children. These were the never realized programs for parents (to encourage engagement with *Sesame Street*), and kits with craft materials that could extend the program's goals beyond the screen and make the learning interactive. The kits would be sold or distributed for free to parents and children in communities that could not afford them. Providing kits and books based on the TV program was seen as a way to grow children's interest in reading in combination with the show. These efforts show that Cooney and the people she had consulted acknowledged the link between structural problems related to poverty and educational achievements. But rather than making a television show where poverty's (racial) bias was addressed directly, the solution was to try to solve the issue—not by speaking about it in the TV program that would later become *Sesame Street*, but by targeting parents and having free kits available for disadvantaged areas. In that way, even if not intended, the show avoided being as controversial to policymakers, the establishment, and middle-class parents as it would have been if it had addressed racial and class divisions directly. Instead, the Workshop's charity model of distributing educational kits and magazines to the disadvantaged addressed only those suffering from the societal divisions, not those factors causing the inequalities.

The Summer Seminars of 1968: No Room for Other Ideas of Childhood

In the spring of 1968 the federal government, the Carnegie Corporation, and the Ford Foundation agreed on a grant package for the Children's Television Workshop and the TV program it would produce. After the money was secured, the learning goals that Cooney, Morrisett, and the funders had agreed would be the core of the show were discussed and defined at five seminars taking place during the summer of 1968. These seminars were part of the initial planning for the show. In charge of them was Gerald Lesser, a professor of developmental psychology and education at Harvard. Lesser was a friend of Lloyd Morrisett and later served as chair of the Workshop's advisory board. At the seminars, the Workshop's small group of staff picked the brains of child development specialists and others.[42] Nothing was seemingly left to chance at these meetings. Academic participants were screened by Lesser so that the Workshop was sure that they made a positive contribution. People who would challenge the Workshop were actively weeded out, because it was believed that critical voices would disturb the group dynamics at the seminars and presumably complicate the baselines the Workshop already set out.[43]

The composition of the seminars hugely favored psychologists. The seminars would therefore emphasize their ideas of childhood and television's role in children's lives and suppress alternatives, just as in Cooney's initial study. Two-thirds of the people in the seminars were academics, most of them from fields with universal, quantifiable understandings of children (e.g., psychology and psychiatry). The other third comprised preschool teachers, children's book authors and illustrators, artists, filmmakers, and people from the television community. Those who did not come from academia had very different experiences of working with children and interacting with children's media than the academics. Even in the carefully controlled space of the seminars, these different approaches led to clashes. Especially the teachers—a number of whom were Black—had a difficult time at the seminars as their professional backgrounds meant that their experience with and understanding of children's needs and wants differed from that of the academics.[44] Entrenched lines between experts' definitions of universal models for teaching and learning and teachers' inclination toward a contextualized approach to education played out at the seminars.

In his report from the seminars, psychologist Daniel Ogilvie commented on how teachers' viewpoints were dismissed. Ogilvie described how these educators wanted to contribute to the seminars by describing their knowledge of children in the "target population" with whom they work every day.[45] Such empirical experiences did not interest Lesser, who saw the teachers' contributions as "an attempt to answer the 'unanswerable question of what is a disadvantaged four year old really like,'" to which he would argue that "since the terms 'lower class' and 'disadvantaged' mean so many different things to so many different children, it was a false issue."[46] Instead of engaging with these teachers' experiences, Lesser wanted the seminars to focus on abstract ideas of four-year-old children, not seeing that such a standard model would potentially be biased against certain groups. The dismissal of the teachers' voices at the seminars reflected how Lesser found it pointless to construct a model of what the Workshop had promised its funders would be its particular "target child": a child from a disadvantaged background, despite having participants who had experience in this area at the summer seminars. Lesser believed that there would be huge variations across this group, but perhaps more importantly, his focus on psychology's universal models meant that he was not interested in exploring the structural social-level problems that underprivileged children might have in common, such as classist and racist biases in the educational system.[47] As the person in charge of the seminars,

Lesser directed efforts away from identifying the root problems of the target audience's lower achievement in the educational system. Instead, he wanted the seminars to focus on creating a television program for all preschool children that he believed would be of universal benefit. Educational needs thus became decoupled from the child's social realities, diminishing the need to listen to teachers' or children's own understanding of their needs and wants. The division between these contrasting perspectives—recognizing the importance of underprivileged children's actual lives and experiences as opposed to assuming universal models of childhood—would later be amplified when the Workshop tried to establish co-productions of *Sesame Street* abroad.

Lesser's planning of the summer seminars along with Morrisett and Cooney's initial ideas left limited room for critically discussing children's educational needs and television's role in fulfilling them. Affective and social competencies—such as self-awareness, the ability to navigate independently and in groups, creative thinking, and emotional awareness—which were highlighted in progressive preschool education were thoroughly downplayed in favor of perceived cognitive needs.[48] The former were considered too difficult to define, teach, and test efficiently.[49] The discussion also affirmed the questionable preliminary claim that there was no need to consider the particular needs of the target audience of underprivileged children: psychometric models of children and their educational needs were believed to be universal.

The idea of stimulating underprivileged children in particular, but using a universalist model and a mass medium that would ideally reach all preschoolers, became an Achilles heel of the Workshop. After all, how could it claim to help the disadvantaged especially, if all children gained the same amount from the program, thus perpetuating the achievement gap, albeit on another, slightly higher, level? Later tests showed that the gap could not be narrowed and create equality of opportunity, such as was promised at the Workshop's launch in early 1968.[50] What mattered to the educational outcome for viewers according to tests at the time was how much children watched; the more they watched, the better they were at learning the narrow set of facts and school-type skills according to tests developed by the Workshop and the Educational Testing Service.[51] The promise to close the achievement gap was questioned by Cooney herself already in early 1970, and later officially abandoned by the Workshop in a US context because it simply could not prove that this outcome would take place.[52] Yet the claim of *Sesame Street*'s production design and emphasis on school-type learning goals as a way to ensure particular gains for underprivileged children was still used in promotional efforts abroad. When the show was marketed in Latin America and Europe, the promise of closing the achievement gap was part of the sales pitch.[53]

Entertainment, Aesthetics, and Diversity

The Workshop was committed to being popular with a large number of viewers, following the success criteria of commercial television: good ratings.[54] This was partly a self-imposed goal for the Workshop and partly a restriction that resulted from the American experience of a highly commercialized broadcasting system. Reaching a large audience in a medium that commercial broadcasting had long dominated required conforming to the expectations of viewers who habitually watched the commercial networks.

Cooney was explicit that she did not want the show to be boring, something she believed was an unfortunate hallmark of American educational television. She was convinced that the show had to be entertaining to draw in viewers, and it had to enthrall not only the target audience of children but also siblings and parents:

> In order to appeal to preschoolers it would also have to appeal to older brothers and sisters (something for the entire family like *Batman* or *Laugh-In*). Otherwise, the members of the household who would most likely control the dial would not be interested in turning to the workshop production.[55]

To appeal both to preschoolers and other family members, the show had to introduce entertaining elements that would be broad and universal. Given the commercial character of American television, the Workshop felt they had to compete with and imitate successful commercial producers of children's entertainment. Notably, Disney had long learned how to appeal to this broad audience. This was a contrast to public service television in Europe, where such commercial competition was rare, allowing public broadcasting to cater to a tiny viewer group like small children without having to reach a wider audience as in the United States. The Workshop's attempt to please an older audience was emphasized by bringing in celebrities more likely to be better known by non-preschoolers.

The idea of manipulating children to learn while being entertained by imitating the aesthetics and persuasive allure of commercials led to production of a rapid-paced sketch-style show. There were four kinds of sketches: street scenes (also called wraparounds,[56] made in a studio version of an inner-city street with actors, Muppets, and children), puppet sketches (with the Muppets), animated cartoons, and live-action short films (see Figures 1.2 to 1.5 for examples). Each element had to incorporate one or more of the teaching goals from *Sesame Street*'s official curriculum. The sketch format was found to be a great way to keep children's attention, a behavior that the Workshop's research department strategically measured using ideas from experimental psychology with a device it invented called "the distractor."[57] This device was aimed at measuring whether children were so caught up in the program that they could not be distracted. Just as with commercials, the idea was that to get the full educational effect, children had to keep their attention on the screen and not tune out and do something else. The show's content was then optimized based on data collected during the distractor studies. For instance, when researchers found that children were easily distracted during the semirealistic street scenes, Big Bird and Oscar the Grouch were added to these scenes because the researchers knew that viewers enjoyed Muppets elsewhere in the program.[58] The producers also dropped the idea from Cooney's original proposal of having children make arts and crafts on the show, as that was not seen as entertaining enough.[59] The focus on entertainment meant that the final show would, besides its focus on teaching school-type skills, also feature other elements like music, animals, urban environments, storytelling, and comical sketches.

The Muppets served not only as entertainment. In the Workshop, ideas from cognitive psychology were also used to justify having more Muppets than real children. Lesser believed the unrealistic puppets would serve as ideals for portraying exaggerated and clear roles and personalities.[60] In that way, the Workshop avoided any messiness and political undertones that might come from portraying conflicts within families, difficult interactions between "real" people, or children's actual everyday lives. Real children were predominantly used in the role of "ideal learners" on the show.[61] This perspective was portrayed through child-narrated voiceovers or their participation as actors on the set. Again, we see ideas from cognitive psychology about modeling child conduct through identification with children on *Sesame Street*, aimed to make television have a very specific and desired effect on the

Figure 1.2 Street Scene with Gordon, Sally, and Big Bird (wraparound). *Sesame Street*, episode 1, airdate 10 November 1969.

viewers that would conform to existing norms in the educational system and society more broadly.

The aesthetic style and production mode of commercial broadcasting were assured when *Sesame Street* recruited staff from commercial television. As with the Workshop's research, there was no room for beginners in or errors from the production department. For example, Cooney hired a former producer at the popular *Captain Kangaroo*, David Connell.[62] The focus on retaining viewers was addressed with a toolbox producers already knew, again making sure that the experiment of *Sesame Street* was not too experimental; it would draw on known visual and narrative formulas from mainstream US entertainment culture. Producers were accustomed to thinking of children's needs in terms of what they knew entertained them, assuring that ratings would be high. As a self-declared "McLuhanist," producer Robert Davidson believed that his and other producers' knowledge of the medium was sufficient to make good children's shows.[63] Thus, rather similar to the psychologists' approach, the production staff planned its work according to an abstract model of children and their needs based on numbers and tested

Figure 1.3 Puppet sketch with two Muppets. *Sesame Street*, episode 131, airdate 9 November 1970.

methods; the producers, though, focused on viewer satisfaction as expressed in ratings. For the production staff, the model viewer was a child whose satisfaction and contentment could be measured in rating numbers, while for the psychologists, the viewer's learning could be measured using a checklist of narrowly defined academic aims. As with all other viewer groups in the commercial system, satisfaction with *Sesame Street* was equated with high viewership (even if actual data were sketchy), and children's interests were seen as being served, as long as they kept watching the show because it was educational. As such, aside from the educational purpose, there was little involvement with questions of what potential roles children's television could fulfill in viewers' lives beyond that offered by the fast-paced and facile model of commercial television.

The alignment with mainstream entertainment culture was evident right from the beginning. *Sesame Street* had to be "more *Laugh-In* than *Play School* and *Romper Room*," in Davidson's words.[64] *Play School* (1964–1988) and *Romper Room* (1953–1994) were two slower-paced shows for preschoolers, produced by the BBC in the United Kingdom and by Claster Television in the

Figure 1.4 Animated cartoon about the letter W. *Sesame Street*, episode 1, airdate 10 November 1969.

States, respectively. Both programs differed from *Sesame Street* in that they focused on traditional kindergarten education, stimulating children's emotional and social skills with a mix of songs, games, and storytelling as well as arts and crafts projects that could inspire viewers to be creative and actively engaged at home. Perhaps not incidentally, *Sesame Street* would compete with these two shows in the international market and attempts to make its show different would thus help create a distinct Workshop brand.

Another way the Workshop marked itself as different from other preschool shows—and indeed children's television in general—was its commitment to diversifying on-screen representation. *Play School* had a team of presenters one of whom was Black, but minority representation in children's programs was as much a rarity in Europe as in the United States. It was a true innovation when the Workshop chose to include Black actors among the lead cast for *Sesame Street* from the beginning. Ensuring diversity in the cast was the main way that the Workshop attempted to cater particularly to underprivileged Black children on screen. It took very seriously the importance of children

Figure 1.5 Live-action film teaching numbers 1 and 2. *Sesame Street,* episode 131, airdate 9 November 1970.

within its target audience being able to see themselves represented on screen and for white kids to see children of color depicted in positive ways. In the street scenes and live-action films, Black adults and children appeared in the first season; and in later seasons, after criticism from other minority groups, the cast included people with Asian and Latin American backgrounds.[65] Still, just as the educational ideas behind the show catered to a traditional view of education, the depiction of race on the show also avoided any direct confrontation with mainstream (read: white) ideas of how to solve problems rooted in structural racism. *Sesame Street* portrayed perfect racial harmony; it was colorblind and nonconfrontational—the epitome of American liberalism.[66] When conflicts were portrayed, they were superficial and interpersonal (never ideological), and could easily be solved with a joke, a smile, or the gentle interference of a well-meaning adult. The studio set was built to look like a typical New York street, with brownstone houses, stoops, and trash cans (see Figure 1.6). This was an innovation in US children's television, which mostly had cozy, domestic decors. However, the social life depicted at

Figure 1.6 Image of Muppets in the urban cityscape of 123 Sesame Street.
Allstar Picture Library/Jim Henson/Alamy Stock Photo.

123 Sesame Street was an idyllic paradise socially and culturally.[67] Again, the
Workshop managed to find a balance between innovation—and in this case,
even being progressive with its multiracial and urban vibe—and not challenging the mainstream. The experiment stayed inside the box.

When later sold abroad, the Workshop would partly abandon its claim
that part of the *Sesame Street* concept was to serve minority children's
interests by representing them on screen. The representation of diverse social and cultural backgrounds in the countries overseas where the English-
language version was sold was never raised as an issue in the international
marketing of the show; the only important point was its perceived universal educational benefit. In an interview concerning the introduction of
Sesame Street to Australia, where the interviewer raised the question about
the lack of representational diversity germane to Australian children, Joan
Ganz Cooney simply replied that for "good or ill the whole world is being
Americanized and paced by '*Laugh-In*' and other US shows."[68] In her logic,
because of American cultural dominance, it did not matter if only the social
reality of children in the United States was represented on screen because it
would be recognizable everywhere. There was no need to acknowledge the
needs of children from Australia to see themselves represented on the screen.

The Workshop's claim of universal appeal, therefore, really meant that as long as American hegemony could be upheld, *Sesame Street* would be relevant in all cultural contexts.

Making a Business of Keeping Funders, Parents, and the Middle Class Happy

From the very beginning, it was clear that the Carnegie Corporation would not be financing the new show alone. Other resources had to be found, so Morrisett with his many connections to the US establishment looked for other funding sources. While *Sesame Street* later became identified with public service broadcasting and anticommercialism groups like Action for Children's Television, this was not a given from the outset.[69] In the late 1960s, everything was considered, including commercial television and production companies. Morrisett tried commercial networks like CBS and production companies like Disney.[70] When the US Office of Education came on board as a financial backer, the pressure to try commercial outlets grew. Louis Hausman, the Workshop's contact point at the Office of Education, had a background in commercial television. He wanted to air *Sesame Street* on commercially run networks to prove to the world that the show had an appeal beyond the narrow audience of educational television and thus demonstrate that the networks driven by profit could also make shows like *Sesame Street*.[71] By attempting to appeal to these networks, Morrisett and Cooney again were limiting the experimental nature of their program. However, in an era of mass broadcasting, it was difficult to find commercial backing for an educational preschool program aimed especially at underprivileged kids because the prospect of great viewer numbers and possible sponsors was slim.[72] *Sesame Street*'s first seasons, therefore, ended up being sponsored by private foundations and government money, even if Cooney and Morrisett had clearly shown themselves to be comfortable with a broad range of options.

Even so, to satisfy its funders, the Workshop needed to prove that it was educationally effective and could reach large numbers of viewers in the selected target groups of underprivileged preschoolers but also preschoolers in general. To measure its teaching effectiveness, the Workshop brought in the Educational Testing Service. The goals that could not be measured—or were difficult to measure, such as social and emotional skills—were dropped.[73] The choice of funders also meant that *Sesame Street* could and should not be "controversial to anybody," but remain a show of both mainstream education and conventional popular public appeal, something the middle-class public favored even if a few educational experts did not.[74] Middle-class public opinion, to which the funders were accountable, counted more than listening to differences about educational opinions, especially because the Workshop already had secured the backing of many like-minded experts through the summer seminars. Later, when selling *Sesame Street* abroad, the Workshop would also favor popular opinion over the beliefs of local educational experts. Anything that might push American middle-class parents or funders away was off the table.[75]

In December 1968 the Workshop had arrived at a statement of instructional areas.[76] These were (1) symbolic representation including letters, numbers, and geometric forms; (2) cognitive processes, relational concepts, classification, ordering, reasoning, and problem-solving; (3) the physical environment, including general information about natural phenomena, and (4) the social environment, including the ability to identify the role of family members and institutions and understand social rules. These four areas were not equally weighted. The first two were by far the most important to the Workshop, broken down and divided into detailed teaching goals that had to be represented in each episode of the show. Everything would neatly fit within any traditional school curriculum; there were no challenges to any established ideas about what formal education should contain. The emphasis on letters and building toward reading skills strengthened the connection of the show to classroom learning and the medium of the book. Even if not intended, this seeming encouragement of children to read books carried many more positive connotations for funders and parents than watching television.

The foundation in cognitive psychology, the inclusion of academic experts, and the alliance with traditional schooling all worked to make *Sesame Street* uncontroversial, even conservative, in its choice of educational content. Emphasizing the ABCs and 123s sent a strong signal of being "useful" in a traditional educational sense, as opposed to more elusive aims such as encouraging social skills. It meant that the Workshop would likely be able to count on a large group of parents and teachers to recognize *Sesame Street*'s content as of value in their children's education. Furthermore, decontextualized numbers and letters were not difficult to learn in a purely instrumental sense, and children's recognition of them would be easy to measure; demonstrating *Sesame Street*'s educational effect in this area therefore almost assured success, if education was defined in this narrow sense.[77]

To ensure a close alignment between *Sesame Street* and theories of children's cognitive development, the Workshop had created a powerful narrative to convince funders and the public of its seriousness. Cooney and Morrisett wanted to experiment with television for educational purposes, but they needed to show current and potential funders that it had a realistic chance of success. Hence, scientific and high-profile research institutions like Gerald Lesser's Harvard signaled funders that they were serious and competent. Emphasizing numbers and particularly letters, which connotated reading and fighting illiteracy, gave government sponsors confidence that the Workshop could make television a positive force in children's lives, rather than just entertainment, as commercial children's television offered. Combined with the later attachment to a public-service, anticommercial agenda, the Workshop became perfectly positioned to address the anxieties of middle-class America as it demonstrated television as a wholesome, educational force in their children's lives. The focus on easily recognizable formal education markers such as numbers and letters also distinguished the show as different and more educational than other contemporary preschool programs such as the commercial *Romper Room* and *Captain Kangaroo* and the public service television rival *Mr. Rogers' Neighborhood* (1968–2001) that offered a traditional preschool education approach in the form of emotional and creative play.[78]

Besides laying a foundation for the Workshop's work, the sheer volume of research produced during its first years also helped distinguish *Sesame Street* from other children's programs at the time. The US Office of Education paid for a grant that resulted in five volumes about the making of *Sesame Street*, all published in 1970.[79] Along with documenting the program's production, the research had several other functions: it solidified the Workshop's work as serious because it was research-worthy; it helped to promote the knowledge of *Sesame Street* in academic circles; and as the research was done partly by the people who worked at the Workshop, it was not surprising that these volumes were sympathetic toward its aims and production. Writing its own history, the Workshop also took part in controlling the narrative surrounding its legacy. This production of research about *Sesame Street* continued within the Workshop, helping to retain an academic interest in its work, controlling the narrative of its development over time, and adding to its purpose of standing out as the "serious" alternative to other children's programs.

The potential to become a darling of parents, educators, and children was, however, not enough to keep *Sesame Street* going. High ratings could not generate money from commercials when it was distributed through a public service network. Even though the funding for the first two seasons had been generous, with $8 million (about $61 million in 2022 dollars) in total, relying on noncommercial income sources from foundations and the government left the Workshop with an ongoing funding shortfall. Unlike television in Europe, which was fully funded as a public service, ironically the Workshop had to go commercial. Foundations and the government were interested in funding research and experiments, not the day-to-day business of what was basically a television production company, even if an innovative one. Almost all US broadcasting was commercial and paid for by sponsors and commercials; there were no viable public service funding models to build on.[80] Having committed itself to first being broadcast by the National Educational Television network and a year later tied to the new Public Broadcasting Service (PBS), the Workshop had gained a lot in terms of its image in being a nonprofit alternative to commercially driven television. Still, the result was limited possibilities for raising revenue in the United States because PBS worked like a program distributor, not a network. Public service broadcasting had only just begun in the States and had not yet found stable and reliable sources of funding, let alone any that could take on a commitment the size of the Workshop. In contrast to Europe, there was simply no long-term commitment to full funding of public service broadcasting. With a new US president in 1969, securing public funding in the long run became even less likely as the Nixon administration was opposed to the idea of paying for PBS. In a highly commercialized media system, there were very few solutions other than selling merchandise, raising money from licensing, and pursuing foreign sales, just as other production companies like Disney, Hanna-Barbera, and Warner Brothers did.

Merchandise and foreign sales indeed became a solution to keeping the Workshop and its many initiatives afloat. One example was the 1971 negotiations with Commissioner Sidney Marland from the US Office of Education, where the Workshop's funding problems and possible solutions were discussed in depth. In a meeting, Cooney floated the idea of offering *Sesame Street* to commercial stations if sufficient funds were not made available.[81] Nevertheless, she and the Workshop also wanted to demonstrate that another long-term plan was in place that could support continued public broadcasting in the United States. She proposed that in the 1974–1975 fiscal year, half of the Workshop's budget would come from nonbroadcast material and sales overseas.[82] The plan was that revenues from abroad would help defray the cost of annually reproducing the two domestic series, as the Workshop's portfolio now included *The Electric Company*.[83]

An added bonus to the US government with the overseas expansion of *Sesame Street*, the Workshop argued, would be the enhancement of America's image internationally.[84] This suggestion fit within the existing soft-power strategies of the US government.[85] The foreign involvement converged with the bigger schemes of US global engagement that "helped" foreign cultures develop and American influence grow, as the Workshop's efforts would "develop new expertise and commitments concerning the application of television technology to improve the quality of life in those countries."[86] By supporting the Workshop's domestic productions, the Office of Education would then help not only the continued production of shows to US preschoolers but also the government itself in its search for cultural influence around the world. It was a brilliant piece of promotion for American liberalism through universal educational preschool television. An example of this strategy was the proposal for a Latin American version developed in the latter half of 1970, where existing TV programs according to the Workshop were "anti-educational and non-aesthetic, provoking mental 'abulia' rather than stimulating mental and cognitive development."[87] Exporting *Sesame Street* to the region would presumably change this. In fact, the Workshop was projecting its understanding of US educational problems and its answer to them onto a completely different context with the help of money it hoped would come from Coca-Cola and the US government's Overseas Private Investment Corporation scheme that helped advance American foreign policy.[88]

The Workshop knew that the alignment of general US cultural interests with its own was a dangerous way to go in a global media market where cultural elites feared the influence of American culture.[89] This was particularly true for children's media products, where commercial US entertainment, particularly in the form of "Disneyfication," had been intruding in Europe for decades on local children's productions.[90] To assure its advisory board that it was aware that it might be accused of cultural imperialism, the Workshop claimed that it "only introduces [*Sesame Street*] in response to requests for it and is concerned with helping each country find the modifications required to adapt it to its own needs."[91] Even if this claim was far from true, as the following chapters show, the Workshop would stick to it consistently. There was within the Workshop an obsession with the idea that it was different from Disney and other commercial producers of children's programs. It would use this idea to promote its domestic image as an anticommercial, nonpredatory alternative to commercial companies. To potential international buyers, it would use it to show why it was much more sensitive to the values of foreign countries than other US companies that had expanded abroad.

The Workshop's worry about its image related not only to foreign sales but also to merchandise. The income from non-broadcast products, books, parent-teacher guides, and recordings was a difficult field for the Workshop to maneuver when they expanded abroad, but it was problematic even in the States. Before the first broadcast in 1969, the Workshop entered a merchandise deal with Time-Life publishing. In 1970 Time-Life's director reflected on how he had found it difficult to strike a balance between preserving *Sesame Street*'s image as an educational show that was an alternative to the commercial network's profit-driven entertainment and its marketing merchandise that would help raise money for the show.[92] An example of these difficulties showed in the "terrible image gaffe" that occurred when Time-Life launched a $19.95 book and poster kit (about $147 in 2022 dollars) for the Workshop, whose brand was all about noncommercialism and being accessible to underprivileged children. However, the idea of being an educational show attracted so many largely middle-class parents that the book kit sold thirty-five thousand copies, and in 1971 the expected royalties from the Time-Life collaboration were $500,000. The Workshop had indeed been right to identify its show as an educational alternative, winning middle-class American parents. In fact, Time-Life estimated that *Sesame Street* was a bigger commercial success in terms of merchandising than *Captain Kangaroo* and Dr. Seuss's books in the early 1970s.[93] This demonstrated that at least in the United States, it was possible to use the Workshop's image as nonprofit and educational in a very successful marketing strategy and draw on the long-term success of toy companies like PlaySkool and Fisher-Price in merchandising "educational" playthings.[94] However, this was trickier when moving to markets abroad that did not have a tradition for financing television productions with related merchandise.

As earlier American merchandisers of educational toys had succeeded, the Workshop appealed to a largely middle-class audience of parents intent on giving their offspring an educational advantage. The show's alleged relationship with academic performance suggested the show's link to book culture and school, a selling point for an American middle class that had valued education as the child's primary occupation since the mid-nineteenth century.[95] Despite the attractive notion that *Sesame Street* toys were better for children to play with than other toys because they educated them while playing, the Workshop privately recognized that showing just how their merchandise was educational was difficult. Its research department had at first insisted on careful studies of the merchandise's educational effects, but that had become a hindrance to making immediately salable products that could capitalize on *Sesame Street*'s success.[96] The conflict between the research department and the nonbroadcast merchandising department led to a relaxation of standards. Instead of being proven educational and tested in the same way as the program, the toys and other commercial products licensed with *Sesame Street* characters were deemed educational if they could be called "educationally sound, durable, inexpensive, of continuing interest ('non gimmicky') and entertaining."[97] In practice, "educational" came to mean whatever matched middle-class parents' expectations for education.[98] The semantic elasticity that the word "education" had in the Workshop's merchandise ventures and its promotional efforts did not necessarily work as well when the Workshop entered new and less commercialized markets. Here "educational" could not necessarily be used as a shorthand in the same way for "good" or "appropriate." Because merchandise based on children's television programs was an alien concept in the first place, European broadcasters were not convinced that just because *Sesame Street* merchandise was claimed to be educational, it was not exploiting children's vulnerability for commercial gain.

To keep the goodwill of parents and funders, the Workshop put a lot of money and effort into improving and sustaining its public relations.[99] This meant that the alliance with public service broadcasting was important, as was the affiliation with the anticommercial Action for Children's Television. As an organization that challenged commercialized children's TV and advertising to kids, Action for Children's Television embraced *Sesame Street* and its ideals of using television for a positive educational aim.[100] This group and the middle-class suburban parents who supported it no doubt approved of Cooney's speech at their symposium in 1972. In it, she condemned the commercials on the big networks for sugared cereal and drinks as well as noneducational toys, saying they led to "bad teeth and warped value systems," and also to "psychological damage" to children who wanted things their parents could not afford to buy.[101] On the whole, selling children things on TV was "dead wrong," she argued, even if she was the top person at an organization that sold tons of merchandise each year. Because of the "educational value" of *Sesame Street* merchandise and because *Sesame Street* did not advertise licensed products (other than the Workshop's own), this was apparently no problem. The fact that *Sesame Street* was aired on PBS and was a nonprofit company seems to have been enough to make it stand out as the appropriate educational alternative to commercial broadcasting, even as Cooney's business model of merchandising licensing and foreign sales essentially echoed Disney's and Mattel's.

The Vulnerability of the Workshop, *Sesame Street,* and the "CTW Model"

The limitations that the Workshop itself, its funders, and the commercial structure of the US broadcasting system had put on the *Sesame Street* experiment left very little room to maneuver. The Workshop might have called itself experimental for more than a decade after it began, but in reality, once the foundation was built, only minor things could change. There were some shifts in curricular objectives over the years, but the commitment to the rigid "CTW model" for production and testing remained, based on a cognitivist psychological perspective where educational goals were expressed in bite-size curricular objectives (see chapter 2 for details about the CTW model). And even if the Workshop made a few other shows, they were not as successful and received none of the energy and resources as *Sesame Street*.

Because the success of *Sesame Street* to a large degree rested on sustained public approval of its carefully crafted production and the ideas behind it, the Workshop became very vulnerable to criticism. It was a costly operation compared to other productions of children's television, with a research division, many puppets and puppeteers, production and curriculum staff, as well as elaborate films and studio street scenes. The Workshop had its own administration and multiple divisions for merchandising, licensing, lawyers, and so on, and all of this had to be paid for with the money *Sesame Street* could bring in either from grants or sales of the broadcasts or merchandise. Morrisett, Lesser, Cooney, and all the employees at the Workshop had built much of their reputations, hopes, and dreams on the show. Staff and affiliates like Lesser were sensitive to any attacks on the show, particularly its basic philosophy—which was inseparable from its brand and reputation in the United States. Because everything in the *Sesame Street* concept was so tightly knit—the aspirations to help underprivileged children, raising the bar for US preschool television, its foundation in cognitive psychology, the education-through-entertainment concept—if one part of this package failed, the whole project might be in danger. This explains why the Workshop fought any criticism bitterly, sticking doggedly to all elements of its basic beliefs.

The way in which the Workshop tackled domestic criticism is important because it foreshadowed its reactions to some of the backlash it met in Europe. Most critics were ignored, or their credentials were questioned in an effort to make their critical points seem wrong, ridiculous, or of minor importance. For example, consider how the Workshop's Lesser responded to the criticism of John Holt, whose books on unschooling sold more than a million copies, when he wrote a blistering review of *Sesame Street* in the *Atlantic* in mid-1971.[102] Holt's review raised interesting points, many of which aligned with the critique the Workshop was facing from European broadcasters, particularly the BBC, at the same time. He criticized the deficit approach of the Workshop, pointing out how he saw the educational system as rigged against the poor, and that *Sesame Street* offered nothing that would alter that situation of systemic bias. Holt thought television for children should show them the real world:

> We could show one or more children exploring different parts of the city, using the city as a resource far richer than any school could possibly be. . . . On a recent show we had a puppet child telling a puppet policeman that he was lost. Why puppets? Why not show a real child looking for a real policeman, and the ways and places in which real policemen are to be found? If a poor black kid who is lost can get kindly help from policeman, let's show it happening. If he cannot, let's skip the whole idea and not sweeten it up with puppets. Better show children instead how not to get lost, how to read and use maps."[103]

However, there was no room in *Sesame Street* for this gritty reality in which children maneuvered on their own. In his 1974 book, Lesser brushed off Holt's criticism as the personal beliefs of "a perceptive commentator of teaching practices," who, however, was not qualified to criticize the sophisticated educational ideas and methods that *Sesame Street* embodied.[104] This dismissal of Holt and other critics was a typical Workshop reaction.[105] Lesser simply believed that *Sesame Street* delivered the best kind of preschool television possible. Because the Workshop's research tried to avoid normative issues in education, it tended to reduce criticism that raised these questions to a debate between other's opinions and its science, even if the Workshop's choices were as much based on a particular view of childhood, television, and education as those of its critics. Moreover, as this chapter has shown, *Sesame Street* and the Workshop were hardly pure exemplars of innovative and scientific educational programming. They were deeply invested in the methods and ideas of US commercial media culture; traditional, formal education; and established, academic psychology.

Sesame Street was an American solution to claims of a lack of cognitive stimulation in preschool education and home environments, tailor-made for the overwhelmingly commercial broadcasting landscape of the United States. On the international scene, the Workshop had a far different audience to convince of how *Sesame Street* would solve social and educational problems. It was broadcasters who came from other cultures and other broadcasting systems where ideas of childhood, education, and even television itself did not match that of the States. In fact, these factors were very different, especially in Europe, where US media products had long been consumed, but also feared, especially those aimed at easily impressionable children.

The Carnegie Corporation had already been in contact with preschool producers from the United Kingdom when Cooney first began her research for the show in 1966. Later, with a publication in 1968, Cooney made sure that the Workshop's ideas were promoted to a pan-European audience in the International Central Institute for Youth and Educational Television's journal *Fernsehen und Bildung*. The next chapter explores some of the initial international sales efforts that followed after *Sesame Street* had first aired in the United States in 1969. *Sesame Street*'s mixture of education and entertainment became an opportunity to market the show, but the narrow definitions of what children needed, determined by cognitive psychology and ratings, also became a hindrance.

To a large extent, it would be the Workshop's *vision,* its so-called philosophy, for preschool television that met substantial resistance. The program itself did contain segments that focused on less classroom-directed elements, such as music, animals, urban environments, storytelling, and comical sketches. However, these features were not emphasized in the international sales effort, even if they overlapped with the content of European children's television and were the areas in which Europeans were most interested. The overseas marketing of *Sesame Street* emphasized instead how the production rested on highly researched educational efforts and was based

on universal psychological models of educational progress that could prepare privileged and underprivileged children better for school and deliver
quantifiable results. Thus, even if the Europeans liked the show's music, advanced production techniques, sophisticated animation, and, above all, humorous sketches with Bert and Ernie, this was not what the Workshop would
try to sell. Rather, it promoted a product that rested on a view of education
and childhood that clashed with those of Western Europe. Furthermore, the
Workshop's entire business model, selling a long-running, fixed concept,
went against the ways in which public service broadcasters abroad produced
children's television.

As we shall see in the following chapters, the differences between children's
television in Europe and *Sesame Street*, in terms of production, content,
and research, would prove both an opportunity as well as an obstacle to the
Workshop. The uniqueness of its product gave it an advantage as it filled a
gap in the market, but at the same time it needed to convince potential takers
that they had a need for *Sesame Street* and its elaborate production model. It
required a lot of market research, networking, and the development of a sophisticated, efficient sales strategy for the Workshop to conquer not only the
European market but that of the entire world.

2

Ensuring Early Success

Strategies to Conquer the International Market

"We are like the British Empire. Someday the sun will never set on Sesame Street," Joan Ganz Cooney told *New York* magazine in April 1971.[1] Cooney, the president of the Children's Television Workshop, had been the head of the organization from the very beginning and continued to be its public face. At this point in time, her dream of colonizing all the world's television sets with Bert, Ernie, and Big Bird seemed right on track. With 50 percent growth in sales of the English version from 1970 to 1971 and new foreign-language co-productions on the way, *Sesame Street* seemed unstoppable. What were the reasons for its rapid international success? In an interview given six months earlier, Cooney had explained quite clearly that there was "no question of [*Sesame Street's*] universality," because even when shown to children in India who had never seen television, it was a "smash hit."[2] *Sesame Street's* innate ability to capture all preschoolers worldwide, simply because of its brilliance, was, and still is, a story often retold by the Workshop to explain its success.[3] It was never acknowledged that these children might have been fascinated by the idea of watching television and any program might have done the trick— or that the Workshop's intense marketing campaigns might have worked the wonders for which it had hoped.

The Workshop's fixation with *Sesame Street's* universal appeal fit nicely with its rapid domestic success across a multitude of demographics. But attributing the worldwide breakthrough to its universal appeal obscured the vast efforts the Workshop put into making *Sesame Street* a globally recognized brand. This explanation not only downplayed all of the work, time, and money it had poured into making *Sesame Street* a new standard for educational preschool television in the United States; it also downplayed the vast resources deployed to persuade the rest of the world of this idea.

Persuading foreign broadcasters to perceive *Sesame Street* as a new global standard for educational preschool programs was a highly demanding

Sesame Street. Helle Strandgaard Jensen, Oxford University Press. © Oxford University Press 2023.
DOI: 10.1093/oso/9780197554159.003.0003

process. The Workshop understood that if it wanted to create a long-lasting international hit by advancing its ideals for preschool television, it had to spend time and money upfront. Its success depended on a regular and sustained exchange of programs, ideas, and people between the different contexts over time—just like in any other global transformation process.[4] Money had to change hands, new ideas about the education of preschoolers through television had to be spread, and overseas broadcasters had to be convinced to buy *Sesame Street* and the Workshop's idea of what role television should play in preschoolers' lives. In a year, from mid-1970 to mid-1971, the Workshop's elaborate marketing strategy for *Sesame Street* largely helped to establish the show as a challenge to existing expectations about what role television could fulfill in preschoolers' lives. The forceful promotion of the show ensured high demand for its product.

The time and resources the Workshop spent on becoming a global hit were not purely matters of choice. As we saw in the previous chapter, limited access to public resources in the long run meant that the Workshop had to make money from sales of programs overseas, develop co-productions, and sell merchandise if further programming was to air in the United States. To survive as a nonprofit organization in the United States and preserve its domestic image as anticommercial, it had no choice but to try and achieve a profit by making *Sesame Street* a long-lasting hit with children in places as far apart as Kenya, India, Mexico, and Japan—which required an aggressive sales strategy.

The Workshop's strategy was founded on a dual wish. It wanted to make sufficient revenue to fund future domestic English-language versions of *Sesame Street*, and at the same time it wanted to preserve its integrity as a nonprofit organization with an altruistic interest in advancing a new idea of educational television for preschoolers. It was difficult to combine international commercialization with the claim of domestic anticommercialism. In the Workshop's archives, this is reflected in hundreds of documents, many of which form the basis of this chapter, where workshop staff discussed this strategy of selling without appearing to sell and instructing the European sales agents on exactly how to promote the show in this spirit. In my exploration of the early attempts to promote and sell *Sesame Street* both as an entirely new idea and as an alternative to existing preschool shows, the entanglement between personal networking and the Workshop's economic motivations take center stage, as this was a crucial interconnection for its international advancement.

This chapter explores the early worldwide efforts to sell *Sesame Street* in 1970 and 1971 and the mid-1970s development of the first spin-off concept, Open Sesame. In the case of *Sesame Street*, sales to the important, affluent, and established European market were deeply intertwined with the Workshop's global sales strategies. The Workshop's particular focus on Western Europe concurs with what historians of the rise of American cultural dominance in this period have stressed as to how Western Europe was where the United States consolidated its power as the global trendsetter in modern consumer culture.[5] American businesses, with the help of the government, did so by challenging and on many accounts successfully overturning cultural hierarchies set by the European bourgeoisie. And because of European influence over regions that had been part of European empires, winning Europeans to American living and thinking would also influence attitudes elsewhere: in matters of mass consumption, convincing Europeans was key to settling as a global leader.

Taking *Sesame Street* global called for a range of activities. It began with the German-based Prix Jeunesse Foundation, whose festival and research activities became an important transfer hub for *Sesame Street*, as the Workshop was very skilled in navigating the different opportunities the foundation provided. From 1970 it included the hire of sales agents in the United Kingdom and France that extended the Workshop's network in international broadcasting, both to sell the English-language version and to explore the feasibility of co-productions. This eventually led to the spin-off concept Open Sesame, a semilocalized, economy version of *Sesame Street*. Together use of the international hub and employed agents were ways in which the Workshop labored to transform *Sesame Street* into a central reference point in the global production of television for young children—all unfolding in a worldwide market in which preschool television was a rising stock.

Prix Jeunesse International: Exposure to the World

One of the best places to promote a new television show to an international audience in 1970 was at festivals as options to see foreign shows were limited. Producers who wanted to review programs from other countries had three choices. One was to travel to another country to have access to the terrestrial network. Another was to have copies sent by mail, a long and complicated process because different countries' technical systems were often incompatible. The third was to participate in international screenings at festivals or conferences.

One such festival was the children's television festival Prix Jeunesse International, an initiative in southern Germany by the free state of Bavaria, the city of Munich, and Bayerischer Rundfunk, the Bavarian broadcaster. Established in 1964, Prix Jeunesse International had quickly become a popular biennial event with screenings of children's television and a prize competition. As one of the world's few forums dedicated to gathering producers of children's television, it was a much-welcomed meeting point for people to seek inspiration, promote their own shows, and look for new content for their own schedule.[6] Screenings went on for days, mixing with network events (see the 1970 schedule in Figure 2.1). Prix Jeunesse International was, in other words, the place to be if you had a children's television program to promote, a fact the Workshop did not overlook.

The Workshop had been aware of Prix Jeunesse as a possible place to promote their project ever since it had been made official in 1968. The festival

Programme: Prix Jeunesse International 1970

	MORNING	AFTERNOON	EVENING
Thursday June 4, 1970	10.00 Constituent Meeting of the Juries	14.00 Working Session of the Juries	
Friday June 5, 1970	9.00 Inauguration of the Contest 9.30 Showings	14.30 Showings	20.00 Reception given by the Intendant of the Bavarian Broadcasting Service
Saturday June 6, 1970	9.30 Showings	14.30 Showings	20.15 Showings
Sunday June 7, 1970	9.30 Showings	14.30 Showings	
Monday June 8, 1970	Excursion (Do not forget to bring your swim suits!)		Social Evening for all participants
Tuesday June 9, 1970	9.30 Showings:	14.30 Showings	20.15 Showings
Wednesday June 10, 1970	9.30 Showings	14.30 Showings	20.30 Reception given by the Bavarian Minister President
Thursday June 11, 1970	9.30 Showings	14.30 Visit to the site of the Olympic Games	20.15 Showings: Non-competing contributions
Friday June 12, 1970	9.30 Showings: Non-competing contributions 10.30 Press-conference	13.00 Showings of the prize-winning entries	19.30 Final evening with awarding of prizes

Subject to alterations!

Figure 2.1 Schedule from Prix Jeunesse 1970. *Prix Jeunesse International.*

was part of the Prix Jeunesse Foundation, which also had a research center for children's television, the International Central Institute for Youth and Educational Television (IZI). Already in 1968, Cooney had contributed to the institute's journal, *Fernsehen und Bildung*, with a piece on the Workshop and its main ideas for the show that would become *Sesame Street*, and Edward Palmer, the Workshop's head of research, had had a second piece published in the journal in early 1970.[7] The journal was in German, a widely read language in Europe at the time, and had extensive abstracts in English, French, Spanish, and Italian. Writing these pieces, the Workshop had made sure that the international community of children's television broadcasters had access to information about their work long before it would be realized and presented at the festival.

In 1970 the Prix Jeunesse festival had 213 participants from forty-one broadcasting institutions located in thirty countries across five continents. Participants came mostly from Western Europe, but there were also producers and other representatives from institutions in North and South America, Eastern Europe, the Soviet Union, Asia, and Africa.[8] Among the festival participants in 1970 were Palmer and the vice president of production and executive producer of *Sesame Street*, David Connell, both ready to promote *Sesame Street* to some of the most influential people in their key overseas markets.

Entering *Sesame Street* into Prix Jeunesse International turned out to be a great win. In the category "Children's Programmes up to Seven Years," *Sesame Street* won jointly with the Norwegian Broadcasting Corporation's *Husmusa og Skogsmusa* (The house mouse and the forest mouse).[9] The prize committee for the preschool category praised the show for being what the Workshop had aimed for—a playful mixture of entertainment and information, as the verdict stated:

> The jury awarded the prize for the attractive way in which the program succeeded in making use of television to communicate with young children, and for its successful combination of entertainment and information. The jury commended the high standard and professionalism of its production techniques and the careful balance of the many different elements of the program. These were combined with humor and vitality in presenting the infectious quality of enjoyment and fun.[10]

This statement not only gave the program the maximum possible positive exposure, but it also emphasized many of the qualities of the program that the Workshop wished to promote.[11] Its ambition to create international demand for *Sesame Street* was off to a great start.[12]

Sesame Street was very different from the twenty other entries in the preschool category. Its editing pace was faster, its run time was much longer, and it featured explicitly educational content.[13] Frequent changes between animation, films, puppet sketches, and in-studio street scenes inspired by the aesthetic of commercials made the program's rapid pace stand out compared to existing children's programs. Its one-hour length also set it apart from other programs entered in the same category, of which the longest lasted no more than thirty minutes and many ran fewer than ten. The aim to teach school-type skills and facts, such as numbers and letters was also a brand-new thing in preschool television. Most existing programs would only overlap with *Sesame Street* in its aim to teach social skills, and other shows would do this very differently. Finally, the dual address where an adult audience's taste was addressed with references to American pop culture—especially upbeat pop music, sketch-show comedy, and use of celebrity appearances—also set it apart. Notably, the prize committee mentioned the "mixture of entertainment and information," but not the program's explicit school-like educational content, which must have stood out. In the 1960s, television for preschoolers in the rest of the world did not teach academic skills but contained a mixture of playful learning with an emphasis on social and cultural education.[14] Consequently, *Sesame Street*'s visual style, episode length, and elements of formal education represented a new take on what role television should and could fulfill in young children's lives.

One reason the committee perhaps did not want to praise *Sesame Street* for its instrumental use of television for school-type skills training might have been disagreement on whether this was a good idea. Indeed, Prix Jeunesse was a forum that represented a rather different take on children's television than the Workshop's. In a Prix Jeunesse context, the conceptualization of children's television was rooted in the organization's view of the connection between children, television, and society at large.[15] Rather than supporting children's enculturation into the norms and values of the educational system or the adult world, Prix Jeunesse emphasized a so-called children's perspective. From its beginning, those who participated in the organization's development had emphasized Prix Jeunesse's ability to set an agenda for children and young people's civic education with television programs that made them independent and empowered them by promoting programs that represented the views of children, not adults.[16] This meant that the organization worked to encourage broadcasters to let the wishes and interests of children themselves act as the point of departure for productions, rather than what various educationalists, television producers, or other groups of adults thought was best for children. The research branch of Prix Jeunesse, the IZI, had been crucial support in the acquisition of knowledge about children's interests, the lives they led, and how this related to their television consumption. The Workshop's representatives do not seem to have picked up on this very different approach to children's television.

The Workshop's later reflections on the outcome of the festival made it clear that *Sesame Street*'s positive reception had boosted its confidence. When top management considered entering its second show, *The Electric Company*, for Prix Jeunesse in 1972, the sense of superiority that Palmer clearly felt led him to send Cooney a heads-up about possible consequences. He told her that

> when "Sesame Street" was entered a year and a half ago, it so overwhelmed the competition that it threatened the morale of European contestants. In fact, the Prix Jeunesse board felt it necessary to offer a special second award in the same category in which "Sesame Street" was entered in order to encourage less well-endowed production groups from other countries to strive for high quality within their own means.[17]

To be sure, the practice of dividing the preschool prize into programs aimed at "information and instruction" and offerings that focused on "play and entertainment" had also been employed at the festival in 1968. However, Palmer apparently did not know this when he claimed that only division of the prize would give others a chance in the competition. For him, it was a testament to *Sesame Street*'s superiority. The statement is a clear illustration of the Workshop's confidence in having a unique program on its hands. Winning the Prix Jeunesse International galvanized the trust in its product when it came to the international market. Rather than seeing the difference between *Sesame Street* and the other programs screened at Prix Jeunesse as a possible expression of different ideas of what television should offer children, it was taken as an opportunity to sell its program on a market with a big room for improvement.

Besides the large amount of positive exposure *Sesame Street* had gained at Prix Jeunesse, the trip had also provided Palmer and Connell with plenty of networking opportunities. Like many other television and film festivals, Prix Jeunesse International was not only an occasion to win prizes and see what other producers had on offer; it was also a time for networking during the many social events. Dinners, receptions, and excursions (including river rafting, see Figure 2.2) provided ample opportunities for meeting future business partners, co-producers, journalists, and the occasional mass media expert. Palmer and Connell had certainly recognized the many possibilities for networking and knew this to be a prerequisite for selling the program on the international market.

Many of the broadcasting people with whom the Workshop would be in business in the years that followed had attended the festival. In August 1970 Palmer made sure to follow up on several conversations he had during the festival by writing to his new acquaintances. One of them was Mogens Winkler from the Danish Broadcasting Corporation.[18] This contact resulted in a trip to Scandinavia in the autumn of 1970, during which Palmer and Connell discussed possible collaboration with the Danish and Swedish broadcasting corporations.[19] Palmer had also met Peter Lewis from the Independent Television Authority, an institution that later became important in the Workshop's fight to gain a footing in the UK market.[20] Besides

Figure 2.2 Participants from the Prix Jeunesse Festival in 1970 river rafting on the Isar. *Prix Jeunesse International.*

making available these possible buyers of *Sesame Street*, the festival also enabled Palmer to connect with other researchers.

Building on Research but Avoiding Scientific Discussions

One of the things that made *Sesame Street* stand out from other preschool programs was its deliberate use of formative and summative research to advance the impact of its educational elements.[21] In relation to Prix Jeunesse and the potential international market it represented, this innovation was both a way for the Workshop to market *Sesame Street* and a potential way to expose it to criticism because this modus operandi was different; claiming it to be scientific potentially opened up complex discussions of methods and theory.

As described in chapter 1, the Workshop's research setup and its direct link to production ("the CTW model") was believed to help optimize *Sesame Street*'s education of children in precisely the way they needed from the point of view of cognitive psychology. The use of formative research meant that during the production phase, *Sesame Street*'s efficiency in teaching a set of clearly described set of educational goals was tried on a test audience. The final version was then adjusted accordingly to maximize the educational effect. After the program aired, the so-called summative research investigated the degree to which these goals were met among the actual audience. Not only in North America was such instrumental use of research for program optimization new.[22] The strategic use of preschool television to teach a fixed set of formal educational goals, as well as the investigation into the efficacy of television in teaching them, was one of the things that made *Sesame Street* stand out from the children's television programming then being produced in Europe and the rest of the world.

The Workshop's innovative approach combining production, content, and research caught the interest of Prix Jeunesse. However, as would later be clear, the Workshop was not similarly interested in the research done by Prix Jeunesse that presented a real challenge to the Workshop's own design. European broadcasters also had research departments or commissioned research from external institutions, but their research strategy had very different aims. The difference was rooted in the different premise for producing children's television within European public service broadcasting. Ratings and the ability to "sell" programs to sponsors or grant givers were not important. Research could therefore be experimental and driven by a wide range of shifting interests among researchers and broadcasters whose producers participated in research projects from time to time. Consequently, European broadcasters had a more sociological and cultural interest in their programs' impact. They were interested in children's understanding of and preference for various programs, not their efficacy in some specific educational area or the metric of viewer numbers. Rather than being integrated into the production phase, this research provided insight into child viewers more broadly and their reception of programs on a general level.[23] Thus, while the Workshop's research was instrumental, strategic, and mainly quantitative—modeled on research in experimental psychology, psychometrics, and audience satisfaction—the European research was more exploratory and used qualitative methods to get at the cultural implications of programs and programming more generally. An excellent example of the European research agenda was the British media researcher James Halloran's pan-European study for the European Broadcasting Union published in 1968. In the study, he and his team explored the cultural reasons for the variation in the European countries' different provisions and production of children's television. Halloran's interest was focused on developing a critical sociological approach that put asking questions ahead of gathering data in a positivist fashion.[24] When he led studies for Prix Jeunesse in the early 1970s, Halloran continued this line of research.

The different view of what kinds of research were needed in relation to children's television is symptomatic of the bigger differences in North American communications research and European media research traditions. The North American tradition focused largely on trying to objectively measure media effects based on the researcher's definitions of the viewer's needs as defined by experts (independently of the viewer's own experience). In the European tradition, the viewer's own experience was an integral part of mass media studies. This also meant that children's benefits from media content were assessed very differently: as something adult researchers could measure on a large scale from a natural and objective starting point, or something that needed to include children's perspectives based on, for instance, interviews and observations that took the research subject's social and cultural setting into account.[25]

The differences in research methods and aims gave the Workshop scope to deploy its broadcasting research to market *Sesame Street* as innovative because it tested the show's efficiency in teaching school-type skills using quantitative (and supposedly objective) methods. However, the difference also made it difficult for the Workshop to engage in Prix Jeunesse International's research projects. On the one hand, being part of comparative international research projects presented the Workshop with yet another opportunity to promote its work. On the other hand, the difference of European research was that it could challenge the ideas behind the CTW model and undermine its assumed superiority.[26] A difficult situation ensued for the Workshop, therefore, when Prix Jeunesse wanted to initiate its own study of *Sesame Street* by an internationally assembled research team.

The Prix Jeunesse Foundation sponsored research on programs that had won prizes in the festival's prize competition.[27] The results of these research projects were disseminated through regular academic channels and at the festival and were, in essence, transnational media studies projects using the prizewinners as comparative cases.[28] The great interest *Sesame Street* had generated at the festival in 1970 led the head of the foundation to propose an international study on the program by teams of researchers from different countries.[29] Despite the exposure this would have generated for *Sesame Street*, the Workshop declined. It was troubled by the suggested study, which was very open-ended, and the Workshop therefore wanted the "methodology developed in much greater detail" before even considering a collaboration.[30] Apparently, any form of research that might have the slightest negative impact on its brand, like the proposal's interest in studying "side-effects not intended," was out of the question for the Workshop even if it styled itself as an organization that was part of a cutting-edge research environment. An undesirable outcome of the research project could damage international sales, as it would make any critique of *Sesame Street* visible to a wide public. Given its uncertainty, the Workshop declined to make *Sesame Street* available for the foundation's project, believing it was already doing the needed research itself better and in greater depth.[31]

The decision not to allow the international research collaboration to study *Sesame Street* demonstrated a high degree of reluctance on the part of the Workshop to engage with others' ideas and potential criticisms about its program and production setup. The Workshop's dislike of research such as that Halloran represented—which considered cultural-social issues using qualitative social research—was a consistent pattern, also seen in the case of how it reacted to criticism in the United States.[32] Its behavior in a European research context fits the general pattern of impe-rialistic claims of American social (communication) science. Producing a large amount of strategic research on *Sesame Street* in-house was a strategy that allowed control of the show's brand in relation to potential overseas buyers. While it welcomed screenings of the program for a wide audience, as had happened at festivals, the Workshop found the prospect of allowing actual research by foreign research teams risky. Mass media researchers were often well connected with foreign broadcasters, and were they to find anything to criticize, this could seriously harm sales as the outcome of such research on *Sesame Street*'s reputation was unpredictable. The Workshop clearly saw little or no value in having others do research on their program, even if they were keen to sell to the markets where the research was being done.

Contrasting the varying successes that the Workshop was exploiting with Prix Jeunesse as a transfer hub demonstrates the range of opportunities and limitations this hub provided. For the Workshop, the festival and *Fernsehen und Bildung* were great ways to let the world of children's televi-sion know about its work. However, as its fixed concept could not be altered because of all the investment intellectually and economically in its core de-sign in the United States, Workshop staff was reluctant to enter the areas of Prix Jeunesse's work that would challenge its production methods and convictions.

Despite the failed collaboration between the Workshop and European researchers in Prix Jeunesse, the launch of *Sesame Street* at the 1970 festival had helped advance the agenda of preschool television. At the Prix Jeunesse festival in 1972, one of the two special research items on the agenda was pre-school television. Also, the overlap of people who attended the festival and re-search seminars at Prix Jeunesse and were part of the European Broadcasting Union's (EBU) subcommittee for children and young people strengthened the interest in *Sesame Street* and preschool television even further. In 1972, the EBU committee dedicated a four-day meeting to discuss the positive and negative ways that television might influence young children (see Figures 2.3 and 2.4).[33]

Besides the more abstract and theoretical interest in preschool televi-sion from a research perspective, another reason for the continued interest in *Sesame Street* was the Workshop's massive sales push. Since Palmer and Connell's attendance at Prix Jeunesse International in 1970, the Workshop had made a massive effort to sell *Sesame Street* worldwide.

Figure 2.3 The 1972 meeting of the European Broadcasting Union's subcommittee for Children and Young People's Programs. *Box 1, 8017503291, Series '1965–1981 Internationalt,' Børne- og Ungdomsafdelingen, Danmarks Radio 1187, The Danish National Archives.*

Finding a Subtle yet Efficient Sales Pitch

The highly profit-driven motivation behind the promotion of the show to markets outside the United States meant that the Workshop was in a very different position in its promotion internationally than at home. As *Sesame Street* was taken abroad, making a profit from sales of the broadcast and nonbroadcast items (books, magazines, and toys) came to the fore in a much more explicit and forceful way. At home, the Workshop had used the fact that it was a nonprofit entity supported by the government and large foundations and broadcast on the new public service network to distinguish itself from other children's shows. Not only the US mainstream media but also many parents and educators had in large part been receptive to this narrative of the show as bringing forth an unprecedented and unique way of using children's television for efficient preschool education as opposed to sales. The commercial motivation for the Workshop's overseas activities meant that

Figure 2.4 The 1972 meeting of the European Broadcasting Union's subcommittee for Children and Young People's Programs. *Box 1, 8017503291, Series '1965–1981 Internationalt,' Børne- og Ungdomsafdelingen, Danmarks Radio 1187, The Danish National Archives.*

this important part of the domestic branding strategy had to be somewhat rethought as the show went beyond US borders.

In 1970, few broadcasting markets were as highly driven by commercial interest as was the United States. Most countries' broadcasters were at this point national institutions governed by a board of directors or directly by the state and funded via taxes or license fees. Even in countries such as the United Kingdom and Japan where commercial broadcasters operated, there was a strong public service tradition and strict control over the commercial networks.[34] Branding *Sesame Street* as progressive because it was an alternative to commercial broadcasting, as the Workshop had done in the United States, was therefore not easy elsewhere, as children's programs for domestic markets were seldom made with the intention of turning a profit. The Workshop, therefore, had to emphasize *Sesame Street*'s innovative educational aspects, particularly cognitive skills training, and elaborate research setup to highlight its novel nature.

But still, it also had to promote itself as an alternative to commercialism in the United States and try to disassociate with claims of American cultural superiority and commercial predatory behavior in its global marketing. Fear of US economic and cultural influence was strong as the Soviet Union and the States battled for ideological dominance in much of the world during the Cold War.[35] In Europe, this was connected to the US influence on Western European societies in the postwar period, where it had risen not only in the form of hard cash from the Marshall Plan for reconstruction, but also with an influx of Hollywood movies and American comic books, music, clothing, and food culture. With the growth of the medium in the 1960s, US television programs were added to the list. While large parts of the population embraced these cultural products, there was also substantial fear about the ways they might threaten national cultures and European authority in what was established as good taste.[36]

A range of United Nations Educational, Scientific and Cultural Organization (UNESCO) reports from the late 1940s and 1950s on children and mass media had put the young at the center of these fears.[37] In particular, children's lack of knowledge and experience was believed to make them more vulnerable to the onslaught of American comics. The fear of American capitalism preying on innocent children was, however, not contained to comic books. Cartoons, cheap children's books with dozens in a series, movies, and television programs were to a greater or lesser extent suspected of not serving children's interests, however loosely defined, because their producers were believed to put profit above all else, always looking for the lowest common denominator to maximize sales. This fear of commercial exploitation of children meant that the Workshop once again would need to position itself as an alternative to commercial culture—a tough task when it at the same time had to sell Sesame Street and related merchandise to as many foreign broadcasters as possible.

To do the hard work of (re)branding and selling Sesame Street in foreign markets, the Workshop employed sales agencies abroad. Collaboration with these agents made a significant contribution to the global recognition of Sesame Street in 1970 and 1971, but sometimes keeping control over the Sesame Street brand proved difficult. The agencies were independent, highly commercialized firms that usually sold television programs or films to broadcasters. Working as independent companies detached from the broadcasting corporations, they were accustomed to measuring success by how many shows they could sell at the highest price, something that did not align well with the Workshop's anticommercial image. It wanted to build a business empire but not be viewed as a commercial predator, yet it was hard not to cross that line and even harder to not have the sales agents do it.

The Workshop's overall strategy for the international market was two-pronged. The first route was simply to sell the English-language version produced in the United States in as many countries as possible. Not permitting any changes to the program except for a limited amount of voiceovers (not dubbing) allowed the Workshop to maintain the integrity of its program as a well-tested educational design for the universal preschool child.[38] The second route was to allow foreign broadcasting companies to be in charge of co-production and financing, even if still carefully monitored by the Workshop. Here some compromises could be made over content and production if these were deemed necessary by local broadcasters who had the need for and means to make cultural and educational adaptations.

Fame over Gain: The TIE and the English-Language-Version Sales Strategy

The United Kingdom served as an important hub for the sale of the original English-language version. In the first place, getting the British Broadcasting Corporation (BBC) to take the show was a priority for the Workshop because many Continental broadcasters looked up to the BBC and followed its lead, the topic of chapter 3. But not only as a potential customer was the UK market itself interesting. Distribution companies located here were a natural entry point to the British Commonwealth, an enormous market for English-language productions. The UK-based distribution company Television International Enterprise (TIE) became the Workshop's ally in reaching this large audience. Though usually a highly commercial company, the TIE was crucial in developing a successful sales strategy that branded the Workshop internationally as a company seemingly more interested in making *Sesame Street* available to a wide audience in need of preschool education rather than reaping big profits. Despite the vital role it played in the early global transfer of *Sesame Street,* the TIE—and its important role in sales, branding, and revenue generation for the Workshop—is not included in any official histories of the show.

The Workshop hired the TIE in the autumn of 1970 with the intent of reaching as many markets with the English-language version as possible. The company already had considerable expertise in selling English-language television programs for production companies worldwide, with offices in London, New York, and Beirut, along with associations in Jeddah, Kuwait, Paris, Sydney, Tokyo, and Toronto. The sales director placed in charge of *Sesame Street* was Peter Orton, who later became a Workshop employee in charge of international distribution.

As soon as the TIE was on board, the Workshop invited Orton and the rest of the TIE staff working on *Sesame Street* to New York to receive a thorough introduction to its organisation.[39] In New York the Workshop made sure that the TIE fully understood the idea and production setup behind *Sesame Street* so that the agency could use them in marketing the show. Orton assured the Workshop management that the TIE could "interpret" the Workshop's idea of preschool television in any territory toward which the Workshop might wish to direct it.[40] He was convinced that the Workshop's philosophy of catering to preschool children's need for school-type skills training would set *Sesame Street* apart from all other children's television programs. The claim that the program was capable of teaching skills such as numeracy and literacy to preschoolers worldwide, just as it claimed to do in the United States, became the cornerstone of the TIE's marketing strategy and an inseparable part of the *Sesame Street* brand.

In view of *Sesame Street*'s claimed universality, the strong efforts exerted by the Workshop to drill the TIE staff in the Workshop's philosophy are interesting for two reasons. First, they demonstrated the Workshop's interest in crafting a coherent narrative that conveyed a core idea of everything from research to production to content, making sure that what the agents told buyers was consistent with its own ideas. That there was a need to teach the TIE's personnel all this undermines the claim that *Sesame Street* had built-in appeal: using a television show to formally educate preschoolers was not automatically considered a good idea. Second, the need Orton saw to "interpret" the philosophy again when selling it shows his awareness of differing cultural needs and wishes in different markets, challenging the universalist claim. Even if *Sesame Street* was supposed to be universal because it was based on a standardized psychological model of children's intellectual development, Orton nevertheless recognized that the program had to be marketed by someone with knowledge of regional differences in broadcasting and educational traditions. *Sesame Street*'s value was not self-evident; it needed to be promoted and sold.

The TIE's strategy to make *Sesame Street* known in markets outside of the United States involved a lot of in-person traveling to persuade broadcasting executives to buy the program. Sales agents went to work right away in the early autumn of 1970, going first to English-speaking parts of Africa.[41] Agents went there again in December of that same year, where in addition to selling *Sesame Street* to more countries, the TIE wanted to collect feedback from countries where Season 1 had already run in order for the Workshop to measure the show's popularity and develop new audiences.[42] Another aim was to collect the payments from the broadcasting companies that had aired Season 1, although payment was a second priority. The main short-term goal was to gain a foothold in new TV markets rather than immediately earn a profit.

Knowledge gathering about how the show was received and collecting money both proved rather difficult, as the African broadcasters lacked sufficient funds and the data collection efforts were not systematic enough for the Workshop. However, the strategy of letting broadcasters air *Sesame Street* before the TIE had received payment seemed like a good idea, as those that had aired Season 1 were all very interested in Season 2 (and willing to pay for Season 1). And even if the research data were flawed, the mere act of collecting it meant that *Sesame Street* became associated with seriousness and accountability.

The TIE followed up its global marketing by expanding to new regions in early 1971, as Orton traveled to Japan.[43] Based on his interpretation of the Workshop's philosophy, Orton successfully made it his mission to ensure that *Sesame Street* would be bought and broadcast by the public service broadcaster, Japanese Broadcasting Corporation (NHK), rather than the commercial Nippon Television. This sales tactic, distancing the Workshop from commercial stations, became one of the TIE's contributions to the success of *Sesame Street*'s brand as an educational and less commercially driven show. Following his trip to Japan, Orton insisted on the sales strategy of separating *Sesame Street* from any commercial broadcasting—and from the highly commercial trade in television—as central to the global marketing of *Sesame Street*'s English-language version.[44] This, he argued, would preserve the Workshop's image as an alternative to commercial children's television and the exploitation of its audience, something it needed if it wanted to avoid the stigma of the ruthless commercialism of other US cultural products for children.

In a detailed report from February 1971, Orton outlined how he wanted to develop his sales strategy for Season 2.[45] The report shows how much effort Orton exerted on getting *Sesame Street* out to every corner of the world by transforming into a global sales strategy the Workshop's philosophy of how television could serve the universal educational needs of preschoolers. Orton's report was a testament to the success the TIE had already had in promoting *Sesame Street* in much of the world. By this point, twenty countries had bought Season 1 in the original English format from the TIE, including broadcasting markets as diverse as Ireland, Greece, New Zealand, and Ethiopia.[46]

The high speed with which TIE had secured a wide reach for *Sesame Street* was possible because the English-language version had been sold with great flexibility, allowing the scheduling mode to deviate extensively from the original. The Workshop's claim of *Sesame Street*'s educational efficacy in the States was premised on the show's one-hour duration and that children would view it frequently throughout the week. However, when it was clear that the TIE would not be able to sell the English-language version show abroad without compromise, those standards were abandoned. Foreign broadcasters were not obliged to buy all 145 episodes of Season 1. To keep costs down, Ireland and New Zealand chose to buy just enough to broadcast two episodes per week, a frequency that in the eyes of the Workshop must have reduced the claimed educational effect to a minimum. To establish a presence in as many markets as possible, the Workshop allowed the TIE to sell it with sufficient flexibility—shorter seasons or airings only twice a week for half an hour, for example. This flexibility grew sales and helped gain a firm footing in developing markets—including readiness to take over more of the schedule should the possibility arise.

Besides the flexibility, the fame-over-monetary-gain foothold strategy was continued in the TIE and the Workshop's worldwide promotion strategy. From the beginning of the collaboration, the agreed-upon approach had been to "introduce 'Sesame Street' to as many foreign markets as possible within a short period of time and not to try to collect large license fees from individual markets, but . . . ensure that 'Sesame Street' begins telecasting."[47] This strategy, prioritizing market domination over immediate gain, had been extremely successful, so it was continued. It had already ensured that *Sesame Street* was broadcast in many countries and well known in many more. The strategy made it easy to claim the show as a new and globally recognized standard in preschool television, even if for many broadcasters it might have been simply a cheap option for filling their schedule. Making the show famous and forwarding the idea that this particular kind of educational television was beneficial for preschoolers in as many markets as possible was more important to the Workshop than the limited returns to be gained in the short run. No wonder this strategy was a success. From the mid-1960s, shows like BBC's *Play School*, CBS's *Captain Kangaroo*, and Claster Television's *Romper Room* had stimulated an interest in preschool television; in competition, the TIE was offering a well-produced, prize-winning *Sesame Street* under rather favorable conditions. The Workshop even had a range of research reports supporting their claim that the program could teach preschoolers—at least those in the United States—a fixed set of school-type skills.

The classic strategy of gaining hegemony or monopoly in a market where fame over gain was prioritized in the short run was one method for selling *Sesame Street*. Another was to brand *Sesame Street* as a show that was unique, educationally progressive in its use of television, and different from all other kinds of preschool programs. This mirrored the Workshop's promotion of *Sesame Street* in the United States and at Prix Jeunesse. To express this strategy, entirely new marketing approaches were explored.[48] Rather than just offering it directly to broadcasters like any other show, Orton planned to approach ministers of education in targeted countries, a strategy he had already had success with in Japan. The program's volume (145 episodes in Season 2) made it an expensive purchase that demanded significant airtime compared to other children's programs, even if it was offered with flexibility in terms of volume and at a relatively low price per episode. However, because ministers of education commanded a budget for funding educational programs, *Sesame Street* could (potentially) be paid for with public money, something that locally produced preschool programs with a less school-like educational purpose could not propose. This appeal to government funding gave the Workshop a substantial market advantage as it allowed access to vast public resources and the appearance of being nonexploitative at the same time.

The TIE's marketing strategies ensured *Sesame Street*'s fame on the global children's television market in late 1970 and early 1971. The long-term plan initially didn't generate much revenue, but meant that the Workshop was present in many markets and could thus claim worldwide interest in response to questions from potential buyers, journalists, and other interest groups. Thus, at the moment when local educational authorities or broadcasting corporations had the available means to expand or consolidate their preschool television schedule, *Sesame Street* became the number-one choice rather than producing a local show or buying, for instance, the BBC's much less advertised and researched *Play School. Sesame Street*'s underlying idea—that all preschool children everywhere shared common educational needs and that *Sesame Street* was the only program proven to deliver them effectively—was a perfect fit for a global sales pitch. The marketing strategy ensured that a wide international representation could confirm this fit.

There were, however, some contexts where the Workshop recognized that it might not be able to sell the original English-language version. Not that this fundamentally changed the belief in *Sesame Street*'s universal appeal or that all preschoolers basically needed the same type of school-type and social skills delivered in the same way, but the Workshop did realize that more had to be done to reach these markets. This is where co-productions became an avenue for the organization to explore.

Big Bird Bucks: The Lure of International Co-productions

Already in 1969, the Workshop planned to make co-productions of *Sesame Street* with those broadcasters in overseas countries that were unlikely to buy the English original.[49] Unlike the English-language version sold abroad, these co-produced versions were to some extent intended to cater to local cultures. The intent was to localize *Sesame Street* mainly by producing it in another language, but also to a minor extent by responding to local educational needs—as long as any changes stayed within the narrowly defined understanding of education set out by the Workshop. To lead the international effort of co-productions, Norton Wright, a former member of CBS's *Captain Kangaroo* production team, was hired to head the Workshop's international division.

The Workshop had set its eyes on a Spanish version for Latin America as the first co-production, believing that South and Central America would benefit greatly from the show's educational resources, as broadcasters there had, in the Workshop's view, virtually nothing of its own to offer children.[50] Treating Latin America as a sphere where US-based organizations could exercise influence was at this point still presumed in the States.[51] The production of *Plaza Sésamo* in Spanish and *Vila Sésamo* in Portuguese (intended for Brazil and Portuguese-speaking countries in Africa) began in 1970, airing in 1972.[52] The financial backing to enable the Workshop to make the pan–Latin American version had come from the Mexican commercial broadcaster Televisa and the US-based Xerox Foundation, after an original proposal to fund the production with money from Coca-Cola and the US government's Overseas Private Investment Corporation had failed.[53] Rather than Televisa acting as a full partner in the co-production, however, as broadcasters would later do in the European context, the Workshop controlled the production and its finances as it had secured the large grant from Xerox.

The Workshop went into production with the expectation that co-productions in Latin America would become highly profitable.[54] Not only did they want $350,000 ($2,3 million in 2022) in the budget for the Spanish-language version that would go toward the Workshop's general funds, but the Workshop also expected lavish income from nonbroadcast sales and sales of the version produced in Mexico to other Latin American countries.[55] As such, despite using a local team in Mexico (led by a US citizen) and inviting a small number of Latin American consultants to two meetings in Caracas, the Workshop controlled the operation very carefully. It was ultimately a Spanish-language production of the US program rather than something self-contained, as scripts were closely modeled on the English-language original and consultants from the Workshop oversaw research and production.[56] Actual production of the show was downscaled from the New York version, and tapes were sent to the Workshop for editing. Nevertheless, *Plaza Sésamo* was promoted by the Workshop as what it called a "latinized" version, where the curriculum had input from regional educators, local actors, and two new Muppets for the 30 to 50 percent that was produced in the studio in Mexico.[57]

Despite the many attempts to carefully replicate the original show and its success, the Latin American version fast became an economic disappointment. It generated nowhere near the expected profits, as the production costs were too high compared to what the Latin American broadcasters could afford. Already at the end of 1970, the Workshop knew it needed another setup in the rest of the world to avoid the troubles they had with the Latin American version, both in terms of funding and control from the United States.[58] The Workshop encountered so many problems raising money for the Latin American version that they were not prepared to do this again: the urgent need for stable income to support production of the US show was too high to take this risk elsewhere. The strategy for international co-productions outside of Latin America had to be different.

In late November 1970, during a visit to France, Joan Ganz Cooney asked the co-director of Compagnie Française de Co-production International (COFCI), Eric Rochat, and his wife to join her and the Workshop's new vice director, Michael Dann, for dinner in Paris. The meeting was a success, and in the beginning of December, both COFCI directors—Eric Rochat and Claude Giroux—visited the Workshop's offices in New York to discuss a French version of *Sesame Street*.[59] Giroux pressed for a new meeting and emphasized the need for speed, as other companies were exploring the possibility of making a domestic French equivalent to *Sesame Street*.[60] Preschool television had become a hot commodity, not least because of the Workshop's heavy promotion of *Sesame Street* through Orton's efforts at the TIE and its promotion at Prix Jeunesse.

Not wanting to miss out on any potential profit by losing to European competitors in the preschool television market, the Workshop acted fast. The contract between the Workshop and the COFCI was signed in February 1971.[61] It is a fascinating document that reveals just how much the Workshop was interested in not only a French co-production but also for Rochat and Giroux to quickly start exploring the potential market for other co-production possibilities, creating foreign versions in Europe that could also be sold in Africa and French Canada. This again contradicts the otherwise much-publicized claim that the Workshop would always wait for foreign partners to contact them and never pursued any markets on their own accord.[62]

The contract also demonstrates the Workshop's awareness of the many issues that might affect the possibilities of co-producing in Europe—not only how it might need to act differently in different markets, but also how so-called foreign versions should be created to reuse material to be profitable, and how best to make money from the versions by using their potential to promote *Sesame Street*–related merchandise. Based on a long list of questions linked to all these sales issues, Rochat and Giroux were to figure out how the co-production could be made available to as large a market as possible in the most cost-effective way. Sensitivity toward local cultures thus worked to ensure the Workshop's presence in a specific market with the aim of making a decent profit.

Once they were hired, Rochat and Giroux came back to New York to receive a thorough introduction to the Workshop's entire operation.[63] The two-day trip was packed; they went through the same meticulous drilling that the TIE staff had. The French consultants' schedule was crammed with meetings, working lunches, and dinners, during which they met with Cooney, two of the Workshop's now four vice presidents, in-house researchers, and the editors of *Sesame Street* magazine. They also met with Norton Wright, who briefed them on his work with the international division and the Latin

American version, the Workshop already trying to use its experiences from business adventures on one continent in a new setting.[64] This careful preparation of agents shows just how important it was that they, as the Workshop's extended arm, could represent it in the right way. This was, as always, especially important because of the fine line between maximizing the Workshop's international influence and sales and at the same time having to preserve its image—and its sales pitch—as an anticommercialist company providing serious education.

Rochat and Giroux's first report in March 1971 confirmed a Western European interest in *Sesame Street*.[65] The two agents reported that they had been in contact with educational and television authorities in France, Belgium, Switzerland, Germany, Italy, and Scandinavia, and outside of Western Europe, French Canada. Providentially for the Workshop, all of the countries had reported a growing interest in preschool programming, and *Sesame Street* was already very well known. Apparently, the exposure at Prix Jeunesse and similar venues, as well as the TIE's strategy of favoring fame over money (in the short run), had paid off. However, it also painted a picture of a competitive market where other broadcasters were already in the process of developing their own international competing programs or, like the BBC, selling bits of their programs to foreign markets. Rochat and Giroux warned that these other preschool shows could potentially outcompete *Sesame Street* even before the Workshop got it off the ground.

All of the people Rochat and Giroux had talked to said that if they were ever to consider co-producing *Sesame Street*, they needed a version that expressed specific national social environments.[66] Being used to a high degree of programs produced locally, the European broadcasters thought that *Sesame Street*'s distinct US agenda concerning urban poverty and civil rights did not fit a European reality.[67] The Workshop's take on these matters seemingly did not appeal to broadcasters in Western Europe, because most of them only had eyes for an audience of middle-class white children, just like the big US commercial networks. Inequality and structural racism were problems in Europe at the time: though less racially diverse than the United States, Western European countries had significant communities with minority backgrounds who suffered under conditions not dissimilar to those afflicting Black, Indigenous, Hispanic and other minority communities in the United States. But in European broadcasting, problems in representations of ethnic minorities were largely ignored, which is probably what led Rochat and Giroux to conclude that the social orientation of *Sesame Street* had to be rethought. They recommended that for any co-productions to be successful, nationally specific (but unspecified) ethnic and social problems, as well as educational differences, needed to be incorporated into the development of foreign versions. This recommendation for national versions that would cater to cultural differences, however, ran contrary to what Rochat and Giroux recommended in much of the report, which was versions divided according to languages, not national cultures.

In the rest of their report, they focused on versions following different languages, but the tension between the needs that would be served in the "language versions" and "national versions" was never resolved. Contrary to national versions, language versions would cover more than one nation-state (e.g., a German-language version for West Germany, Austria, and German-speaking parts of Switzerland and Italy). The differences between the two kinds of versions are important because they highlight different priorities in localization strategies. In Latin America, the Workshop had itself pursued the language-versions strategy with one co-production for Portuguese-speaking Brazil (also intended for Portuguese-speaking African countries) and another in Spanish for the rest of the continent. This strategy made much sense, as it resonated with the scientific beliefs of the Workshop in which cognitive psychology emphasized the fundamental similarities and same educational needs of children across race, class, gender, and nationality— linguistic differences being the only real difference any production would need to address.[68] The so-called locally produced scenes in these language versions were believed to cover the needs of countries as different as Mexico, Chile, and Colombia, not to mention a variety of different ethnic groups and dialects within the individual countries. National versions, on the other hand, would have presumed that children had different needs because of differences in national cultures.

Aligned with the Workshop's own convictions of language versions as the way to adapt to environments where the English version could not sell, the majority of Rochat and Giroux's report focused on the possibilities for three different language versions: French, German, and Italian versions of *Sesame Street*. These language versions were linked to broadcasting institutions and networks in France, Germany, and Italy, but only as representatives of producers within a certain language domain, not culturally specific national organizations. This language-version strategy, like the localization efforts in Latin America, aimed to tackle cultural differences only through linguistic diversity, not considering nationally specific issues. This excluded obvious national differences in educational systems (for instance, in Austria and Germany, or France and French-speaking parts of Belgium); differences in conceptualizations of childhood and the role of television in children's lives; and the political and colonial implications of standardized language versions produced by former colonizers (for instance, in French-speaking parts of Africa).

Rochat and Giroux's ignorance about issues of representation went hand in hand with the Workshop's own emphasis on *Sesame Street*'s "culture free" outlook in its international marketing. With their proposal's failure to take into account the intricate questions of nation, language, and power, Rochat and Giroux ended up confirming the Workshop's effective commitment to diversify on the basis of language, not nationally specific cultural or social needs. All in all, this implies obliviousness toward the subtle form of liberal imperialism upon which the ideas behind *Sesame Street* rested, strongly aided by the universality that stemmed from the Workshop's narrow take on cognitive psychology.

To make concrete suggestions for the language versions, Rochat and Giroux took a closer look at the possibilities of producing these in France, West Germany, and Italy. Their report showed that preschool television was now a focus area in French broadcasting, and the Workshop had to act fast if it wanted a footing in this market, as a potential competitor had used growing European criticism of *Sesame Street* as a lever to promote its own programs.[69] As France only had one television network, this could be devastating for Sesame Street's chances because there just was room for one preschool program in its schedule.[70] The limited schedule time set aside for children's programs thus made for a very competitive situation in which the Workshop would have to beat local initiatives. In the West German case, Rochat and Giroux had talked to representatives of both the nationwide networks. In Italy, the consultants also had detected a considerable interest in *Sesame Street*, but funding seemed to be an obstacle.[71]

The immediate action that Rochat and Giroux advised the Workshop to take was to retain influence by securing airtime in France, West Germany, and Italy.[72] This was a low-risk route, as it did not present any immediate obligations. It was nevertheless vital because airtime was limited in these networks and therefore a key component in entering the market and beating potential local or foreign competitors. Once the time slots were already filled by another preschool television show, it would be much harder for the Workshop to enter the specific market. For Rochat and Giroux, just as for the

TIE, the priority was to secure footing in as many markets as possible. What the Workshop actually wanted to do with it could follow at a later stage.

Rochat and Giroux's concluding remarks emphasized the need for the Workshop to act sooner rather than later. *Sesame Street* had shown itself to be a highly successful format, but also one that many other broadcasters were keen to develop on their own:

> In essence we need now, because of the time pressure, and ironically enough, because of the success of *Sesame Street* as a new format, to get commitments from the television stations regarding the airing of our to-be-developed international program, while keeping complete freedom and control over the content and utilisation of such a program.[73]

The report ended with the consultants urging the Workshop to authorize them to proceed with securing airtime in order to continue their survey so that they could take steps toward the production of international programs. Now it was up to the Workshop to decide what strategies it wanted to follow to secure its footing on the European market. The difficult thing was that it had to do its selling while keeping its brand intact as an educational, more sophisticated alternative to other American players on the international media market.

Keeping Control of the Agents, Keeping Control of the Brand

The Workshop's vice president Michael Dann became concerned for the branding strategy of *Sesame Street* in Europe when he saw Giroux and Rochat's ideas for the Workshop's next moves on the European market. Dann was a former vice president of programming at CBS who had quit his job in mid-1970 to work for the Workshop and, using his many contacts, help with international sales. In a telegram sent shortly after the arrival of the French agents' report, Dann reminded the two consultants of their relationship with the Workshop and what their limited purpose was. He stated somewhat patronizingly, "I know that you both realize your sole function is to gather data on the various European countries and under no circumstances imply commitment to anyone until specifically authorized to do so by the CTW."[74] Keeping their agents in check was a serious concern for the Workshop, as personal relationships were key to conquering international markets, especially as it wanted to refrain from pursuing more explicitly aggressive marketing strategies.

In an attempt to resolve the growing conflict, Dann met with Rochat and Giroux while in Europe.[75] But he also asked the TIE's Peter Orton for help. The TIE was only meant to sell the English-language version, but Dann had already begun to consult Orton on other issues related to the European market behind the backs of Rochat and Giroux.[76] Even if Orton in the TIE and Rochat and Giroux at the COFCI were supposed to focus on different aspects of the Workshop's overseas sales strategy, their roles as the Workshop's representatives to foreign markets sometimes overlapped. What became clear from these conflicts was that the two agencies represented different routes to worldwide sales, which could have consequences for the Workshop's reputation. Orton was playing the long game whereas Rochat and Giroux—who were concerned about *Sesame Street* being outcompeted—were applying an aggressive strategy. One place where tensions came out in the open was at the annual television festival—the International Market for Content Development and Distribution (MIP)—in Cannes in 1971, an important place for buyers and sellers of television programming on the global market.

MIP was a leading worldwide venue for television sales, an equivalent of the city's famous film festival. It was, therefore, very important for those who wanted to sell programming to the global market.[77] Rochat and Giroux had told Dann that they wanted to represent the Workshop at the event with a big promotion stand and invite Cooney to talk to potential buyers, but Dann was afraid of having *Sesame Street* there because he did not want to be associated with other US institutions selling their programs in syndication. Seeing the festival as a syndicators' convention, he argued that *Sesame Street* should not be "hawked . . . to foreign broadcasters" at the MIP like "*Lucy* or *Beverly Hillbillies*," clearly wanting the show to appear classier and the Workshop more civil than the regular commercial shows and their production companies.[78] In fact, he was very concerned that the ideas Rochat and Giroux had in mind for their presentation of *Sesame Street* would ruin the Workshop's "perfect record . . . in establishing the fact that people seek us out rather than our being peddlers."[79] Dann was therefore much more reassured by the TIE's Peter Orton representing the Workshop, as Orton assured him his strategy was to "expose 'Sesame Street' to all buyers without appearing to sell it."[80] Orton thereby positioned himself as the ultimate advocate of the Workshop's strategy to expand *Sesame Street*'s market share while avoiding being seen as a cheap huckster. The disagreement over the Cannes festival's nature, and its possible importance for *Sesame Street* sales, was intertwined with negotiations over how to present the show as a progressive, serious, and proven educational alternative to other products on the television market of the time—and the Workshop's image as not driven by profit. And even if the two agencies represented their differing interests on the global market—the English-language version versus co-productions—they were also in competition over their influence at the Workshop, and over how they should sell *Sesame Street* to the world.

Moving On: A Possible Format for Co-productions

The bad chemistry between Dann and the two French agents threatened to jeopardize the Workshop's strategy for co-productions in Europe. However, Cooney stepped in and handled the situation, and in early May 1971 Tom Kennedy, the Workshop's vice president of finance, took over the communication with Rochat and Giroux.[81] Ultimately, the solution was to involve Rochat and Giroux in only the French-language version of *Sesame Street* aimed at audiences in Canada, France, Belgium, Switzerland, and Africa with 180 units of twenty-four minutes. The twenty-four minutes were to contain two-thirds material from the original English version of *Sesame Street* dubbed into French, plus one-third material developed specifically for the French-language version. Most of this would be co-produced and shared between broadcasters in the French-speaking consortium, but a short, nationally specific wraparound could also be produced locally to satisfy a request for national localization.[82] This idea for a framework became extremely influential for the foreign versions going forward. The modular construction had, at least on paper, the promise to encompass both the profit-maximizing needs of the Workshop and the ability to be localized enough to outcompete shows produced by national broadcasters.

Having a small local team like Giroux and Rochat in charge of the Francophone version made the collaboration around localization similar to the arrangement the Workshop had in Latin America, even if the Workshop had wished to move away from exactly such a setup. The problem with these teams was that they were not directly embedded in a single institutional framework.[83] Negotiations of what a localized version should look like did, therefore, in the first instance, not include the broadcaster that would buy and air the program, as would be the case in, for example, the negotiations with West Germany and the Scandinavian countries. Localization issues were solved between the Workshop, its Paris-based sales agents, and a producer they had hired. This situation was easy for the Workshop to control but complicated in terms of sales because the French national broadcaster, Office de Radiodiffusion–Télévision Française (ORTF), was the only potential buyer, and Rochat and Giroux were not attuned to its demands in terms of localization and financing. These complications eventually led to the development of the generic Open Sesame format, which was later sold to Spain, Italy, Portugal, and Sweden. Key to this format's development was the length to which the Workshop was willing to minimize the idea of what it meant to "localize" production in order to sell *Sesame Street* in France.

On the Workshop's behalf, Rochat and Giroux had to obtain financing and production facilities for a French version of *Sesame Street* with two possible localized wraparounds, a so-called Parisian and a Canadian.[84] In 1972, they teamed up with a possible producer, Christoff Izard, who visited the Workshop early that year.[85] During Izard's visit, it was agreed that the three Frenchmen were to submit a production proposal to the Workshop, following its detailed instructions. Like in Latin America, a pilot had to be developed, experts for a French advisory board assembled, and a report written that formally presented the case for the French version's market potential. Everything related to the production of the pilot was under the Workshop's meticulous control and supervision. Similar to the Latin American version, the French-language version was meant for a large geographical area, including France, French-speaking Canada and Switzerland, Luxembourg, Belgium, Monaco, French overseas possessions, and former French colonies. The Workshop expected Rochat and Giroux to contact broadcasters in these countries to find out if there was a market for their program. The Workshop only deemed it necessary to set up advisory boards with local educational experts in France and Canada; the other countries' individual educational needs were apparently not as important.[86]

In early spring 1972 Izard began the production of the so-called Parisian French pilot, titled *Rendezvous Rue Sesame* (Meet Sesame Street). A thirty-minute program was to be based on 50 percent material from the American *Sesame Street* dubbed into French, and the other 50 percent produced by a local team. Izard's pilot had a locally produced introduction, closing segment, and wraparound based on American scripts, as well as two French-produced films—one about a girl and a flower, teaching different perspectives, the other about the Eiffel Tower as an example of a man-made environment.[87] No new curriculum was developed for the pilot, and the advisory board for the French version had not assembled before the pilot's production plan was finished, only after, making the advisors' feedback merely a theoretical exercise with no consequences for the pilot.[88] This sequencing seems to be a result of the Workshop's early, somewhat ad-hoc efforts to create foreign versions, but it also shows that having this local board of experts determine the needs of "local" children was not necessarily important to the Workshop.

With the pilot being completed in the summer of 1972, all that was left was to sell it to ORTF to finance the production of the first series. This, however, was not easy. A domestic preschool show, *Le Jardin Magique* (The magical garden), had already been developed, and its producers were also approaching ORTF to finance its first series. An article in *L'express* told an amusing story of how the two production teams courted ORTF trying to win them over for their respective shows.[89] In December 1972, ORTF decided not to buy *Le Jardin Magique*, but still no final decision was made about *Rendezvous Rue Sesame*. A reshuffling of ORTF personnel caused by the French election in spring 1973 seems to have put all plans on hold.

As a result, the Workshop shifted its efforts in France. There seems to have been a problem raising the large amount of money (estimated 7.7 million francs, about $1.8 million in US dollars in 1973, and $12 million in 2022) that it would cost to produce a series with 50 percent new, locally produced French-Parisian material.[90] This would explain why the Workshop suddenly made plans for what it called an "economy-styled" production for France in the summer of 1973. This less expensive solution was estimated to cost one-tenth of a full-blown co-production.[91] This solution became the Open Sesame concept, *Sesame Street*'s first spin-off.

The Open Sesame Concept

Open Sesame was envisioned as assembly line for relatively cheap, semilocalized productions. Instead of creating new segments and having local experts provide input on defining local needs, the Workshop would provide blocks of programming extracted from the American original along with generic curriculum sheets. These would not have any of the street scenes, only films, animations, and Muppet sketches. Local teams, like the one Izard led in France, would not produce anything new but would be in charge of technical issues and dubbing. There would also be no local advisory boards. In the Open Sesame model the Workshop was paid a generous fee and had all expenses reimbursed.

The decision to shift strategy—from selling the *Sesame Street* concept as a co-production with a mix of content produced by the Workshop and a local broadcaster, to selling it as the generic concept of Open Sesame— challenged the Workshop's understanding of its business.[92] When first conceptualized, Open Sesame would be a twenty-seven-minute show of English material dubbed into French and the languages of other in- terested broadcasters. This compromised an early decision made by the Workshop not to allow shortening the sixty-minute English version; as mentioned, the Workshop thought the show's educational benefit was tied to how much children were exposed to it. In reality, the idea had already been compromised by the way that the TIE sold the show: not demanding five showings a week and turning a blind eye when broadcasters decided to cut episodes in half and air them only two days a week. With official sanctioning of the Open Sesame format, the Workshop was merely con- tinuing a practice where its early educational ideals were bent in order to turn a greater profit on the international market. However, ORTF made the Workshop reconsider even further what length of the show was defen- sible from an educational viewpoint. The French broadcaster was only in- terested in a thirteen-minute-long show, possibly because it would allow for a combination with another, domestic French program that together would constitute a twenty-eight to thirty-minute-slot for preschoolers.[93] Within the Workshop, discussion took place about the dangers of revising their policy. These discussions were curiously not about compromising ed- ucational effectiveness by shortening the program, but about money and branding strategies.

One of the problems foreseen with Open Sesame was that even if it might raise money immediately, when the Workshop desperately needed it, it would hurt the *Sesame Street* brand in the long run.[94] The Workshop's Michael Dann feared that selling past content as "bits and pieces" would harm po- tential future sales of more lucrative kinds, that is, the co-productions.[95] The Workshop, therefore, restricted the Open Sesame format, making it less at- tractive as well as culturally less flexible than a co-production. Open Sesame would not allow local production of any wraparounds tagging onto the block of the US-produced material. The episodes were designed by the Workshop's production and research team so that twenty-seven-minute episodes could be halved into two segments of thirteen minutes, thirty seconds, and no dele-tion was allowed. Despite this minimalistic setup, the Workshop still insisted that Open Sesame's thirteen-minute, thirty-second blocks offered an "enter-taining, educationally balanced" show that basically delivered what *Sesame Street* did.[96] It was cheap, but also strictly a Workshop product with no inter-ference from the buyers.

The downsizing of ambitions worked for the Workshop in France, as it managed to sell the Open Sesame concept as sixty-five blocks of thirteen minutes, thirty seconds.[97] As the concept was developed for streamlining international sales, the Workshop hoped to repeat this success elsewhere in Europe.[98]

In September 1974 the first episodes of the French version based on the Open Sesame concept were ready to air on ORTF. In its English-language newsletter, the Workshop presented this version, which was indeed just dubbed episodes, as a short block of the American *Sesame Street*, but adapted carefully to fit French cultural needs:

> They look like Bert and Ernie, those brash "Sesame Street" puppet characters, but they *sound and act like a pair of Parisian night club comics*— which is just fine. Rechristened "Bart" and "Ernest," they join 17 other Muppet regulars on "*Bonjour Sesame*," a new French-language version of TV's *Sesame Street* which makes its debut on French national television this month. *Bonjour Sesame*, which premieres September 16, is the first of a new kind of Sesame Street offspring: a version made up entirely of an "in-ternational library" drawn from the original English-language series and *adapted to another culture*. The new version is devoid of "street" scenes—no Gordon, Susan or Big Bird, for example—and there are no sequences that depend on the English language or American cultural nuances.[99]

The Workshop, of course, had introduced no cultural adaptation, as claimed. Moreover, the newsletter quoted its own international develop-ment director, Jack H. Vaugh, saying that Bert and Ernie acted like they were French: "*Bonjour Sesame* looks so French it's hard to believe the show is an American product. . . . Bert and Ernie are very French—the gestures and actions are perfect."[100] In fact, the only change from the American original was the dubbing. An article in *L'express* from before the show began repeated the Workshop's evaluation of its own adaptation efforts.[101] The French press simply assumed that the experts who had been consulted for the pilot of

Rendezvous Rue Sesame had also helped with the adaptation of Open Sesame even if they had not. This product was purely American.

The Importance of Brand Recognition and Merchandise Sales

The Workshop's problems with localizations did not end with *Bonjour Sesame* on the air. The Open Sesame block in *Bonjour Sesame* was transmitted together with a show that Izard had produced called *L'Ile Aux Enfants* and listed in the television program as a single block as *L'Ile Aux Enfants Présente Bonjour Sesame* (The children's island presents hello Sesame) and credited only Izard. The Workshop believed this presentation would tank the program's success and harm nonbroadcast sales, as viewers would not recognize the *Sesame Street* brand.[102]

Brand recognition was extremely important to the Workshop insofar as a large portion of its income from overseas markets came from nonbroadcast *Sesame Street* merchandise because the Workshop was the rights holder. To bolster brand recognition and thereby strengthen nonbroadcast sales, the Workshop wanted to have any other segments that were part of the same timeslot as theirs, such as *L'Ile Aux Enfants*, presented as secondary to *Bonjour Sesame*. A case that demonstrates why the brand recognition that led to merchandise sales was so important is the Workshop's difficulties in airing some version of *Sesame Street* in Italy.

In Italy the issue of nonbroadcast sales put negotiations about a possible Italian-language co-production on hold for six years. Radiotelevisione Italiana (RAI), Italy's national broadcaster, feared that children were especially vulnerable to commercial influences and should be shielded from them—criticism similar to what the Workshop itself had offered about commercial networks' merchandise sales in a US context. The nonbroadcast business linked to *Sesame Street* encouraged "premature commercialism," RAI argued.[103] The broadcaster insisted, therefore, on a yearlong suspension of sales of *Sesame Street* merchandise in Italy if it was to air the program. The Workshop's legal counsel and products group objected, as merchandising was an important part of its business model. The Workshop "counted on non-broadcast income for survival," in the words of its vice president of finance, Tom Kennedy.[104] Because of the vital role that merchandise sales played, the Workshop wouldn't accept restrictions on merchandise and insisted that RAI would have to compensate the Workshop for the loss of income by making a much larger payment for the broadcasts than originally agreed.[105] The conflict clearly demonstrated the Workshop's need to sell licensed merchandise; linkage to the program was an important vehicle in this process.[106] Despite its stated opposition to commercialization, the Workshop held firm, revealing how little it cared about what Cooney in a US context had said about the "dead wrong" hard-sell of merchandise.[107]

In France, Izard's failure to make the *Sesame Street* brand properly recognizable was however, not the Workshop's only objection. The Workshop also believed that Izard had breached their contract because he deleted segments from the thirteen-and-a-half-minute blocks that he did not find appropriate for a French audience. Consequently, the Workshop threatened Izard with a lawsuit.[108] To smooth things out and hopefully not have to take him to court, Izard was invited to visit the Workshop in New York in May 1975.[109] Here the Workshop supplied him with a script, lead sheet, lyrics, and band track for a short opening film, which the Workshop wanted him to produce for them. This was a French version of the American introductory segment, "Can You Tell Me How to Get to Sesame Street?" This idea of a localized version of the theme song was later implemented in all Open Sesame formats sold in Europe. This was a great feature for the Workshop because it helped distinguish its show from other children's programs. Also, because the short opening films were produced locally—although with approval needed from the Workshop—they added to the sense of effort to localize the show.

In New York, Izard and the Workshop also discussed what it would take to make a co-produced series that would incorporate cast members from *L'ile Aux Enfants* (the puppet Casimir and a cast of humans) into French-produced street scenes for a French version of *Sesame Street*. Internal correspondence about a possible co-production indicates that this mode of collaboration was seen as ideal as it would raise the Workshop's revenue and, with changes in the contractual relationship, give them more power over *Sesame Street*'s presentation and influence in the French broadcasting landscape: "In the long run a co-production would . . . be a better financial venture for CTW. At best we only break even with the continuing arrangement [the Open Sesame concept]. Whereas, a co-production would cost us less money and give us greater control."[110] The long-term plan for the Workshop was hereafter a full co-production with the newly formed French public service institution, Télévision Française 1 (TF1), but with greater Workshop control over the French production team.[111] A French co-production with the Workshop aired for the first time in 1978 with the title *1 Rue Sesame* (1 Sesame Street) and ran until 1982.

An Empire Ready for Battle?

In mid-1971, when Cooney expressed her ambition for *Sesame Street* to rival the British Empire in its advance across the world, the program's global reach could be attributed to much more than just the show's claimed universal appeal. Prix Jeunesse had been an important hub for the Workshop's exposure to the world, and it had formed a close relationship with two sales agencies, notably the TIE, which continued to find new markets for the English-language versions. Together, Orton, for the TIE, and the Workshop had settled on a sales strategy that ensured maximum exposure for *Sesame Street*, while keeping intact its reputation as a nonprofit entity. This was done by taking the time to find networks that fit their brand, working with ministries of education, and grooming an image of superiority to other preschool shows by emphasizing researchers' role in developing the show, as well as being careful not to appear too eager to sell *Sesame Street* to the highest bidder.

Co-productions in other languages were also moving forward. The Spanish version for Latin America was on track, and at this point, the summer of 1971, Rochat and Giroux had just been charged with making a pilot for the French version—no one yet knew the many complications that would arise along the way. A West German co-production now also seemed feasible. In August 1971, the Workshop had serious talks with the public service network ARD's Hamburg branch about a German-language version.[112] The TIE also had detailed plans for the Workshop to turn a greater profit from nonbroadcasting and foreign versions.[113] It seemed all parts of the Workshop's empire were now in place so that the Workshop could profit from *Sesame Street* without fear of the brand being damaged as an educational alternative to commercial broadcasting.

For all the care taken to protect and nurture its brand as an educational nonprofit entity deeply interested in localizing its product if needed, the Workshop was to meet increasing pushback from late 1971 onward. Even with the advice of its agents, the Workshop was not able to fully anticipate potential disagreements with some of the major European broadcasters and educators over television's role in children's lives. The rigidity of the production setup and the need to keep *Sesame Street* intact as an easily recognizable brand that could support marketing and broadcast sales meant that the Workshop had difficulties adapting to the demands of the well-established, highly independent European market. In this market, the Workshop would be confronted with potential buyers' and co-producers' views of childhood, educational traditions, and modes of production that were radically different from its own. This meant that the Workshop faced a possible loss of control over its brand, as well as potential income, to which it reacted fiercely. Because of the global scale of its operations and its commitment to an image as an alternative to other, commercially driven American companies, the Workshop was convinced that if one co-production went wrong or resulted in a dilution of its brand, it could potentially damage its entire operation—a pattern we have already seen in this chapter. But whereas the sales and promotion activities in this chapter were fundamentally under the Workshop's control, this was not the case with the partners it tried to engage in Britain, West Germany, and Scandinavia.

The following chapters address the Workshop's advancement in these key markets. Together they reveal a substantial resistance toward *Sesame Street* because of diverging views of education and the role of television in preschoolers' lives—completely different traditions informing children's TV programming. The chapters also show how the Workshop tried to navigate these situations by pursuing new forms of partnerships, attempting to streamline its approaches to collaboration with all foreign broadcasters, and sometimes using rather heavy-handed methods—all to protect the work they had done to craft the concept of *Sesame Street* and the CTW model.

3

Ban and Bother

The Workshop's Troubles in the United Kingdom

On September 8, 1971, a front-page headline in the *New York Times* read, "BBC Orders Ban on 'Sesame Street.'"[1] It was an intriguing story. How could the world's most respected public service broadcaster, the British Broadcasting Corporation (BBC), ban an educational and prize-winning show that had received so much praise in the United States and been broadcast widely in other parts of the world? Children's television rarely merited front-page news, but this story was mindboggling enough to make for really good copy.

As with so many front-page stories, the BBC's alleged ban on *Sesame Street* was not as straightforward as it seemed to the reader who only skimmed the headline. The BBC had not banned the show, it had just refused to buy it and had chosen to explain why at a press conference because of the growing pressure the organization faced to justify this decision. In a press release published ahead of the conference, the head of the BBC's children's department, Monica Sims, had been quite direct in her description of *Sesame Street* as a show that prepared children for school, but not for life: it focused on making viewers school-ready rather than offering social and cultural stimulation. In particular, she expressed worry over "the programme's authoritarian aims. Right answers are demanded and praised and a research report refers to the programme-makers' aims to change children's behavior."[2] With a hint at fears of mass media propaganda in Europe following the Second World War, she reflected that *Sesame Street* might be indoctrination and "a dangerous extension of the use of television," as it did not encourage children to think for themselves, but rather reproduce the answers adults wanted.[3] Despite Sims's perhaps somewhat unfair description of *Sesame Street*, the BBC and the Workshop definitely represented different approaches to children's television. These were rooted in opposing views of childhood and education, and the vast differences in the media landscapes in the United States and the United Kingdom.[4]

Sesame Street. Helle Strandgaard Jensen, Oxford University Press. © Oxford University Press 2023.
DOI: 10.1093/oso/9780197554159.003.0004

The fundamental opposition on ideological issues, as well as a more cov-
etous competition between the BBC and the Workshop over co-production
rights with the affluent broadcasters in continental Europe, led to a bitter
rivalry that set the scene for *Sesame Street*'s advancement in Britain. In the
end, the rivalry with the BBC meant that, contrary to the Workshop's initial intentions, the United Kingdom's commercial network, Independent
Television (ITV), ended up transmitting the show. This chapter describes
Sesame Street's localization history in the United Kingdom, showing how
competition in the local broadcasting market, differences in views of preschool education, the Workshop's obsession with its image, and potential
conflicts over foreign sales all influenced why the show only became partly
successful there. From a cultural transfer perspective more broadly, the
chapter demonstrates how quality productions and strong policies regarding
children's television on the local market made success difficult for an outside company that lacked detailed knowledge of—or even apparently interest
in—local conditions rooted in broader, longstanding cultural traditions.
Drawing on a global history approach, the chapter also shows how sales and
branding interests in the wider territory of continental Europe that went
beyond the narrow territory in question (the United Kingdom) heavily impacted how the involved parties, especially the BBC and the Workshop,
maneuvered here.

The UK market for children's television at the end of the 1960s was unlike
many others in the world. The BBC, the world's oldest public service broadcaster, had already established a tradition of producing preschool programs
whereas others had none or were only just beginning to consider such an
addition to their children's schedule. The BBC's preschool production was
embedded in an educational tradition very different from the pedagogical
and educational principles behind *Sesame Street*.[5] State primary schools in
the United Kingdom had been moving toward a child-centered, progressive
education that stood almost in direct opposition to the educational principles the Workshop relied upon, which favored rote learning and focused on
a fixed set of skills.[6]

The embrace of progressive education in the United Kingdom had been
cemented with the Plowden Report, commissioned by the minister of education in 1963 and published in 1967. In this form of nonutopian progressive
pedagogy, adults played a guiding role in the child's development.[7] This approach heavily favored social and developmental psychology and sociology
as its scientific basis, urging education based on discoveries and curiosity

where adults guided children in *finding out*, rather than *being told*.[8] The progressive educational climate was an important factor in children's television production in the United Kingdom, and subsequently affected the discussion around *Sesame Street*'s (in)appropriateness for a British educational environment. As the Workshop began to approach that market in late 1969, it seemed to either be unaware of these differences in educational approaches between itself and the BBC, or simply more interested in the potential economic gains from signing up the BBC than *Sesame Street*'s adaptability to local educational frameworks.

Looking to secure a steady source of income to keep US production of *Sesame Street* going, the Workshop had contacted the BBC just after airing the first episodes in the States in 1969. The United Kingdom was by far the biggest and most affluent of all the international markets at the time. In the mid-1960s there were nearly ninety-five million TV sets in use outside of the United States. Of these, a little less than half were placed in Western Europe, with one-third in Britain alone.[9] Selling *Sesame Street* to the United Kingdom would secure a steady source of considerable income. In fact, the Workshop estimated the net revenue of UK sales to be worth almost 10 percent of the production costs of the US season.[10] Securing a five-day-a-week broadcast in the United Kingdom would thus make a huge difference in the Workshop's financial stability.

The UK market was attractive for the Workshop for reasons other than the income it could provide. Even though they ended up selling to the commercial ITV network, the Workshop had first wanted to see *Sesame Street* aired on the BBC because of the organization's global reputation as the gold standard for public service broadcasting. European broadcasters looked up to the BBC and followed its lead in making new programs or trying out new genres. Having the BBC's seal of approval would be more influential with the rest of the world's broadcasters than any promotional efforts the Workshop itself could make. Losing that approval, however, could potentially harm its further expansion. Affiliation with the BBC would also help the Workshop further its brand as an alternative to commercial broadcasting. The conflicts between the BBC and the Workshop about children's television and preschool education that led to the alleged "ban" in 1971 were thus more than just about the buying and selling of a television program. Succeeding in the United Kingdom, and especially with the BBC, would have been a significant step in securing financial stability for the Workshop and potentially the key to the affluent European market. The story of the Workshop's long journey to strike a deal with the BBC and later ITV told in this chapter demonstrated how the Workshop recognized Britain's, and especially the BBC's, possible function as a gateway to the European market—a gateway the Workshop went to great lengths trying to secure, applying along the way a not insignificant amount of pressure on people who had a say in the outcome.

The UK Broadcasting Market and Existing Offers to Preschoolers

Since the early days of broadcasting, the United Kingdom and the United States have represented two different ways of broadcasting in terms of economics and regulation.[11] Britain was a heavily regulated market that offered highbrow programming (with some concessions to middlebrow) favored broadly by the middle classes. The United States was a highly commercial market, with little oversight or influence by a "cultured elite," broadcasting popular programs heavily laced with advertising. This meant the premise for success was very different in the two markets. In Britain, the Workshop could not claim itself to be a new educational alternative to commercial programs. The BBC was already that alternative. Coming from the United States, the Workshop could easily be tainted by association with a commercial, entertainment-focused media culture. Combining highbrow snobbery and middle-class anxiety, British observers feared that American entertainment was ruining British culture, and to many, *Sesame Street* was just another expression of American commercialization.

At the beginning of the 1960s, there were two nationwide UK networks: the BBC and ITV. The BBC was a national public service broadcaster and had one channel. Its content was paid for by license fee, and no commercials or sponsorships were allowed. It operated as an independent institution overseen by a board of governors who approved policy and strategy and ensured that the institution provided a balance of education, information, and entertainment. The governors also oversaw complaints, such as the one that would be filed on the Workshop's behalf in 1971 because of the alleged ban on *Sesame Street*.

The second network in Britain, Independent Television (ITV), was launched in 1955 under the auspices of the Independent Television Authority (ITA). ITV was a commercial network with fourteen local stations working as companies that together covered the country within the network's regional federated structure. Given the general British fear of commercialization, the ITA was a powerful regulatory body that selected the regional companies that transmitted on the network's regional stations and controlled the output to ensure a proper balance of high-quality information, education, and entertainment, just as the BBC offered. However, ITV stations' increased import of American entertainment led to questions of whether the ITA was regulating the network properly. When an investigation of the UK television market, known as the Pilkington Committee, in 1962 recommended that a third channel go to the BBC, it also criticized the ITA for the poor job it had done regulating the commercial network's offerings. The report led to a strengthening of public service in UK television, at ITV as well, where stations had to transmit serious drama, news, and current affairs at peak times.[12]

The cultural preferences for domestic public service, as opposed to imported American entertainment, had a significant and direct impact on the Workshop's attempts to get *Sesame Street* on ITV when a deal with the BBC fell through, as the ITA had imposed restrictions on programs imported from other countries. Each regional company was only allowed to import a maximum of 13.5 percent out of the fifty-three-and-a-half hours they broadcast per week.[13] Most of the quota was used to present US-produced fiction, and *Sesame Street* would thus have to outcompete these programs to secure a place on the schedule.[14] None of the companies in the ITV network produced any programs for preschoolers, even if the ITA had expressed such a wish since 1968.[15]

The BBC, on the other hand, had a long tradition of producing television for a very young audience. It had offered brief television segments for this cohort as far back as 1953.[16] From 1955 onward, these were collected under the title *Watch with Mother* that had five daily strands aimed at very young children, spanning a total of about fifteen minutes.[17] This segment included fiction series such as *Andy Pandy*, about a little puppet, sometimes accompanied by a teddy bear; simple songs and movements; stimulation of fantasy world and language; looks into family life and the world outside; and ideas for making little arts and crafts projects. Some of the segments were sold to broadcasters in other European countries and Australia and had given the BBC an early start on the international market for children's television.

Programs produced with the direct aim of supplementing and supporting preschool education had begun with BBC's *Play School* in 1964. As with *Sesame Street*, *Play School* was also embedded in a discussion around insufficient preschool education, due to the failure of successive governments to implement the 1944 Nursery School Act. *Play School* was the first television program in the United Kingdom and Europe directly seeking to provide a preschool experience for children at home and tried to "give them something that the best nursery schools would provide."[18] It was transmitted daily, Monday through Friday, for twenty-five minutes. Recognized for its innovative take on television for the preschool-age group, *Play School* received an honorary mention at the Prix Jeunesse in 1966, and thus also enjoyed wide exposure to a European audience like *Sesame Street* did in 1970.[19] This meant that at the time when *Sesame Street* was introduced in Europe, *Play School* was already a well-known program and had paved the way for educational preschool television, even if its pedagogical ideals were very different.

Contrary to *Sesame Street*, the focus in *Play School* was not on a fixed set of school-type and social skills in the form of a fixed checklist curriculum, but a set of loosely formulated social and cultural lessons. The program had no stated learning goals or a fixed policy statement. The preschool ideal found in *Play School* was a child-centered focus on stimulating the child's sense of self and their surroundings, supporting cultural and social skills, imagination, and activity by introducing children to games, stories, arts and crafts experiments, and more.[20] The cast was a group of adults, often a pair or three of them working together on the screen. The setting was minimalistic, resembling a nursery with cupboards, drawers, and lots of arts and crafts materials. There were also toys, some of which the presenters would treat as children treat their own toys: pretending they were alive and speaking with them. The arts and crafts sections strongly suggested that viewers play along, using things they might find at home—feathers, newspapers, cardboard, leaves—to make creations of their own.[21] In line with the BBC's longstanding policy for their children's programs, this was supposed to stimulate children to engage in activities away from the screen.[22]

The program was planned to also introduce children to what was called "hard work"—teaching numbers, days of the week, seasons, and such—but not in a systematic manner. The connection to any school-type skills was ambivalent and not foregrounded.[23] Thus, even if there were in fact some overlaps in the actual content of the two shows—*Play School* did occasionally teach things with "right answers" such as numbers, time, and relational concepts, and *Sesame Street* also had slow-paced segments that focused on children's play and social world—the pedagogical ideologies behind them were different. Gently guided by the adult presenters' model behavior, *Play School* focused on deepening the child's experience of their everyday world here and now, whereas *Sesame Street* focused on making the child fit into the formal requirements of the existing school system it was to enter later. As the competition and conflicts between the BBC and the Workshop grew, these ideological differences, deeply rooted in different moral views of childhood and preschool education, were enhanced and exacerbated by the two organizations' representatives when they argued for their own show's superiority, as this chapter shows.

Sesame Street and *Play School* differed not only in terms of educational ideology; the ways they were produced and scheduled were also different. In contrast to *Sesame Street*, the production of *Play School* was a very small operation within the bigger children's department at the BBC.[24] Far fewer people and resources were directly involved in the production of *Play School* than *Sesame Street*. However, it also meant that *Play School* was part of a schedule approach: a comprehensive plan assembled by the department that included several other offerings to the same age group, such as cartoons and live-action drama.[25]

Play School was also different in how it drew on experts. These were not the Workshop-favored psychologists but people with practical experience with preschoolers, such as nursery school specialists, primary school teachers, and art, dance, and drama advisers.[26] A specialist in nursery school education, Nancy Quale, oversaw programs, reading scripts and discussing them with the production team.[27] Mostly, however, the ideas for content, what the interest of the target group might be, and so on were based on the team members' experiences with similar kinds of programming traditions for making children's television and, moreover, the institution's collective experience with broadcast production. As in the rest of Europe, this tradition was based on institutional traditions and practices, not expert-driven research and systematic audience testing like *Sesame Street*.

Play School had not only been the first nursery school program in Britain. Internationally it had also paved the way for other programs of this kind, being the first and, until *Sesame Street*, the only preschool-style program for the international market produced outside the United States. In the global market it competed with the American *Romper Room*, which also ran on some local ITV stations.[28] The BBC itself considered *Play School* a more substantive alternative in a market it believed was dominated by fairy tales and stories featuring cute little puppets.[29] As such, the BBC believed *Play School* was a shoo-in when overseas broadcasters in the late 1960s began to look for alternatives that would provide children with something other than the fictional worlds that were usually the focus of their programs. This move was inspired by new psychological and educational discoveries at the time, which had prompted many broadcasters to look for ideas on how to best strengthen the healthy development of desirable social and creative skills children needed in their everyday lives.[30]

The new interest in preschoolers' development and television's possible assistance in this process meant increased international interest in *Play School*.[31] BBC Enterprises, the commercial arm of the BBC, had sold the first programs to ABC in Australia in the autumn of 1965. The Australians bought the entire series, but other sales models customized to non-English-speaking countries had evolved. Sales to Italy had begun in 1966; Switzerland in 1968; Norway, Austria, and New Zealand in 1969; and Canada, Israel, and Spain by 1971.[32] This was a very different, much more loosely structured co-production model than the Workshop would insist on with *Sesame Street*. *Play School*'s scripts were sold rather than recordings of it, versus an entire production concept, as with *Sesame Street*. The scripts purchased from the BBC could be adapted rather loosely by the foreign broadcaster, as they played an inspirational rather than prescriptive role.[33] The BBC's success with *Play School* meant that when the Workshop approached the BBC, *Sesame Street* was not just a potential new offering the broadcaster needed to consider as a replacement to its own program domestically, it was also an international competitor.

The BBC's experience with preschool television had made Joan Ganz Cooney contact the *Play School* team in October 1967 when she did the second draft of her feasibility survey of *Sesame Street* for the Carnegie Corporation. This early exchange of ideas about preschool television demonstrates some of the main similarities and differences in the Workshop's and the BBC's views on the role of preschool television in children's lives long before the two organizations began to argue over *Sesame Street*.

It was Molly Cox, a *Play School* producer, who answered when Cooney sent her report, "The Potential Uses of TV in Pre-School Education," to the BBC for feedback. Cox's response showed a genuine interest in and admiration for Cooney's copious research. However, Cox's up-front politeness and words of wholehearted agreement with the findings were followed by severe criticism challenging *Sesame Street*'s fundamental assumptions—that preschool programs should primarily be used to teach a set of skills.[34]

Cox vividly disagreed with the pedagogical approach of Carl Bereiter and Siegfried Engelmann that Cooney had employed to argue for using television to teach children via drill routines. Based on her experience, Cox simply did not believe that television could prepare children for school, as Cooney had proposed, because the child viewer group was so vast and diverse and would need different kinds of stimulation than the Workshop offered. Cox warned that only "the over pushed middle class toddlers" would watch this kind of program, not the main target group of underprivileged children whose needs Cooney in particular wanted to serve. Contrasting Cooney's belief that television could tell children what they needed to know, Cox explained that the BBC had tried to "encourage [children] to think up alternative ideas to express themselves their own way."[35] Cox essentially saw television's role as supporting children in expressing themselves and exploring the world around them, a sharp difference from Cooney's idea of using television to help children improve themselves to do better within the educational system. Unfortunately, we know nothing about Cooney's response to Cox, if one was delivered at all.

Another early encounter between the Carnegie Corporation and the BBC is illustrative of the conflict between the Workshop's research-based approach to television production and the BBC's more practice-based approach. Alan Pifer, head of the Carnegie Corporation in New York, visited the BBC in the autumn of 1967. Though never directly involved in the work leading up to the Workshop, Pifer's reaction to *Play School*'s production processes is telling in terms of the difficulty the Workshop's first funder would have in understanding the British point of view. During his visit, Pifer had apparently been taken aback that the BBC had made *Play School* without first doing years of research, such as Cooney was performing for the nascent *Sesame Street*.[36] He apparently did not realize how the long institutional tradition of producing children's broadcasting might have prepared the *Play School* team for the task ahead. While *Sesame Street* was constructed anew based on educational theory, *Play School* built on a treasure-trove of institutional knowledge the BBC had from decades of producing broadcasting for children and adults. Coming from an organization that focused on using academic research to improve educational results, Pifer might have underestimated the quality that could result from applying practical experience and institutional traditions not based on quantifiable scientific research or constant monitoring.

From its perspective, the *Play School* team did not see their interaction with the Carnegie Corporation as something that might affect it or indeed threaten its leading position in preschool production in the United Kingdom or abroad. In a document from 1967, the *Play School* team concluded that the program Cooney was considering was no competitor to *Play School*, because even if America was "beginning to wake up to the possibility of using TV as an entertainment/information medium for pre-school children," the *Play School* team was "obviously four years ahead of them."[37] What the team failed to understand was that the preschool show Cooney was developing would include things like numeracy and literacy training that promised an early educational advantage for children that many parents favored over hard-to-define progressive educational goals.

Selling *Sesame Street* in the United Kingdom:
A First Attempt

In the summer of 1969 it became obvious to the BBC that the Workshop was now ready to present a model for preschool television that was not only very different from the BBC's, but also a strong rival in terms of financial backing, production quality, and public relations.[38] The BBC's collaborators from the *Play School* unit at the Australian public service broadcaster, ABC, had reported to the BBC news of *Sesame Street*'s progress after one of its representatives had been invited to visit the Workshop in New York in mid-1969. Thus, when *Sesame Street* was first offered to the BBC in January 1970, it knew that this was not only a potential addition to their own programming, it was also a competitor in the United Kingdom and abroad—indeed one that had already been offered to Australian ABC as a possible replacement to *Play School*.

In January 1970, Joan Ganz Cooney and David Connell traveled to Britain to promote *Sesame Street*. They showed the program to a number of groups, including UK journalists and the BBC. Press reactions were positive, with several newspapers carrying good reviews of the show.[39] The press's positive reaction meant that Monica Sims, head of the BBC's Children's Department, felt under some pressure to buy it.[40] However, little more than month after seeing the program, Sims confided to a friend that no one in Britain was likely to buy *Sesame Street* as it was "too American."[41] Pointing to *Sesame Street*'s origins, as Sims did here, seem to have been a not-so-subtle shorthand for British perceptions of the shallowness of commercial broadcasting culture in the States and its inappropriateness in a public service context.

Despite Sims's judgment of the program as a whole, she was keen to buy segments with the Muppets or exchange them for some of the BBC's natural

Figure 3.1   Monica Sims with Humpty, a toy from *Play School*, 1968. *Photo by Evening Standard/Hulton Archive/Getty Images.*

history film clips that she knew the Workshop wanted.[42] Sims even expressed interest in co-production with the Workshop. The fact that she entertained the idea of a possible co-production demonstrates that she did not at this point perceive the visions for *Sesame Street* and *Play School* as irreconcilable. Six months later the BBC formally requested to buy Muppet segments and the exclusive broadcast rights for the British Isles.[43]

The Workshop declined the BBC's offer. The rejection made sure to mention how Canada, Australia, New Zealand, and a number of Caribbean islands had purchased *Sesame Street* in its original format, indicating that the BBC would before long probably regret their choice.[44] While Sims might not have regretted it, the Workshop was right; its vast international success became a lever when people questioned the BBC's rejection of the show.

Not having success with the BBC, the Workshop turned to the commercial network, Independent Television (ITV). The Workshop already had a connection at the Independent Television Authority (ITA), the institution overseeing ITV. The ITA's Brian Young had seen *Sesame Street* in October 1969 on a visit to the Workshop in New York.[45] Another ITA employee saw *Sesame Street* at Prix Jeunesse, after which he talked to and later corresponded with Edward Palmer, leading to a number of screenings of *Sesame Street* for ITV producers and advisers throughout the autumn of 1970. Then in November 1970, Young had dinner with Cooney and told her of ITA's interest in *Sesame Street*, but also briefed her on the problems the Workshop would be facing because of ITV's quotas on foreign material.

As part of the ITA's Schools Committee, Young had been involved with informal discussions about *Sesame Street*, which had begun as it was becoming increasingly likely that one or more of ITV's companies would wish to buy the program. For years, committee members had wished to see an ITV contribution to the preschool field.[46] Young might have told Cooney that the committee was much divided in its opinions about *Sesame Street*, and was especially conflicted over its explicit educational goals, the emphasis on facts, and its overall educational approach which some of its members feared would be too different from the progressive British approach to preschool education. Some members were, however, most positive toward the show.

Given the ITA's internal disagreements about *Sesame Street*, the Schools Committee decided that more people, including "parents, children and educationalists," should see the program and form their own opinions.[47] The ITA therefore allowed a trial screening.[48] This gambit may have been to win over the public with the program's appealing mixture of Muppets and popular music and thus persuade British television executives to ignore the objections of progressive educational experts. The news about the ITA's trial screening of *Sesame Street* let to a renewed interest in the program from the British press. On December 7, 1970, the BBC current affairs program *Late Night Line Up* devoted a segment to a comparison of British and American educational techniques, and *Sesame Street* was taken as an example of the latter.[49]

The renewed interest in *Sesame Street* put pressure on Sims to defend her decision not to buy the program. She even confessed to her boss, the BBC's director of programs, David Attenborough, that she was tired of replying to the many inquiries from the public about her reasons for not purchasing it.[50] So when *The Guardian* printed an extraordinary positive article about

Sesame Street and a lengthy interview with Joan Ganz Cooney on December 16, 1970, Sims wrote a letter to the editor defending her decision and explaining why she did not think that *Sesame Street* should "become a daily television fare" for children under five.[51] This letter became the beginning of a long controversy between Sims and most of the British press, ITV, and the Workshop. The question of whether *Sesame Street* should be broadcast in Britain became a fight over preschool education, ideals for children's television, and the power that the BBC was accused of holding over the entire UK television market.

In her letter to *The Guardian*, Sims argued that because *Sesame Street* was made for a particular US context, it was unfit for British children. Gone were any ideas about possibilities for co-productions. All she focused on was opposing educational traditions and approaches to children's television. Playing on British skepticism of American culture, Sims argued that, unlike American children, British children had *Play School* and other high-quality programs and therefore did not need the "commercial hard-selling techniques" *Sesame Street* used. With a broad, deep-rooted public service suspicion toward the commercialized American media landscape, Sims believed that *Sesame Street*'s fast-paced, mesmerizing format was only needed because "[American children] will not watch anything quiet or thoughtful" because of the commercial makeup of the US broadcasting market. British programs discouraged "passive box-watching," Sims said, and British children therefore did not need something that kept them focused on the screen for sixty minutes. She thought it more valuable for children to watch twenty minutes of programming that provided "imaginative and intellectual stimulus" and encouraged "creativity and activity," rather than "be hypnotised into gazing for an hour." While it was a crude description of *Sesame Street*'s approach, Sims's description touched on some key differences in how the BBC and the Workshop aimed to relate to children and with what effect.

To realize *Sesame Street*'s intended educational effect, children were supposed to concentrate on the program, taking in the lessons presented. The goal of capturing the attention of presumably easily distracted children was tested by the Workshop using a "distractor" device, as described in chapter 1. In the BBC's programs, children's own input and participation were encouraged, as the BBC aimed to stimulate the audience's engagement with their social world. One example of the Children's Department's so-called child-centeredness[52]—understood as an interest in children's lives here and now—was the constant encouragement of children to send in pictures and drawings and sometimes participate in writing screenplays. Two examples from 1969 were the six thousand stories that children ages four to sixteen had written for the *Jackanory* program, and the three hundred thousand drawings of reindeer the department had received for a competition to visit the Arctic Circle.[53] Encouraging audience contributions and inclusion was very different from the Workshop's carefully planned, research-led, school-centered lessons that were supposed to help children do better later in life. *Sesame Street* was not based on ethnographic research of what children did or liked; rather it was carefully planned on experts' ideas of children's needs.

The differences in the approach to television's role in preschoolers' lives were also apparent in Sims's criticism of *Sesame Street*'s teaching methods. With the echo of an entrenched skepticism of authoritarian upbringing among European educators following World War II, she found alarming the emphasis on teaching facts.[54] Such didactic methods, she held, were inappropriate for a mass medium like television, especially if not followed up by teachers who stimulated children individually. Moreover, she did not believe television should dictate what children should learn. Again, her argument drew on deep European fears of the uses of mass media for propaganda and indoctrination that had been the focus of European-led studies by the United Nations Educational, Scientific and Cultural Organization (UNESCO) on mass media and children in the 1940s and 1950s.[55] All television produced by her department should and could do, in her view, was enrich, stimulate, and entertain. *Play School* accomplished this, she believed, and was therefore a much better program for British children under five than *Sesame Street*.

Stacking up the arguments against *Sesame Street*, Sims also drew on scheduling and financial problems. It was very important to the BBC to give children a mixture of programs that, like the BBC schedule for adults, provided a variety of alternatives that together offered a balance of different genres and programs.[56] Thus, already having a dedicated preschool program and a mix of other programs for children in that schedule, Sims was not prepared to skip over *Play School* and many of the other programs the BBC produced to make room for a daily *Sesame Street* broadcast. The American program by itself would take up half of the total weekly hours of *all* children's television and much of the budget currently paying for local productions. Keeping the schedule as it was enabled the department to provide give entertainment and educational content for children, but in separate programs. Sims preferred this to the mixture of genres in *Sesame Street*, she told a mother in reply to a letter sent to the BBC a few weeks later: "I believe it is much more dangerous to make use of the commercial techniques of a 'Scooby Doo' in the educational context of 'Sesame Street' than to show it as we do straightforward easy entertainment with no pretensions of being educational."[57] Disguising education as entertainment as in *Sesame Street* was in Sims's view dishonest indoctrination, because it was deceiving in its aim to teach specific skills and facts, but hiding it behind entertainment.

Despite this harsh criticism, the Workshop took very little notice of Sims's *Guardian* letter. In Britain, however, it was a different matter, and the letter helped Sims gain support among the educational establishment and people within the BBC.[58] The question of what educational value, if any, *Sesame Street* could offer to preschoolers in a British context became salient in the next rounds of the Workshop's attempts to secure the sale of *Sesame Street* for five-day-a-week transmission in the United Kingdom.

Was *Sesame Street* Educational? Testing *Sesame Street* on a British Audience

Harlech Television, which controlled the ITV network in Wales, was the first company to air *Sesame Street* in Britain. The ITA had allowed a screening of ten episodes, Monday to Friday in late March and early April 1971.[59] Negotiations for this trial transmission had been difficult. The ITA had no prior experience with buying foreign educational material and the ITA's Schools Committee was hesitant as it doubted *Sesame Street* would be suited for the UK educational framework, especially since Sims had already publicly questioned this point. Besides, there was also the question of scheduling rules. Any ITV company that wished to carry the show would have to devote almost all of its foreign quota to it, *and* special permission was needed for an early-afternoon broadcast that would extend its local schedule beyond the allowed eight-and-a-half hours a day. The permission for an extended schedule had to be made by the Ministry for Post and Telecommunications, and such dispensation had only ever been given to educational programs meant for use in schools. The ministry, however, agreed to allow an extension for a trail period.[60] This time would be used to decide if *Sesame Street* was "education" or "entertainment" in a British context, and only if it were deemed "education" could it be exempted from the scheduling rules in the future. The decision on the educational benefit of *Sesame Street* for British children henceforth became the core question that could make or break it for *Sesame Street* in the United Kingdom.

The educational value of *Sesame Street* was to be determined by a small-scale study that monitored children's reactions to the programs. Ultimately, the Workshop and its supporters hoped that if the arguments in *Sesame Street*'s favor were strong enough after the trial period, both the ITA's scheduling rule and the allowance for more foreign broadcasting could be "bent or altered."[61] The study was headed by Frank Blackwell, director of the Primary Extension Program of the British National Council for Educational Technology, who some years later became a Workshop employee. For the study, ITV and Harlech jointly installed television sets at a number of preschool playgroups, nursery classes, and infant schools in Bristol and Cardiff and prepared questionnaires for the adults in charge to complete. Parents were asked to respond by telephone and letter, and some home monitoring was also done.[62]

Initial notes given to the study group show how *Sesame Street*'s focus on "letter learning goals" was conceived almost as a gimmick meant to convince parents of the show's quality, and that its educational effect was boiled down to its "holding power."[63] In his introduction to the researchers who took part in the study, Blackwell felt it necessary to point out how *Sesame Street* "may been unfairly criticized for the importance it gives to letter learning goals," likely trying to mitigate the hesitation among British educators toward introducing school-like learning in a preschool setting. He asserted,

> These [letter learning goals] were chosen not for their prime importance in the pre-reading and reading skills, but for their value and connotation with educational success by parents and adults in the homes of the viewers. Incidentally, too, letter recognition and the learning of the alphabet is an attainable goal by most children, and therefore represents a possible achievement for the bulk of the viewing audience.[64]

This description reveals how some of *Sesame Street*'s content was not primarily included for educational reasons, but as a kind of signaling to adult viewers of the show's traditional educational intent. The UK survey confirmed this effect; parents responded that they liked *Sesame Street* because it (presumably) taught children something because of its focus on numeracy and literacy.

Another goal of the study was to find out how much holding power the program had over children, because it was deemed key to the show's educational effect.[65] A strong premise for the research done during the trial period was that if *Sesame Street* could capture children's interest, they would learn what the Workshop had stated in its curriculum, as the effect on British children was believed to be the exact same as on American children. This premise was deeply rooted in universal ideals of learning, fundamentally assuming that all children went through the same developmental steps and would therefore benefit from learning the same things in the same way, regardless of their social or cultural context or the local educational system. Such an approach disregarded the many differences between the British and American educational systems and how they were shaped by and responded to their respective national contexts. The UK report concluded that reaction to the program was very mixed and inconclusive as to its possible educational effect. The report stated that parents would probably welcome a new program for this age group, but *Sesame Street* was perhaps too American, echoing the general skepticism toward US programming and its cultural connotations.[66]

As soon as it was clear that the first ITA report was going to be inconclusive, the Workshop started lobbying for another trial run in London, as this would increase viewer capacity and possible exposure to members of the press.[67] The idea behind the second trial was still to make the ITA deem *Sesame Street* to be educational and therefore allow it despite restrictions on foreign material and scheduling. The Workshop had already used this strategy in Canada to get scheduling rules dismissed.[68]

To persuade the ITA, the Workshop's chief academic adviser, Harvard psychology professor Gerald Lesser, went to London in June 1971 to meet the ITA's Schools Committee and brief it on his own *Sesame Street* research. Prior to the meeting, the Workshop's sales agent Peter Orton, who also worked for its UK-based sales agency, Television International Enterprises (TIE), told Lesser about the UK broadcasting landscape. He painted Sims as leading the British opposition toward *Sesame Street*, framing the reluctance toward the show a matter of BBC versus ITV, not seeing this as rooted in the Workshop's different educational tradition. Yet in Lesser's meeting with ITA representatives, the head of its Education Advisory Committee, Wendla Kernig, objected to transmitting *Sesame Street* on ITV's network for exactly the same reasons as Monica Sims had. Lesser reported back to the Workshop how Kernig argued for "child-centered education," something Lesser saw as "entirely antithetical" to what *Sesame Street* set out to teach.[69] Despite stating at the beginning of his report that local educational experts would know what was best for local children, Lesser entirely failed to see her points and consequently dismissed her views.

Lesser's chief argument for dismissing Kernig's opinion despite her expertise on local issues was justified in his report's opening paragraphs. Here he claimed to be completely capable of assessing the validity of local experts by judging them on their personality. That Kernig was a woman is likely to have directly influenced his belittlement of her views, as he, before he listed her objections to *Sesame Street*, plainly objectified her by commenting that she looked "not bad," but "rather handsome in a spinster sort of way," and he assured his readers that he had "made no amorous advances."[70] This unprofessional evaluation of Kernig's looks speaks volumes in terms of his (in)ability to separate his evaluation of people's expertise from his evaluation of their personalities.

Despite Kernig's concerns about *Sesame Street*, the rest of the ITA representatives, who were all male, overruled her objections and allowed another trial run for *Sesame Street* at ITV. In July, the two ITV companies covering the London area on weekends (London Weekend) and Northern Scotland (Grampian) were allowed to transmit *Sesame Street* on Saturday mornings for thirteen weeks during the autumn of 1971.[71] As with the first time, conditions were tied to the trial transmissions. Once again, more parents and children's reactions had to be surveyed, but further conditions were also added, specifically directed at the public perception of the ITA's role in the *Sesame Street* trial screenings.

Sparked by the first trial, public debate about *Sesame Street* was growing in Britain. Based on Sims's letter in *The Guardian* from December, the British press, which had many ties to ITV, eyed the chance to dig deep into a conflict between the BBC on one side and the proponents of *Sesame Street* on the other. Old oppositions between the BBC and ITV that ran along entrenched divides of middle- and working-class culture, highbrow public service ideals, and popular commercial programming were renewed through the lens of *Sesame Street*. Even if the show was pitched as an alternative to US commercial culture, Sims and British educators used its American origins to undermine this claim. Trying to stay out of the growing conflict—not taking sides regarding *Sesame Street*'s educational value in a UK context, a key point in the conflict—the ITA made two conditions related to public announcement of the new trial screenings.

First, the ITA staff had to "in any public statement [make] clear that the Committee regarded the educational validity of *Sesame Street* for British children an open question. The Committee was endorsing further experimental transmissions, in order to enlarge the critical debate about *Sesame Street* itself."[72] Second, the ITA wanted the public to know that it "wish[ed] that a British series might in due course be produced," a question that would refocus the debate away from *Sesame Street's* suitability for a British audience and onto possibilities for new domestic preschool productions. The ITA knew its decision was followed closely by the press and the public and could end up in high-pitched and politicized arguments about British culture and education. One telling example could be seen in the *Sunday Times*, which in early August wrote about the new trial transmissions,

> One person who may not be too pleased is Miss Monica Sims, Head of BBC Children's TV. She boldly replied when challenged to show *Sesame Street*, "We believe we can make better programmes for British under-fives." Now she will have to prove it. *Play School* . . . comes over as genteel middle-class pap compared with the vigour of the American show. Daddies can see for themselves this Bank Holiday Monday. It is Useful Box Day, whatever that is, and there's a story, Old Toby and the Hedgehog. Take cover, Miss Sims, the Muppets are coming![73]

Clearly, the journalist assumed fathers would side with the Muppets and Sims would be left to defend her rejection based on a collection of middle-class pap. The press with its many connections to ITV, could, meanwhile, enjoy the possible mistake made by the biggest institution in their national media landscape.

Switching from the BBC to ITV, the Workshop had positioned *Sesame Street* in the middle of a cultural fight about Americanization and protection of British values, which meant that the verdict for or against the program had high stakes for everyone involved. The Workshop's Orton even told his colleagues that the trial broadcasts might make the BBC's executives strip Sims of her power and force her to reconsider, if the public perception was positive enough:

> It would appear that Monica Sims, Head of Children's Programmes at the BBC, has made a major error in taking up a negative attitude towards "Sesame Street" which could be instrumental in seeing some of the very

real power that she now holds in terms of children's broadcasting at the BBC being taken away. When "Sesame Street" Series I is telecast by the Independent Television contractors, the commercial network, many questions will be asked of Miss Sims as to why, having the first option, she did not purchase it. . . . There is a strong likelihood that the BBC will be forced to rethink the Children's Television Workshop and its productions.[74]

ITV trial broadcast therefore could serve as a route to airing *Sesame Street* with the BBC, as the Workshop had hoped all along. This use of ITV as a possible detour to the BBC shows not only how elaborate the Workshop was in planning for the long-term outcomes it wanted. It also demonstrates how important the BBC brand was to the Workshop, but also that it had not understood—or chosen to ignore—the fact that the organization's opposition toward *Sesame Street* did not rest with Sims alone but was deeply rooted in organizational policies and educational ideologies.

The ITA once more put Blackwell in charge of the research. Even if the ITA tried to appear completely open to the question of *Sesame Street*'s educational value in a British context, it led the Workshop to influence the design of the new study, apparently not thinking about how this might effect the outcome. The Workshop's field research coordinator, Patrisha Haynes, met with Blackwell and the head of the ITA's School Committee, Brian Groombridge, to convince them what the parameters for the upcoming research should be.[75] Haynes was also allowed to attend the actual research meeting where the scope and content of the exercise were decided upon and was happy to report back to the Workshop that she had succeeded in getting Blackwell on board with all of her ideas.[76] Drawing upon the Workshop's own research, she had effectively convinced Blackwell's group that since US research had shown that *Sesame Street* was an educational success, the only real question left was to determine if it appealed to British children.[77] All other questions could be covered by consulting the Workshop's own studies. Again, we see how the Workshop used the premise that all children need the same kind of educational stimulation using the same teaching methods no matter the context to argue that the research they did on US children's learning was applicable everywhere else.

Despite the Workshop's intense lobbying, the ITA was not fully convinced that US research on *Sesame Street*'s educational benefits could be applied directly in a British context. The new study, therefore, included a group of British experts on preschool education who were not psychologists of the same background as the Workshop's research and consultants, but a mixture of educationalists and teachers coming at the topic from a more philosophical and practical angle. The British expert group was asked to review the programs to advise the ITA on their findings from a local educational perspective. The Workshop was worried about this group and the importance the ITA placed on its opinions.

Multiple screenings of *Sesame Street* had been conducted earlier in the summer by Sir James Pitman, a frontier in the battle against illiteracy in the United Kingdom, but they had not given *Sesame Street* the positive reception among British educators for which Pitman and the Workshop had hoped. The Workshop therefore put an end to these screenings for the fear of an uncontrolled narrative about their program.[78] To avoid what the Workshop saw as further misunderstanding about its program—not acknowledging that this might be actual opposition and disagreement with its educational methods—it insisted that the group of experts who were to inform the ITA be meticulously briefed by someone from the Workshop on the philosophy behind *Sesame Street*. Blackwell agreed to invite Edward Palmer to do so.[79] Using the advantage of their in-house research and vast resources, the Workshop was thus able to exercise considerable power over the ITA's study and would influence it further by having a chance to convince the experts.

The ITA's allowance of new trial broadcasts led to positive press for *Sesame Street* in which British journalists did not miss the opportunity to scorn the BBC's rejection of the program, following similar framed articles from earlier in the summer.[80] Not only the British press, however, had taken an interest in the British reception of *Sesame Street*. In the autumn of 1971, the American press came to play a central role in the growing controversy between the BBC and the Workshop, provoked by the former's rejection of *Sesame Street* and the latter's attempts to get ITV to carry it.

The BBC's "Ban" of *Sesame Street*

In late June 1971, the *New York Times* carried a story outlining the differences between British and American children's television. Contrary to later articles in the US press, this item displayed a genuine interest in uncovering what made the BBC's sense of responsibility for the child viewer different from the American tradition. Sims, who was interviewed for the article, stated that the BBC had respect for the child's intelligence and was known for treating childhood realistically.[81] The article pitted *Play School* in opposition to *Sesame Street* and showed sympathy for the former's lack of didactic intentions and interest in starting "trains of thought and a desire in the child to find out and learn for himself." The article concluded that even though perspectives on commercialization for the BBC and companies in the US market were very different, the fundamental differences lay in the approach to children's educational needs engrained in the two traditions. This important point would soon be lost in accounts of the BBC's rejection of *Sesame Street*.

With the British press tuned into the possible conflict of the BBC versus the Workshop and ITV, and a new trial transmission period on ITV, Sims thought it necessary to make it plain again why she had refused to buy little more than Muppet segments from the show. Her explanation became much more important for both her and the Workshop in the middle of 1971 than at the time when the decision was made a year earlier. Now, *Sesame Street* and Sims's choice not to buy it held the attention of the press, as well as a large number of British educators because of the ITA's second trial transmission.

To make her position on *Sesame Street* absolutely clear, as preparation for a press conference in early September, Sims wrote a seven-page paper defending her decision not to buy the full episodes of *Sesame Street* when they were offered to the BBC in early 1970.[82] It was meant for the managing director of television at the BBC but also sent to three of her other bosses. Sims was probably trying to reinforce her already strong institutional backing, evidenced by the continued concerns of the vice president of the BBC Board of Governors, Lady Plowden, regarding preschool educational programming.[83] Knowing that this matter had the attention of the governors was not something to take lightly, especially not when Lady Plowden was the same Plowden who had headed the committee that made the influential report on primary education for the government half a decade earlier. Given the attention *Sesame Street* had managed to attract, Sims seemed to have worried about how the BBC would look in light of the new ITV trial broadcasts if its programs were not perceived as a clear alternative to *Sesame Street*. Consequently, she was eager to pick apart the argument that *Sesame Street* could be more or better in terms of its "educational" effects than the offerings from her department and used her paper to argue why *Sesame Street* was not appropriate for children's television in Britain.

Sims's paper was an elaboration of the points she had made in her *Guardian* article from December 1970. It was, however, much more academic in its

outlook, quoting experts critical of *Sesame Street* and referring to empirical evidence of where the program had failed to live up to its set goals. Her
paper shows how she had followed the reception of the show very closely and
done extensive research, drawing among other things on the BBC School
Broadcasting Council's report by Elaine Mee on *Sesame Street*—all to back up
Sims's own opinions.[84] Her paper underpinned her stance on *Sesame Street*
as a wrong kind of televised preschool education for British children because
of its focus on a strict curriculum of intellectual stimulation. With quotes
from American and British educationalists, sociologists, and teachers, she
attacked the program's deficit model; she disagreed with the Workshop's attempt to raise disadvantaged children individually to the level of the middle
class through TV, rather than Americans addressing the structural problems
of an educational system that was biased against underprivileged children.
Siding with progressive American educators such as John Holt, Sims stated
that the educational norms were the problem, not the children who could
not live up to them.[85] Responses to circulation of her paper inside the BBC
showed support within the organization for her decision.

Ready to release the plans for its autumn schedule and defend Sims's decision not to buy *Sesame Street*, the BBC held a press conference on September
6, 1971.[86] At the press conference, Sims directly addressed the way the press,
among others, had represented her as an "arch-enemy of *Sesame Street*" because of her department's decision not to buy the series.[87] She rejected this
framing, saying that she admired many parts of the program, including the
music, the Muppets, and the animation. However, she also indicated that
she did not think that the program was particularly appropriate for children
under five. Referring to unspecified American educationalists, she said that
Sesame Street's educational approach had been questioned because it required
"acquiring knowledge in a passive, uninvolved fashion . . . the programme's
essentially middle class attitudes, its lack of reality and its attempt to prepare
children for school but not for life."[88] Sims stated that she was "particularly
worried by the programme's authoritarian aims. Right answers are demanded
and praised and a research report refers to the programme-makers aim to
change children's behavior. This sounds like indoctrination, and a dangerous
extension of the use of television." Finally, she contrasted this approach with
the BBC's own, which in her opinion tried to

> enrich the lives of our viewers and, especially for very young children, the
> greatest enrichment comes through the enjoyment of finding out through

the use of all their senses. In BBC Children's Programmes, our job is not only to teach a set of facts but to stimulate children's activity and enthusiasm to learn and do things for themselves.[89]

Following this rather black-and-white characterization of the differences between the Workshop's and the BBC's approach to preschool education, Sims applauded the ways in which the publicity for *Sesame Street* had helped to focus attention on the needs of preschool children. But, she warned, it was essential to recognize the limitations in any "packaged" view of education such as *Sesame Street*'s. The criticism of a packaged view of education referred to the Workshop's belief that if education could be made bite-sized and fun, children could learn without noticing, just as they did from commercials. This kind of educational approach did not resonate with British children's television and had also been rejected more widely in the Plowden Report.[90]

If Sims had hoped that her press briefing would be the explanation that would make people understand her rejection of buying *Sesame Street* in full, she was dead wrong. British and American newspapers both widely reported on her press conference, but not in the way she had intended.[91] On September 8, the *New York Times* carried a front-page article titled "BBC Orders Ban on 'Sesame Street,'" as mentioned in the introduction to this chapter.[92] The article reported, mistakenly, that the BBC on September 6 had decided to bar *Sesame Street* because of its "authoritarian aims." While the BBC had refused to buy more than Muppet segments, the rather sensational framing of the rejection as a "ban" and highlighting "authoritarian aims" as the reason, led readers to view the context of the refusal as completely absurd, not a dispute over different approaches to educational traditions in preschool television. Mentioned nowhere were Sims's lengthy explanation of the differences between the progressive preschool education of her department and the more traditional education basis for *Sesame Street*.

The *New York Times* article reported unwavering support for *Sesame Street*. Neglecting the substantial skepticism toward *Sesame Street* among British educators, it used quotations from Sir James Pitman to wrongly imply that all UK educators were angry with the BBC and had urged airing of the program. Drawing on thinly veiled negative gender stereotypes, Pitman called Sims's decision "irrational and emotional," driven by jealousy because the Workshop had produced a program superior to the BBC's shows. The Workshop's vice president Michael Dann had also been interviewed for the piece. Using the same gendered language, he mocked Sims's irrational judgment in choices of content, telling how her department had bought *Huckleberry Hound* and *Yogi Bear* instead of *Sesame Street*. These were, in his opinion, inferior programs to *Sesame Street*. Nowhere did the article explain that these served as entertainment in the BBC's very mixed schedule of programs and that the BBC already had a serious preschool program of its own, albeit based on a different educational philosophy.

The London office of the Associated Press (AP), an American news bureau, also wrote a rather sensational piece about the BBC's decision on *Sesame Street*. Though not framing it as a "ban," the article stressed that the BBC had turned it down because it was "non-democratic and possibly dangerous to little Britons." The item appeared with spectacular headlines in many US newspapers on September 8.[93] This item also reported that BBC had bought *The Further Adventures of Dr. Dolittle* and *The Harlem Globetrotters*. Again, this detail must have stood out as very odd to American readers who did not know that the BBC already had programs like *Play School*, and these other shows were used as entertainment between other types of more educational learning programs. The AP release stated that *Sesame Street* had been shown now in more than forty-six countries, a context within which the BBC's rejection looked absurd. As did the *New York Times* article, the AP's item did not report the praise Sims had for several aspects of the program or contextualize the decision with reference to the completely different educational and media landscapes of the BBC. The omission of this point made the BBC's decision seem bizarre especially if American readers thought that the UK television market worked like the American.

US reporting on the BBC's decisions regarding *Sesame Street* made Sims's decisions look backward, coming almost from a place of ignorance or envy. The US press's response resembles how the American establishment at the time saw many threats to its global advancement. Opposition to international philanthropy schemes by the Carnegie, Ford, and Rockefeller foundations were treated with the same dismissal: criticism was simply seen as rooted in foreigners' misguided and irrational opposition to American politics and culture.[94] By debunking Sims's criticism as merely a matter of misunderstanding and irrational prejudice against American culture rather than acknowledging her expertise in children's television and knowledge of *Sesame Street*, American commentators turned the focus away from her criticism of *Sesame Street*, reducing it to her presumed resentment of American success.[95]

To exploit the attention *Sesame Street* was receiving, the ITV company London Weekend and the Workshop arranged a combined screening and lunch for the press in mid-September attended by Michael Dann and Edward Palmer.[96] The screening led to more press for *Sesame Street*. Though some of it was nuanced and discussed educational politics, most newspapers seemed to take the opportunity to mock Sims and the BBC.[97] The day after the screening the *Daily Express*'s Bruce Kemble wrote, "Pity the poor BBC. It has made a monumental blunder in rejecting what I can only describe as the most exciting children's programme I have ever seen."[98] The *Guardian* reported that the journalists attending the screening were "bewildered because they clearly found it difficult to see what had caused Miss Sims to condemn the programme as too American, too middle class . . . too authoritarian." When a reporter asked Michael Dann about the BBC's rejection, he again indicated that Sims was being emotional and irrational. Dann avoided answering questions about different educational standards by deflecting Sims's argument as being part of an "intramural" British debate. However, he could not resist mocking her comments about the show being middle-class and authoritarian, asking in jest who would argue that teaching the alphabet was dangerous, as if he did not understand her accusation that the show was teaching children to passively abide by the norms that underpinned the educational system.[99]

The widespread reporting on the BBC's rejection of *Sesame Street* also led to interest and follow-up articles in the United States. The *New York Times* published a letter to the editor from the BBC's New York office correcting the paper's report: there had been no actual ban.[100] This led the newspaper to go back to exploring its earlier reporting on the differences on British and American children's television and the pedagogical objections that had led to criticism of *Sesame Street* in both Britain and the States.[101] As part of this new take, the *New York Times* asked Sims to write an article explaining her stance on *Sesame Street* and her standards for children's television.[102] Sims was happy for the opportunity, feeling wrongly accused by some press reports of being chauvinistic and arrogant.[103] However, now naturally cautions because of the negative reception of her press conference, Sims asked her superiors for permission to write the article. In her request, she explained that she wanted to clear up things that had apparently most upset the American press, which was her argument about *Sesame Street* being "authoritarian" and "brain-washing" (which in the *Times* article had also become "antidemocratic").[104] Sims was allowed to write the article, but it was later withdrawn as events in late September led to a direct confrontation between the Workshop and the BBC.

The EBU Meeting That Threatened the Workshop's Advancement in Europe

So far, the Workshop's management had only dealt directly with the BBC's rejection of *Sesame Street* in Britain when it affected the Workshop's affairs with the ITA or when the press asked for comments. No direct confrontation had taken place to date between the Workshop and Sims. However, this changed on September 27, 1971, when the Workshop's director of information and utilization, Robert Hatch, informed his top bosses about a meeting of the European Broadcasting Union's (EBU) Working Party for Children and Young People that had been held in Oslo. Sims's long document about *Sesame Street* was allegedly distributed at this important meeting as part of a press kit from the BBC.[105] In information and utilization director's eyes, she now served "as European distributor of Sesame Street dissents."[106] This information intensified immensely the conflict between the Workshop and the BBC. Soon the Workshop would threaten to sue the BBC, and the chairman of the BBC's board of governors, Lord Hill, would receive an official complaint about Sims from Lord Harlech—the head of the regional ITV company Harlech Television that had first broadcast *Sesame Street* in the United Kingdom. Sims would ultimately be strong-armed to stay silent about her opinions on *Sesame Street*.

The paper that the Workshop had possession of, and that started this hard-hitting snowball rolling, was a slightly longer version of the confidential seven-page paper Sims had sent to her BBC bosses before the September 6 press conference. This version had been extended by two paragraphs, additions she had apparently made before bringing it with her to a meeting of the EBU's Working Party that took place the day after the BBC's press conference. To understand the Workshop's reaction to what they believed Sims had done, and the possible impact they believed this paper might have on the *Sesame Street* brand and potential sales in Europe, one should understand the power this particular EBU working party held in terms of the European market for children's television and the BBC's position within it.

The EBU (established 1950) was an alliance for public service media organizations across Western Europe. The union had different subcommittees, so-called working parties, where representatives from the member states' media organizations discussed policies and programming. Sims was a member of the working party for children and young people's programs. This group's discussions were often frank and open; it was a friendly—but also tough and critical—forum when it came to assessing the programs they screened.[107] The BBC had taken the lead in the group at the end of the 1960s, a role that consolidated during a 1968 seminar in London for producers and directors of children's television. Hosting such a seminar the BBC had hoped to "add to its prestige in Europe," and "increase [. . .] sales by [BBC] Enterprises of children's programmes in the European field." Using the EBU as a forum for sales and policy influence, the BBC eyed an opportunity "to off-set U.S. influence and the market deterioration [caused by] U.S. programmes for children."[108] Sims's predecessor had believed in 1966 that market deterioration was an imminent danger, because "of poor quality and lack of professionalism in much of [the continental] European material."[109] Thus, already before the Workshop had offered *Sesame Street* to Europe, the BBC had identified the EBU as an arena where it might sell its children's programs.[110]

The Workshop was hardly aware of how the BBC had tried to influence the EBU working party a few years earlier, but the Workshop did know how important the forum was for European producers of children's television. Consequently, the Workshop's top executives did not take kindly to the thought that Sims had used the EBU as a forum to spread anti–*Sesame Street* sentiments. France, West Germany, Italy, and the Scandinavian countries were among the most lucrative markets that the Workshop and its sales agents were pursuing at that very moment.

Coinciding with the information about the EBU meeting, the Workshop's top leadership was also briefed about a *Late Night Line Up* program involving Sims critical of *Sesame Street* that aired on September 27.[111] In the morning the next day, just one day after having learned about Sims's actions at the EBU meeting, Cooney heard a tape of the *Late Night Line Up* show. The combined impact of the two events left Cooney "very disturbed," not only because of the serious misquoting she thought Sims was doing, but also because of how widely this was reported, not only in the United Kingdom but also via the EBU.[112] Consequently, Cooney wanted to know if Sims's stance on *Sesame Street* was official BBC policy. She set forth a plan to find out by having the Carnegie Corporation's Lloyd Morrisett contact BBC's representatives in New York, and Orton getting on the phone with BBC in London. Cooney demanded nothing less than "a full apology be written by the BBC and distributed to everyone [in the EBU] who had received a copy of the Sims' critique."[113]

Orton called the BBC immediately.[114] In the call, he made it clear that Cooney felt misquoted and that many of the references Sims had made to experts who had criticized *Sesame Street* were misunderstood and wrongfully represented. He demanded an official apology that addressed what the Workshop saw as serious "misrepresentation, misquotation and inaccuracies" in the paper, and they wanted this apology distributed to the members of the EBU working party.[115] To make sure this happened, the Workshop had already made arrangements with the chairman of its board of trustees to see BBC representatives in the BBC's offices in London and New York.[116] Finally, Orton mentioned the possibility of litigation "unless this [was] cleared up."[117]

The seriousness of the allegations and possible consequences meant that the matter was attended to quickly by David Attenborough, the BBC's director of television. When Sims explained to Attenborough what had happened at the EBU meeting, she claimed never to have circulated her paper, but only showed it to a few people who were interested in knowing why the BBC had not bought *Sesame Street*.[118] As for the paper's wide circulation, Sims said that someone else must have copied it and distributed it to the twenty-seven organizations that the Workshop claimed had it. As proof of her side of the story, she referred Attenborough to the chairman of the working party and an official EBU representative, who confirmed that there had indeed not been a circulation of her paper.[119] Sims also claimed that any accidental circulation of her paper could not have influenced the decisions of European broadcasters on whether to buy the show, as she believed people had already made up their minds. This was indeed not the case, as many were still deliberating and would do so for years, as Sims might well have known.

Sims's account of the events to Attenborough also addressed the press release from the press conference on September 6, to which the Workshop had also apparently taken an exception. She explained that her reason for mentioning *Sesame Street* had been in the BBC's best interest, because

If I had not given some of our reasons we would have continued to look insular and complacent. "Sesame Street's" own publicity campaign has been subtly angled against us for a long time through their supporters in this country and it looks as if they have now silenced me as effectively as they have silenced their critics in the United States.[120]

Sims ended her report to Attenborough saying that she hoped it would eventually be possible for her to release her article to the *New York Times*, as she felt this would give her a proper chance to explain herself.

While Sims defended herself, Michael Dann worked to preserve *Sesame Street*'s positive image and to challenge Sims. He immediately took action by doing three things. First, he went to London to meet Lord Harlech, the head of Harlech Television, who in support of the Workshop assured Dann that he was "quite prepared to make quite an internal fuss" in Britain about Sims and her attitude toward *Sesame Street*.[121] Making good on his promise, Lord Harlech met with Lord Hill, the chairman of the BBC Board of Governors, in late October to discuss *Sesame Street* and Monica Sims.[122] Before the meeting he had made a formal complaint to the BBC about Sims spreading inaccuracies about *Sesame Street* and demanded that the organization would "take action to get the record put straight."[123] Second, Dann started drafting a combined apology and rebuttal letter in Sims's name, which he wanted the BBC, on behalf of Sims, to send to all the EBU members. Third, he called the BBC's Attenborough about the EBU incident to (according to Attenborough) complain

> in the most extreme terms, saying that this was part of a studied campaign by the BBC to destroy *Sesame Street*, that Monica Sims was waging a personal vendetta . . . and that he [Dann] was marshalling all the most influential people in the United States, from the Government downwards, to bring pressure to bear on the British Government and the BBC.[124]

Though Attenborough tried to explain the BBC's side of things, Dann was not mollified, ending the call by saying that the BBC would hear from the Workshop's lawyers. Although Attenborough clearly disapproved of Dann's behavior, he asked Monica Sims to put off writing the article she had promised the *New York Times* to avoid further conflict.

When Dann briefed Joan Ganz Cooney on his three-way scheme to make the BBC pay for their potential harm to the *Sesame Street* brand, he assured her that "the BBC has already put a clamp on Miss Sims and is eager to correct the situation."[125] Dann clearly foresaw a situation where the BBC would not only stop Sims's article, which he was already aware of, but also force Sims to retract the paper they believed she had distributed to the EBU alongside an official apology to the Workshop.[126]

To be sure, Sims's and Attenborough's accounts of this matter see the case from the BBC's point of view, but the Workshop's extreme reaction is clear. The Workshop believed its international reputation was at stake and reacted accordingly. It was not afraid to mobilize its vast and influential network in the United Kingdom and the United States to help put weight behind the threats. However, intimidation was not the only strategy the Workshop tried. After Lord Harlech had met Lord Hill to discuss the Workshop's complaint and apparently had not been able to get an official promise for an apology, Dann tried to switch his method of influence on the BBC from intimidation to luncheons. In mid-October, Dann wrote to the director of television at the BBC, Huw Wheldon, proposing a lunch meeting with him, Attenborough, and the controller at BBC1, in early November. Dann told Wheldon that this was "not to discuss any past difficulties."[127] Nevertheless, even if Dann said this, the London meeting coincided with when the Workshop had drafted an apology-*cum*-rebuttal letter they wanted the BBC to distribute to all the EBU members in Sims's name.

On November 3, the Workshop's draft of the apology letter it had written on behalf of Sims was finished.[128] No one in the BBC had any knowledge of this letter, but Dann is likely to have brought it to his luncheon with Wheldon and the other BBC bosses in London on November 11, as a full version ended up in the BBC's internal archives.[129] Furthermore, even if Dann in his suggestion for them to meet had stated that it was not about past events, later accounts of the meeting described it as tense and difficult.[130]

The Workshop's top people wrote the apology letter to appear as if it came from Sims's own hand. It is an incredible document, not only indicating the length to which the Workshop was going to defend its name, but also that it was willing to do so by ruining the reputation and possible career of a respected individual, as well as to use that ruin to strategically promote its own brand. The letter severely undermined Sims's judgment and integrity, as its introduction indicates:

> It has been brought to my attention by the Children's Television Workshop, that the paper contained several errors of fact which placed the 'Sesame Street' experiment in an unduly harsh light. . . . I regret that the sources I had reason to believe were objective failed to provide me with accurate information and that some of the conclusions drawn from that material on our side of the Atlantic resulted in distortions. I am happy, though, to be able to amend my original remarks and thus set the record straight.[131]

After this introduction, the letter runs five full pages, listing twelve instances where "Sims" admits to have been wrong in her original paper. As a fabrication to display Sims's "realizations" of her wrongdoings, it reads more like a perfect opportunity for the Workshop to defend *Sesame Street* against everything it was ever criticized for, rather than an apology. The letter had her admitting that she was wrong about issues ranging from her judgment of *Sesame Street*'s target group to the ideas behind its composition; that she supposedly knew in fact that there were only very few critics of *Sesame Street*, all with limited credentials; that *Sesame Street* encouraged participation by children; and that only one person had said it lacked real-world connections. Furthermore, the letter has her admitting that she should have known that Cooney only made a remark about the Workshop being like the British Empire in jest, and that requests for the series had come to the Workshop long before it could handle all the attention.

After its first pages, the letter slid more from a staged apology and admittance of wrongdoing into an advertisement for *Sesame Street* and a straight-up criticism of the BBC's own policy. The rest of the letter was used to demonstrate just how inconsistent and careless Sims was in her policy choices and purchase of foreign material. Finally, the Workshop's letter had Sims admitting that she had made a "gross distortion" when she said that *Sesame Street* was intended as a substitute for nurseries, and that she had made "ridiculous" claims about their advertising.[132]

The level of self-inflicted humiliation this letter entailed makes it hard to believe that any recipient would ever believe that Sims herself had written it. In fact, the rebuttal letter was never distributed, even if the Workshop kept pressuring the BBC for some time to do so.[133] Still, its existence shows just how far the Workshop felt it had to go in trying to silence a critical voice. It also shows that the Workshop knew how important the BBC's opinion was to other members of the EBU working party and what an opinion formed about *Sesame Street* in this forum might do to the possibilities for selling the show in Europe. The rebuttal letter goes to great length to explain the Workshop's foreign sales strategies, with "Sims" writing that she knew the Workshop had never pushed for sales of *Sesame Street*. As far as co-productions were concerned, the letter is very humble and underplayed, showing none of the hunger for expansion seen in internal documents. Clearly, the rebuttal was meant as much as a way for the Workshop to save face as an advertisement for possible co-productions with EBU members.

Despite the false rebuttal letter never being circulated and an official apology never being given, the Workshop's anger silenced Monica Sims for good. Even though she did finish her article for the *New York Times*, it was never printed.[134] Sims truly regretted this, because when the American *TV Guide* in March 1972 printed a sensational and very inaccurate story about Sims's handling of the whole *Sesame Street* affair, it was clear from BBC internal correspondence that Sims felt she had to suffer public ridicule without having had a chance to defend herself.[135] The *TV Guide* story and its incorrect claims about Sims's conduct at the EBU event were based on accounts that the Workshop clearly fed to the magazine. The result was that the article made Sims look rude, jealous, and possibly chauvinistic—a pompous British matriarch denying children what they craved, the deranged counterpart to the exquisitely polite Cooney whose show would give working-class families in England what they had wanted. Thus, even if the Workshop never had their false letter circulated, the one-sided stories that it presented to the US press certainly helped destroy Sims's reputation in the States. It also helped to diminish any possible influence the BBC's opinions about *Sesame Street* might have had on the Workshop's other critics. When the EBU working party had a four-day seminar on preschool television in February 1972 where *Sesame Street* was also discussed, Sims's name was nowhere in the official report, and she clearly must have kept a very low profile even if she was on the committee's steering group.[136]

The fact that the Workshop could strong-arm a BBC department head the way it did in this case shows how well connected the Workshop was in the United Kingdom. And the fact that top people at the BBC took the Workshop so seriously even while its production volume was very small in the global television market seems to speak volumes about the Workshop's vast influence.

ITV and *Sesame Street*'s Continued History in the United Kingdom

While the Workshop was having the BBC bosses clamp down on Sims, the trial broadcasts with the ITV companies moved ahead. However, even if the trials had resulted in positive press, they had also resulted in something else: more competition for *Sesame Street* on ITV's own network. As a result of all the debate around preschool television, four ITV companies were in the autumn of 1971 planning to make pilots for preschool series modeled on *Sesame Street*. Subsequently, the ITA's School Committee now asked the special experts' group, which was supposed to consider *Sesame Street*'s suitability for the British market, to also consider what would be desirable elements in a future British series like *Sesame Street*. By November, the British press was writing about how it looked forward to seeing new British preschool shows from ITV companies rather than *Sesame Street*.[137]

The Workshop nevertheless wanted to keep *Sesame Street* on the air alongside these new programs in the hope that it would outshine them. The ITV company London Weekend therefore asked the ITA for permission to continue with Saturday showings of *Sesame Street*. This was a cunning request because it meant that the ITA was pressured to decide on the show's exception from foreign quotas and schedule restrictions before their official report on the trial broadcasts was finished, and a decision would need to be rushed through before ITV's own new preschool shows had aired. When the ITA polled the ad-hoc group of educationalists who had taken part in the evaluation of *Sesame Street*, they decided narrowly in favor of *Sesame Street* being educationally beneficial for British children. However, the ITA's full Schools Committee decided narrowly in opposition. The authority itself decided to overrule its own Schools Committee and allow weekly showings of the series in London and elsewhere.[138] Newspapers such as the *Evening Standard*, the *Daily Express*, and the *Daily Telegraph* all celebrated the ITA's rejection of its own Schools Committee's ruling on *Sesame Street* and again scolded the BBC for its rejection. The narrow votes and disagreement show how *Sesame Street* had come to represent deep tensions over education and children's television in Britain.

Weekly showings in the London area were not what the Workshop had first hoped for when they approached the British market, but it was a partial success for now. Throughout 1972 and 1973, Peter Orton and Michael Dann worked hard on turning this truncated result into a five-day-a-week showing on the ITV network. In 1972 Dann concluded that with Saturday morning broadcasts by four ITV companies that gave them 60 percent coverage in England, the Workshop had "broken the BBC blockade."[139] The Workshop had reason to be optimistic.

When the ITA report on the trial broadcasts in 1971 was finally published in the summer of 1972, there was no firm conclusion as to whether *Sesame Street* was educationally useful for British children. The report concluded in noncommittal fashion, stating that the ITA had been mainly concerned with the response of children and parents. Among educationalists the debate is not resolved and will no doubt continue as long as the series runs, but whatever the merits and demerits of *Sesame Street*, showing it and arguing about it certainly strengthened the interest of British programme makers in producing an indigenous series.[140]

In this way the ITA avoided taking one of the now rather polarized positions on *Sesame Street* that the UK press had featured around discussions of the BBC, preschool education, and what British children needed to learn from television.

The report's penultimate paragraph is interesting because it framed the British response within a larger global context, a perspective that made the UK debate seem somehow misplaced and overblown. The ITA noted that *Sesame Street* had won a number of international prizes, including the Japan Prize, and that it had now been broadcast in more than thirty countries, with co-productions on their way. The report said that other English-speaking countries had not shown the resistance seen in Britain, seemingly wanted the reader to wonder why that was, and in the context of the positive reception elsewhere, that did not make the British resistance look all that well-founded.[141]

The research itself became rather inconsequential for *Sesame Street*'s position in the United Kingdom. The competition was now the upcoming preschool shows made by the ITV companies. To beat them, *Sesame Street* had to stay on the air to prove its superiority. The Workshop assessed that keeping *Sesame Street* on the air during weekends would surely stimulate the British public to demand more and secure a five-day-a-week network showing. The Workshop blamed the failure to achieve a full network showing in Britain on the "defensive tactics of the educational pundits of the BBC and ITA."[142] As the Workshop predicted that ITV's upcoming British preschool shows would be inferior to *Sesame Street*, its 1972 strategy counted on the British public to demand that it replace the domestically produced shows and make the ITA dispense with its strict rules. Such hopes were not completely illusionary, as the Workshop again had used its influential network to lobby its case at a dinner party in London where Joan Ganz Cooney met the minister for post and telecommunications.[143] Alas, not even connections to the minister got the Workshop as far as it had hoped.

The first ITV preschool program, *Rainbow*, began broadcasting on October 16, 1972. This was the beginning of ITV's preschool venture involving four ITV companies for twenty-minute-long shows on weekday afternoons (*Rainbow*, *Inigo Pipkin*, *Mr. Trimble*, and *Hickory House*). After one of the Workshop's representatives saw *Rainbow*, he told his colleagues that it was paced like *Play School* (much slower than *Sesame Street*) and had good, simple animation, but dreadful puppets placed in a usual fantasy world.[144] However, lacking in quality or not, 1972 brought no popular uprising demanding that *Sesame Street* replace ITV's new preschool offerings.

In November 1972 the Workshop concluded that it was not going to get its desired five days a week, but that some progress had been made as three of the ITV companies that together represented 45 percent of the UK market still scheduled *Sesame Street* on Saturday mornings.[145] The Workshop's Peter Orton admitted that the ITA had cleverly used *Sesame Street* to persuade UK companies to produce their own preschool series. Apparently, he was not able to fathom that a British audience would actually prefer productions that looked familiar and that used an educational style that aligned with their own educational system. These productions were "crap," Orton said, but unfortunately they were acceptable to UK educationalists.[146]

Considering the past years' events, Orton saw three options available to the Workshop. It could withdraw from the British market and "publicly take credit for the introduction of pre-school programs in Britain," ignoring the fact that *Play School* since 1964 had been such a program.[147] Another road to take was to be satisfied with 45 percent of the market, which *Sesame Street* currently reached without having any quota dispensations. A third and final road would be to try achieving a daily broadcast by collaborating with a commercial broadcaster and allowing British segments to be mixed with American ones. Orton suggested that the Workshop could even try this route with the BBC, but given the history with Sims, it might be best to first do so with its new program, *The Electric Company*. One reason for going back to the BBC despite the earlier conflict was that, after all, there was "no better partner for the CTW as money, hardware, staff and prestige [went]" than the BBC, and the Workshop could still make good use of all these things.[148]

Putting the former disputes behind them, the Workshop followed Orton's advice and kept pursuing the BBC. The organization's high standing, not only in the eyes of broadcasters outside the United States but also among American supporters of PBS—as well as its financial capacity—was still too big a pull for the Workshop to resist. Thus, Orton began a conversation with Sims about *The Electric Company*, and at the beginning of 1973 Orton, David Connell, and Joan Ganz Cooney met Sims for lunch to discuss a purely commercial venture for the Workshop for which they would like to use the BBC's facilities.[149] The lunch was also used to discuss the new Open Sesame format that the Workshop was considering.[150] The Workshop hoped that this format would give them another chance to create long-term opportunities with the BBC. There was, of course, the possibility that this would jeopardize the relationship with the ITV companies, but in the long term the Workshop was willing to take that risk if it meant a collaboration with the BBC—getting "the BBC seal of approval," which, as Sims saw it, was all they cared about.[151]

In the end, Sims never bought episodes of *The Electric Company* or pursued Open Sesame. The Workshop did, however, eventually achieve a small in with the BBC's Education Department, which aired a number of episodes of *The Electric Company* in May 1975. This might have helped to patch things up for everyone on a professional level as a small incident from the same year illustrates. In a note from April 1975, David Connell wrote to Peter Orton, "I thought you would be interested in this correspondence with Monica. It sounds as though the war is over with us if not the British press. Hopefully, future writers on the subject will take it easier on the poor woman."[152] The note referred to the aftermath from an article from in the *Daily Express*. The article was about *The Electric Company* and had quoted Sims saying that she was unhappy about it, without ever having interviewed her. Sims had therefore sent a letter of chastisement to the author.[153] She also sent a copy of that letter to the Workshop.[154] Sims was still marked by the old dispute and not interested in once again being brought into a conflict. Clearly, one of the most avid critics of the Workshop and *Sesame Street* had been silenced for good. Meanwhile, in the end, the Workshop had only had a little corner of their UK dream fulfilled, with *Sesame Street* being broadcast only once a week and to a little less than half of British preschoolers.

Conclusion: A Market Failure, but a Silencing Success?

The UK television market presented a big challenge to the Workshop. They wanted the income that was possible from a five-day-a-week broadcast, and they wanted the seal of approval that the BBC could give them. The Workshop, however, seemed utterly unprepared to acknowledge the fact that other educational traditions might produce preschool television as valuable as their own. The British valued a child-centered, progressive approach to education. Although a "light-scale," nonutopian progressivism, it was still very different from the educational ideas that guided *Sesame Street*. In BBC's programs children were encouraged to express their own ideas and explore the world while being guided by the adult presenters, the social and cultural lessons slowly enculturating them as good British citizens.[155] British progressive preschool ideals were not questioning adult authority per se, but they were child-centered, looking to support children's pursuit of their own interests and ideas. Some programs in the BBC's schedule focused on educating children on social and cultural aspects of everyday life, while other programs were to satisfy children's wishes for entertainment. *Sesame Street* came from a completely different media reality and perspective on children's needs. The mixture of entertainment and education was intended to satisfy a perceived need for school readiness for preschoolers, as defined in a set of expert-developed school-type skills, whereas the entertaining format was made to please children's tastes and keep them focused on the screen.

The Workshop's emphasis on research that showed the program's improvement on children's school-type skills won over some of the British press. *Sesame Street*'s emphasis on expert-defined bite-size lessons that could be measured and were easily recognized as belonging to a formal school context convinced some journalists of its benefits compared to *Play School*'s much fuzzier and progressive aims. The BBC was arguing for their importance, yet often failed to clearly articulate how this progressive preschool offering functioned within a mixed schedule that had many different programs for children, fulfilling different needs. *Sesame Street*'s focus on a narrow set of skills and facts, the disingenuous letter-learning aim one of them, also convinced many British parents of the need for such a show. Thus, while the BBC's Monica Sims and other British educators had objections to the way the Workshop wanted to use television, they had a hard time conveying the ideas and aims of the British preschool philosophy and *Play School*'s articulation of its merits.

The British broadcasting tradition with its tightly regulated market did, however, mean that the British preschool tradition prevailed. Even if it was easy for the British press to ridicule Sims, who had a hard time explaining exactly what she meant about *Sesame Street* being authoritarian and middle-class, quotas on foreign material and scheduling at ITV—and the BBC's independence and long history of children's broadcasting—meant that the Workshop could not conquer the market easily. It was nevertheless influential and strong enough to silence Sims's criticism, and after the infamous EBU meeting, hinder her participation in strong European opposition to *Sesame*

Street and the Workshop's approach to preschool education. The Workshop's global sales plans thus set the scene for the way it conducted its business in the United Kingdom, as the BBC's actions in particular were believed to affect a wide range of other potential buyers, including the affluent broadcasters in Western Europe.

One thing that helped the Workshop in its UK marketing campaign was its success elsewhere. Journalists, members of the ITA's Schools Committee, and people from the Workshop itself were able to show how big a hit the show was in other parts of the world. Thus, the marketing strategies that Peter Orton first at the TIE and later at the Workshop had planned—where some episodes of the first season were given away for free, just to have them on the air in as many places as possible—paid off as publicity that could be turned into real pressure. Sims looked foolish when so many other broadcasters had embraced the show. Equally, the vast amount of research that the Workshop had done was overpowering in a context like the British one, where television production to a large extent was based on practical experience. Even if the producers of children's programs like *Play School* had much experience, it was difficult to win an argument against the Workshop because all their "evidence" seemed to prove its superior status. The same tradition of quantitative research did not exist in the United Kingdom, and mass media researchers operating there were not working to measure the efficiency of a single show (also, shows were not created to have direct "impact," either educational or commercial). The public service nature of the broadcasting system meant that BBC was simply not prepared to argue for its program's benefit in the same way as the Workshop.

In the United Kingdom the Workshop had tried to sell the original American English-language version. There had been some considerations about a localization first with Sims's idea of co-production (though not proposed officially) and later with the Workshop's offer of Open Sesame that could be dubbed into British English. These options were, however, never discussed seriously as the Workshop was most interested in having the same one-hour, five-day-a-week setup as in the States. In the United Kingdom, the real question was whether the American original would be educational and attractive enough to a wide range of stakeholders—educators, broadcasters, children, parents, critics, and so on—in order to be accepted into the schedule. In areas where English was not the first language and where the program was not used for English-language teaching, the question of localizing the program was different. Here the question of the need for linguistic adaption was entangled with the question of the (possible) need to cater to other cultural and educational preferences. The extent to which a local incarnation of *Sesame Street* needed to change, and why, in order to be accepted became a difficult question for the Workshop and its potential collaborators in West Germany, as we shall see in the next chapter.

4

Negotiating Local Needs

Sesame Street in West Germany

In September 1972, the executives at the Children's Television Workshop watched a second round of newly produced pilots for the West German version of *Sesame Street*: *Sesamstraße*. In a letter to the local producers at the television station in charge of the German production, Norddeutscher Rundfunk (NDR) in Hamburg, the Workshop executives told how they liked the pilots and believed *Sesamstraße* would be excellent both technically and educationally. However, one aspect concerned them deeply: the "treatment of the topic of questioning authority."[1] The executives were alarmed that the local producers would so "clearly encourage the viewing children to question and to defy regulations and restrictions imposed by adults." The Workshop was convinced that West German parents and teachers would not support this encouragement of questioning adults' authority, no matter what the local team and their educational advisers thought. Clearly worried that this type of content would jeopardize *Sesamstraße*'s acceptance in West Germany, the Workshop urged that the pilots be changed immediately.

This incident shows conflicting ideas about localization on two different levels. First was the conflict regarding the content. How much and in what way did the *Sesame Street* concept need to change to satisfy local educational needs? The educational advisers to NDR had defined one of West German children's needs as developing a questioning stance toward adults as a way to become rounded, democratic citizens. This belief was built on the conviction that education that helped children question authority would prevent the kind of obedience that had led to Hitler's success and resulted in the Holocaust.[2] In accordance with widely accepted ideas in West Germany at the time regarding children's need for democratic education, NDR's team believed the development of independence to be an important focus when adapting *Sesame Street* to their local environment.[3] The Workshop staff, with an apparently limited understanding of how the World War II experience had impacted pedagogical thinking in Germany, saw these ideas as

Sesame Street. Helle Strandgaard Jensen, Oxford University Press. © Oxford University Press 2023.
DOI: 10.1093/oso/9780197554159.003.0005

inappropriate for a child audience and perhaps also feared a negative parental reaction, something to be expected in the United States in the wake of the 1960s' youth protests.

Second, the incident demonstrates a conflict over who should judge whether the local adaptation was successful. For the NDR team, the show was a success if it conformed to local educational and aesthetic standards. The Workshop, by contrast, believed that if the local version of the show was popular with the public at large, it had successfully adapted to local needs; the opinions of local experts were less important because *Sesame Street's* basic philosophy already had the approval of many American experts. These two conflicting notions of successful television paralleled the contrasting perspectives of public and commercial television landscapes more broadly. Public television was ultimately supposed to meet the perceived needs of the target group as defined by the broadcaster (its advisers and the cultural elite), even if there was an increasing interest in audience preferences in public service children's television at the time. In commercial television, viewer satisfaction—indicated by high ratings for advertisers—was the ultimate goal. Though the Workshop was not a commercial organization, its criteria for the German version's success were partly rooted in commercial "ratings game" thinking, as it had to sell its merchandise licenses and demonstrate to other potential buyers what a success the German show was. In addition to perceptions of the educational needs of preschoolers, the differences in these overall mindsets in terms of measuring success shaped the development of the West German version of *Sesame Street*.

The adaptation in West Germany was built on the experiences the Workshop had in Latin America, which it tried to process into a general framework for co-productions. Understanding how local adaptations unfolded in specific contexts but were later recycled in others provides valuable insight into how the Workshop's model for sales of its so-called foreign-language versions was developed and the local consequences of such attempts to standardize localization. This sales process differed from the Open Sesame concept because localization efforts went beyond dubbing and making a local version of the intro song. It also differed from the sales campaign related to the English version. In Britain, the acceptance of the English-language version had been a question of whether the program could be accepted as it was. When becoming engaged in foreign-language versions, like Spanish for Latin America and German for West Germany and other German-speaking areas, the Workshop had to balance the degree that it would allow its core concept to be changed with its need to make money from overseas sales of broadcast and merchandise—activities that depended on a highly recognizable brand.

The West German Market

In West Germany, as elsewhere in Europe, there had been an increasing interest throughout the 1960s in the lives of young children and providing preschool to them.[4] Inspired by new theories in child psychology that brought attention to the early lives of children and their later development, pedagogues, sociologists, nursery school teachers, and public intellectuals discussed how best to support children while they are growing up. In West Germany, much of this effort was concentrated on deliberations on how to make children self-aware, stimulate their creativity and independence, and inspire a thirst for knowledge and social understanding, as well as how to navigate and critically assess the norms and rules of adult-driven society.[5]

The German interest in early childhood development and education was, as in the United States, aimed at understanding how a child's social environment affected their intelligence and aptitude. The West German discussions were rooted in a long tradition of pedagogy linked to Continental philosophy.[6] Rather than an educational context like that of Sesame Street, where the focus was elaborate data collection and testing made to detect and solve possible shortcomings in academic achievements, the dominant West German solutions to educational challenges were found in qualitative, analytical approaches, as in the British context. A difference from both the American and UK contexts was, however, the German focus on what was called "democratic" or sometimes "emancipatory" education, where the way to a better-educated and more equal society included questioning traditionally hierarchical adult-child relationships. Thus, even if the core principles of German preschool education at the time overlap somewhat with a progressive education in Britain, the focus on questioning authorities was more pronounced in Germany.[7] The explicit emphasis on social education as a tool to collectively change established norms regarding authority also made German educational thought stand out compared to the British and especially the US contexts, where a more individualistic focus dominated.

Television for young children had been limited in West Germany throughout the 1960s. The protection of small children from audiovisual material was most visible with the 1957 law that banned children under six from going to the cinema, but nationwide television networks had followed suit and only broadcast programs for children eight years of age and older until the end of the 1960s.[8] Watching television was framed as a problematic activity, portrayed as keeping children away from the active use of their bodies and creativity.[9] However, at the end of the 1960s, the interest in preschool education coincided with the growing realization by German parents and television producers that this now decades-old medium was part of small children's everyday life and routines, even if it was not supposed to be. As such, at the very end of the 1960s the dominant attitude became that children needed shows that were appropriate for their age group and would help their enculturation process.[10] The interest in preschool television was evident in both networks that covered West Germany.

The Zweites Deutsches Fernsehen (ZDF) network was established in 1963 and covered all of West Germany with programming on Channel 2. In 1970 it considered establishing a preschool program based on ideas from the BBC's *Play School*. The other, older West German network, Arbeitsgemeinschaft der öffentlich-rechtlichen Rundfunkanstalten der Bundesrepublik Deutschland (ARD) consisted of nine independent regional corporations covering the countries' nine states with a mixture of joint and local programming on two channels (one for national viewing on Channel 1, the other for regional programming on Channel 3). The first program on ARD's network for preschoolers aired in 1969, made by the broadcasting corporation in Munich, Bayerisches Rundfunk, for a national audience. Though the program was not related to the BBC's production, it had the same title, albeit, of course, in German: *Die Spielschule* (The play school). *Die Spielschule* had a total of thirteen episodes that were typical of the experimental, shorter formats of children's shows on public service broadcasters.[11]

Ideas for *Die Spielschule* had been discussed since 1967.[12] The show was based on the ideas of emancipatory education, as it was aimed at giving young viewers a very matter-of-fact impression of West German society and everyday life. It was also supposed to pose questions that would challenge commonly assumed, self-evident facts and rules of the everyday lives of adults and children, and thereby take children's perspectives seriously. Consequently, the show had no studio recordings or fixed location, was largely nonverbal, and made to be "observed"—all intended to encourage children to draw their own conclusions about what they saw.[13] Even if the regional ARD corporation in Munich first produced a preschool program, the emerging genre had gained attention network-wide. Several initiatives were taken to support the production of these programs, including research and a network-wide working group.[14] From 1970 onward, thirty minutes weekly were set aside on the network's Channel 1 for national broadcast of regionally produced preschool programs. *Die Spielschule* aired nationwide in 1970 and was joined by preschool productions from the regional broadcasting corporations in West Berlin (*Kwatschnich* [You don't say][15]) and Cologne (*Lach- und Sachgeschichten für Fernsehanfänger* [Fun and fact stories for TV beginners][16]).

Though based on a very different approach to preschool education than the West German productions, *Sesame Street* arrived just in time to be part of the debate of what television for this age group should offer. Joan Ganz Cooney had already in 1968 published her article about the Workshop's project in the internationally distributed German-language journal *Fernsehen und Bildung*, and *Sesame Street* won the Prix Jeunesse Prize in 1970 at the international festival in Munich—an event that many West German children's television producers attended. The exposure of *Sesame Street* in Germany as well as the Workshop's Paris-based sales agents' relentless efforts, had led to interest from both West German networks, ARD and ZDF.[17]

In early 1971, a joint ARD working group with representatives from all nine of its regional broadcasting companies had been established to develop preschool programming more systematically. This group became very important for the development and expansion of preschool programs in West Germany.[18] The group was expected to follow a policy that outlined plans for child and family programming. The policy that laid the foundation for the group demonstrates the high degree to which *Sesame Street* influenced the ARD's internal debate about preschool programming. Its third point explicitly mentioned *Sesame Street* and offered a positive assessment of its combination of education and entertainment:

> Particularly with a program for small children, it must be taken into account that experience has shown that the attractiveness of a television program suffers if the medium is understood purely as a means of conveying teaching material, neglecting the entertainment and playful elements. Even if the concept of "Sesame Street" cannot simply be transferred to a German context, the design of the series shows that a program can manage without obtrusive teaching, despite its fixed learning objectives, and can indeed be extremely attractive.[19]

Even if there were diverging attitudes toward *Sesame Street* within the ARD working group, it was generally agreed that *Sesame Street* offered an alternative to didacticism. The policy was equally sympathetic to another feature of *Sesame Street*—the need to fill a void for those children who were not able to attend preschool. The proposal also explicitly stated how preschool programs might help eliminate sociocultural inequalities by filling out "a compensatory function to adjust educational opportunities," just as the Workshop wanted *Sesame Street* to do in the United States.[20] The idea of television as "compensatory education" was repeated when the German broadcasters applied for funding from local and federal governmental entities, but eventually debunked by the group of experts who later became the local advisers for the show.[21]

Not everything about *Sesame Street* was seen as ideal or transferable to a West German context. The policy for the ARD working group clearly stated that programs should not focus on "one-sided promotion of the cognitive domain [but instead] aim at the overall development of the child, who should become aware of the world as it is," contrary to what was believed to be happening in *Sesame Street*.[22] Instead of skills that were associated with school-type learning, the policy called for programs that stimulated children creatively, socially, and linguistically. Though it clearly drew inspiration from the Workshop's ideas about developing a set of "learning goals" for program production, the ARD working group wanted these goals to include a much wider range of issues than the Workshop had made for the original version of *Sesame Street*.

With its official status and inclusion of all of ARD's nine regional broadcasters, the working group became the most influential forum for discussions of preschool television in West Germany in the 1970s. It had a vast influence on program policy not only nationally but also internationally through its members' publications in *Fernsehen und Bildung* and participation in Prix Jeunesse and the EBU working group for children and young people. Furthermore, the preschool working group had the power to decide if a program like an adaption of *Sesame Street* to West German broadcasting should be a joint ARD project on Channel 1. This power meant that it had a large influence on the Workshop's success, determining whether it could be a nationally transmitted program (on Channel 1) or only in some regions (broadcast regionally on Channel 3). In making such a decision it would also influence discussions on whether *Sesame Street* was truly the proper program for West German children.

Looking for the Right German Partner

In late March 1971, the Workshop needed to decide with which of the two networks in West Germany it wanted to cooperate.[23] In the summer of 1970, it had already met with Ursula Klamroth, a producer from the local Hamburg-based station of the ARD network, NDR, in hopes of collaborating with her. Gerald Lesser and Michael Dann had been very impressed with her understanding of *Sesame Street*.[24] However, as the Workshop's Paris-based sales agents had initiated talks with the competing German ZDF network, there had been some initial confusion about with whom the Workshop wanted to collaborate. The rather complicated West German broadcasting system—where one network was nationwide and another had two channels that were shared by nine regional broadcasters—does not seem to have made things easier.

Before making a final decision about which network it wanted to deal with, the Workshop prepared a test run of five English-language episodes. These were broadcast at ARD's Hamburg-based corporation, NDR, in April 1971. The test was intended to measure the popularity of their show and hopefully help NDR convince the last eight members of the ARD network to help pay for a West German version that could be broadcast nationwide on Channel 1.

The Workshop was justifiably convinced that the outcome of their dealings with West German broadcasters would influence the fate of the show in the United Kingdom, France, Italy, and Scandinavia as well.[25] The Italian broadcaster's official magazine *Radiocorriere* closely followed the West German test shows as they went on, and Danish newspapers would report on the forthcoming trial runs.[26] Another issue also made the test's success important: the Workshop had learned that the ARD planned to have a daily preschool program ready for national transmission on Channel 1 by September 1972. If this program was not a version of *Sesame Street*, it would be the ARD's own program, probably leaving no room for *Sesame Street* to join later as schedule slots and resources would have been spent on domestic programming.

From the ARD's perspective, the test was a way for members of its joint working group on preschool programs to consider the show's suitability for a West German audience. The program had to be reviewed in its English-language version both for potential use in schools for the teaching of English and to assess if there was a basis for a German co-production with the

Workshop. Like the test broadcasts that ITV had done in Britain, the ARD working group wanted to use these test viewings of *Sesame Street* to survey the opinions of a wide range of groups working with children, including pedagogues, psychologists, social workers, and kindergarten teachers.[27] They wanted to use the feedback to make sure that the educational style of the program resonated broadly with these groups. As in the United Kingdom, viewers were encouraged to send letters to the NDR in Hamburg, letting them know what they thought of the programs.[28] But unlike in the United Kingdom, no formal study was conducted to monitor the German reception of the program, much to the dismay of those Germans who disliked *Sesame Street* and had wanted the same open discussion about the show's suitability in West Germany.[29]

The announcement of the *Sesame Street* test broadcast was widely and grandly promoted, just as it had been when the show premiered in the States and Britain. Articles in big news outlets like *Der Spiegel* and *Die Zeit* were very favorable.[30] A long article in *Der Spiegel* repeated much of the framing that the Workshop itself had set up around its brand, distinguishing it from the purchase of American entertainment shows like the Western *Bonanza*, which was popular with West German children, but not with educators and public intellectuals.[31] The article also tried to forestall criticism of the show's American outlook by telling readers how it would be adapted to a West German television culture, ridding it of its most "American" characteristics and reducing it from sixty to thirty minutes to keep children from too much exposure to the TV screen. To further calm critical voices, Klamroth, who had been interviewed for the article, told how *Sesame Street* was the "most tested program in television history," indicating that the American test results generally proved the show's worth.[32] The article highlighted how three-year-olds who watched *Sesame Street* regularly knew more about their surroundings than four- or five-year-olds who watched infrequently. Again, as in the United Kingdom, research on educational benefits achieved in the United States with an American audience was presented as directly transferable to German children, even if set in a very different social and educational context. This uncritical assessment of the value of American research supported the Workshop's branding strategy.

The test broadcasts were well received by the public.[33] NDR received more than two hundred letters, of which 95 percent were reported to favor a West German adaptation of the program. However, public support was not enough. Because of the significant costs involved in adapting the program to West German standards, the NDR team now needed to secure support from the other regional corporations in ARD as well as from federal and local governments and private foundations. Nevertheless, the popular reception of the test shows made it easy to convince some of the other ARD's regional broadcasters to do their own trail broadcasts.[34] Getting the eight other local program directors to support NDR in buying the program was another matter.

ARD's program directors were to meet in mid-May 1971. Before the meeting, the programming director (a so-called intendant) of NDR in Hamburg had circulated a written statement to the other regional corporations to convince them to take part in his corporation's *Sesame Street* venture.[35] The note presented *Sesame Street* as the most rigorous and successful project in preschool programming. The Workshop was described not only as very successful in supporting the education of underprivileged youth, but also in capturing a global audience of more than seven million children. The statement, referring to the Workshop's own research, noted how the program raised the cognitive skills of underprivileged children by 62 percent in the first year. Intent on arguing for *Sesame Street* as a perfect match for German preschool needs as described in the policy proposal made by the ARD's joint working group, the NDR intendant ignored the discrepancy between the educational aims of *Sesame Street* with its stress on school-type skills and progressive preschool ideals in West Germany. Instead, he referred to a new paper produced by the German government on preschool education to support his positive assessment of *Sesame Street*. However, the paper was, quite contrary to the aims of *Sesame Street*, a testament to the need for a preschool reform based on progressive, emancipatory education that deemphasized formal learning:

> The Federal Republic of Germany considers the expansion of elementary education to be particularly important and urgent and sees this as the decisive dismantling of social barriers. This makes elementary education the first and most important step in school reform. In pre-school education, the aim for children is not to learn "by the book," but rather to make them enjoy learning. They should become independent and practice social behavior in an age-appropriate manner. Above all, this includes growing independence, consideration for others, and recognizing simple problems and their possible solutions.[36]

This government paper emphasized preschool education as an important element in social mobility, a point that of course overlapped with the aims of *Sesame Street*, and so did the emphasis on enjoying learning. However, it did not support the kind of rote learning of facts and school-type skills that *Sesame Street* had, but instead emphasized social mobility and social skills that would make children independent. The fact that NDR's intendant was not aware of this difference—or he ignored it or did not believe it existed— allowed him to align *Sesame Street* to official federal policy in the preschool area. He pointed out that only one-third of West German children between three and six were in kindergarten, and that it would take a long time for this situation to improve. He also argued that *Sesame Street* offered a solution to this problem by providing preschool education to the unserved majority via television and that the ARD's German version, shorter than the original sixty minutes and with 30 percent new material produced locally, would be successful with West German children.

However, despite the best efforts of the NDR intendant, the joint committee of all the intendants that presided over the ARD's program for Channel 1 decided not to buy *Sesame Street*.[37] One reason was the cost. Notwithstanding the promise of subsidies from official and private organizations, adapting the program to fit West German needs was considered too expensive. Second, the intendants found the Workshop's focus on reducing the achievement gap between privileged and underprivileged children irrelevant in a German context, as they did not think the same problems existed in German society. Third, the director of the ARD's Bavarian-based corporation believed that child viewers had to see themselves represented on the screen and therefore questioned whether West German children were best served by a program featuring many Black children.[38] Finally, some intendants worried that buying *Sesame Street* would block homegrown ARD initiatives for preschoolers.

The intendants, however, only had the final word when it came to Channel 1's schedule, not the regional programs on Channel 3. A group of the ARD's directors from regional broadcasting companies with headquarters in Hamburg (NDR), Cologne (WDR), and Frankfurt (HR) could therefore choose to go against this decision. The three companies decided to pursue a co-production of the show with the Workshop and broadcast it regionally on Channel 3, as they would not risk going against public opinion, which was very much in favor of the show after the test broadcasts, not least because of all the positive press. They also did not want to risk the possibility of this popular show being bought by their rival network, ZDF, which they knew had made a bid for it. Thus, a minority of the ARD's regional corporations joined together to make a West German co-production led by NDR's team in Hamburg.[39]

The fact that the three regional ARD broadcasters had gone against the majority was a problem for the joint ARD working group on preschool television. It meant that *Sesame Street*, a major preschool show, would be broadcast on parts of the ARD network, but the working group's members would have no official advisory capacity on the adaptation because it was a regional affair broadcast on Channel 3. However, because of the intertwined nature of the regional and federal levels of ARD, the working group frequently discussed *Sesame Street* at its meetings, and the program affected its work with other preschool programs.[40] For instance, it inspired a massive effort to establish learning outcomes for other preschool shows, even if some broadcasters objected to such a checklist format. The working group was also split in its stance on *Sesame Street*'s qualities or lack thereof. There was no agreement on whether the show could successfully be adapted to fit West Germans' needs and ideals. Likewise, there was disagreement on whether the focus on school-type learning goals—as well as the reliance on drills, facts, and rote memory—was at odds with education aimed at furthering creativity, imagination sensitivity, and spontaneity. A central question was if *Sesame Street* could be made into a program that had the ability to support the child in exploring and questioning established norms, as, for instance, the program *Maxifant und Minifant*. *Maxifant und Minifant* had reached broad consensus when its progressive goals had been presented within the working group:

> Television should not meet the understandable needs of parents and educators for security for the child too much; the moment of uncertainty must be seen . . . as an opportunity for the child to ask questions, be curious or critical. . . . [Television] has to offer high-quality programs as a provider of information and storytelling . . . that challenge children to see their own possibilities.[41]

The agreement of *Maxifant und Minifant*'s goals as important clearly demonstrates that even if the working group disagreed on the value of *Sesame Street* in West Germany, the social learning goals related to independence and freedom that the German version, *Sesamstraße*, would later include were strongly supported in the West German children's broadcasting environment.

Despite the disagreement on *Sesame Street*'s qualities the working group had to deal with the fact that a German version would be broadcast on parts of Channel 3 when the co-production was ready.[42]

Professionalizing the Approach to Foreign Versions

At the same time that the West German co-production was being planned, the Workshop talked to other broadcasters in Europe about similar arrangements. These parallel sales efforts affected the ways in which the Workshop negotiated possible local demands for co-productions. In the spring of 1971, the Workshop also negotiated with Scandinavians in the Nordic Broadcasting Union on how to make a version of *Sesame Street* for Norway, Sweden, and Denmark; it had held meetings with representatives from Radiotelevisione Italiana (RAI) in Italy; and its sales agents in Paris were talking about a French version. Realizing that it might soon have other co-productions to keep track of, in addition to those being developed in Latin America, the Workshop began to systematize its approach to produce what it called "foreign-language versions" in the early summer of 1971. Its unified approach with fixed guidelines was intended to make future co-production efforts easier.[43] The Workshop's International Production Unit was responsible for standardizing the co-production guidelines, drawing on ongoing experiences in Latin America.[44]

The Workshop's co-production guidelines, which were sent to the West Germans in the summer of 1971, had several demands that foreign broadcasters needed to follow. The lead producer had to have extensive experience in television production, be proficient in English, be sympathetic to the Workshop's goals, and have ideas as to how the existing material could be retailored economically to address local needs. The production facilities had to meet the Workshop's expectations in terms of technical ability. Equipment costs were of great concern. Dubbing and producing new scenes locally was a technically demanding and very expensive process, which meant that only a group of broadcasters or a very affluent local organization would be able to participate in co-productions. The Workshop would provide material for the co-production that it believed was easy to dub into a foreign language: this included animated films, live-action films, and Muppet sketches. All these segments matched particular goals in the *Sesame Street* curriculum: numbers, counting, numerical operations, geometric forms, the natural environment, relational concepts, and perceptual discrimination.[45] This material was expected to be repeated eight times per season on top of locally produced segments, with the American-produced material making up at least 45 percent of a season. For the *Plaza Sésamo* production, tapes were sent to Mexico for simple dubbing of Workshop-produced material, sent back to New York for processing, and sent then back again to Mexico for further local processing.[46] This was much more complicated than just normal dubbing. Broadcasters that did not have the resources to make a foreign-language version like this had to settle for the English-language version, as the Workshop did not at this point allow dubbing of entire episodes as they believed the educational effects of the show would be lost; concepts like Open Sesame only came later. The little room left for foreign broadcasters to maneuver on their own in relation to a local airing of the program was rooted in the Workshop's obsession with brand control, seeing every show as possibly impacting their sales to other interested stakeholders. It was, however, also a form of cultural imperialism where only the US way was seen as the right one, and deviations to accommodate local conditions and wishes would cause a substandard outcome.

Correspondence with the West German team at NDR illuminates how unusual the Workshop's approach to co-production was for this period. It was far from standard practice to have local bits patched together with dubbed original material. When shows were sold to foreign markets, the original producers would not be as invested or require as much control when it came to localization.[47] Anyone undertaking a co-production with the Workshop had to consider these new and complicated workflows, including their own cost in time and money. In contrast, co-producing *Play School* with the BBC or buying other formats to be remade in local environments was much less complicated, as the producers of the originals were not as interested in what happened in the concrete localization process; buying and selling formats had not become a formalized process in most of Europe at this point.[48]

The Workshop wanted localized content to closely fit the American content because the US production setup was seen as the best. This meant that at the beginning of the co-production process, foreign scriptwriters were supposed to adapt the "original, USA 'Sesame Street' scripts, motifs, comedy, and educational situations to the lifestyle of the foreign country producing," not write original material. The co-production guideline offered the Latin American version as an example, illustrating how "the writing staff will initially 'Latinize' existent 'Sesame Street' scripts," and only when they had demonstrated that they could reproduce the Workshop's core ideas could they begin to write new material.[49]

To further ensure a high degree of likeness between Sesame Street and local co-productions, foreign producers had to undergo meticulous training by the Workshop in New York to be drilled in its educational philosophy and production methods.[50] This training was not only technical and practical but included careful instruction in how to use Sesame Street material as a model for balancing curriculum goals and production. The foreign collaborator had to demonstrate how the local material supported all of Sesame Street's original four major goal areas and then pass this on in a clear directive to their writers by developing a so-called curriculum assignment sheet.

With these technical and conceptual requirements for co-productions, the Workshop had drawn the contours of what would later become the basis for their export of the Sesame Street concept, the CTW model.[51] This was a complex set of expectations resting on an intertwined relationship between goals defined by educational experts, television producers ensuring high production value and appeal, and researchers evaluating the show's efficiency. Local adaptations to this model would eventually involve a huge amount of oversight from the Workshop. The element of control over the co-productions, was, however, not firmly established when formally agreeing to the first co-production with West Germany. The Spanish version for Latin America was very closely modeled on the American original, largely because the Workshop had technical and financial control. The West German co-production partner was embedded in a big broadcasting institution, technically equal if not superior to the Workshop and part of a strong milieu for preschool education and children's television. This gave the Germans freedom to pursue what they found best within Sesame Street and at the same time follow emerging ideas in German preschool education that were very different from the Workshop's. The Germans' technical independence combined with the Workshop's eagerness to sign a deal that would help its financial situation gave the German partner the strength to push back on specific demands that the Americans made regarding the local production.

Setting Up Production of *Sesamstraße*

Once the test shows at ARD were finished and the group of three regional broadcasters had decided that they would buy *Sesame Street*, three Workshop representatives visited NDR in Hamburg, which would head the project on the West German side. The Workshop's team was supposed to prepare the groundwork for the future relationship on which the co-production would be based and help the Hamburg team on its way to a pilot and a curriculum for the program. The team consisted of Gerald Lesser, the Harvard professor who chaired the Workshop's advisory board; Norton Wright, the head of the International Productions Unit; and Al Dwyer, the Workshop's top lawyer.[52]

Sending Harvard's Lesser to represent the Workshop helped strengthen the association between the *Sesame Street* brand and academic research. Lesser had chosen to combine the visit with a trip to London to convince the ITV to do more test runs in Britain. As in Britain, Lesser was officially sent by the Workshop to help the Germans determine if *Sesame Street* was appropriate for their culture and to gauge how much adaptation was needed.[53] But whether *Sesame Street* was suitable for West Germany was not the real issue; the Workshop needed to sell it to West Germany for financial reasons and to gain a footing in continental Europe. The question was how much adaptation would be needed to have the local audience accept the show.

Lesser's unprofessional interaction with and superficial judgment of local experts on his trip to Germany adds to the impression of the evaluation as a shallow operation intended to lend the Workshop academic credibility but not truly evaluate local interests. As discussed in chapter 3, Lesser's official report to the Workshop from this trip shows that he was very certain of his own ability to judge the competencies of local experts. In no way did he see his limited knowledge of local educational cultures as a hindrance when advising foreign educators and producers. Furthermore, as also discussed in chapter 3, Lesser had an unprofessional way of objectifying women. On his trip to Hamburg, his report to the Workshop—on stylish Harvard letterhead—reveals his indifference and distraction in his interactions with his German counterparts. He mentioned how the "charming young lady" who was interpreting "by whispering quietly in his ear" was "driving him wild with lust at the same time," and for this reason, he had not been able to follow part of the important meeting.[54] Lesser's lack of interest in local discussions clearly shows in this behavior. Based on later disagreements between the production team in Hamburg and the Workshop on the making of

Sesamstraße, he might have done well to take his visit more seriously. His report concluded that the Hamburg team could make an acceptable adaptation for a West German audience without any acknowledgment of differences. It mentioned none of the specific adjustments that the Germans believed they needed to make. It only listed generic ideas about defining a target audience and stating educational objectives, confirming that Lesser with his Ivy League credentials acted more as an academic figurehead to the Workshop in this context than someone whose expertise was used to assess local needs and wants in any detail.

When the Workshop drafted an agreement for collaboration with NDR, control of the *Sesame Street* concept was key.[55] The Workshop wanted the Germans to demonstrate that they had the ability to produce a high-quality pilot and for it to maintain the right to stop the broadcast of any segment or episode of which it disapproved. Within the Workshop, the drafted agreement was very favorably viewed. The Workshop would retain the rights to the German productions (allowing it to sell them to Austria, Switzerland, and other German-speaking regions without sharing any sales revenue), just as had been the arrangement in Latin America with the Spanish version produced in Mexico. Anxious to get this favorable contract signed, Wright still told NDR that the German producers had to prove worthy for a foreign production.[56] Wright had already drawn up a curriculum assignment sheet listing the special social learning goals for the German version, though he admitted in a letter to Klamroth that these were only his best interpretations based on the pilot script for *Sesamstraße.*[57] Later, Wright's lack of understanding of the social learning goals, and the Workshop's arrogant disregard of German programming ideas, would turn out to present a big challenge. As we saw in the introduction to this chapter, German social learning goals, including critical perspectives toward authority, were exactly what these goals would needed address.

In September 1971, three representatives from NDR flew to New York to discuss the draft contract.[58] Included were Klamroth; her boss, Karl-Heinz Grossmann, who would be the person responsible for the broadcast on NDR; and NDR's legal counsel. An important discussion point was the Workshop's right to interfere with and control the production of the German pilot, which the Germans opposed. The Workshop in turn was concerned that a substandard pilot would "harm [its] reputation and good name" in the eyes of other foreign broadcasters.[59] To ease the Workshop's anxiety, it was agreed that it would have the right to review and reject the pilot for approval.

However, the clause that gave the Workshop rights to pre-censor all production was removed. The negotiations were difficult because of the novel nature of this kind of production partnership. Co-productions between German regional broadcasters and between EBU members generally in the area of children's television were not as rigid. The difference is likely to be rooted in the fact that European broadcasters, in contrast to the Workshop, had many different productions for children and therefore were not as invested in the success of a single program with a fixed concept, as was the case with the Workshop and *Sesame Street*.

In October 1971, NDR had a ready pilot. Klamroth sent it to New York together with a thirty-page-long proposal specifying NDR's plans for the German version of *Sesame Street*. In the report, she did her best to convince the Workshop that NDR was a worthy partner, using some of the same arguments that the Workshop itself had used when it raised the first money for *Sesame Street* in the United States. Her first point was that young children who did not have access to preschool education and the children of the country's two million immigrant workers would benefit from the program. *Sesame Street* was seen as important in teaching German children of all backgrounds to "accept people of different race and color."[60] In Germany marginalization was especially a problem related to immigrant workers but also other minorities. It was exactly this group that the show aimed to include and wanted to represent on the screen:

> To integrate the foreign workers into our community it is very necessary that children within [our target audience] get used to the inhabitants of *Sesame Street* and to have children of foreign workers participate in the German version.[61]

The idea that children's television could play a positive role in favorably representing immigrants or minorities, and that it might help them do better in the educational system, was inspired by the American version and adjusted to fit a West German context.

Klamroth also noted that NDR recognized how *Sesame Street* would help achieve the federal government's aims of reforming preschool teaching to emphasize independence and social behavior and make learning enjoyable. However, unlike the program director of NDR who had glossed over the differences between West German preschool education and *Sesame Street*'s goals, Klamroth's report made sure to specify what these differences were and why German experts on preschool education met *Sesame Street* with skepticism. She went to great lengths to explain the Germans' reluctant attitude toward the show's emphasis on skills training like "counting [and] schematic recital of the alphabet." They would much prefer a program that promoted "education to emancipation, social relationships to the environment of the target audience and systematic exercises of social conduct," all of which they believed were neglected in the English-language version.[62] According to the NDR, a German version needed sequences that promoted the freedom of children as well as segments that showed man-made environments in Germany to help children orient themselves more independently in society at large.

Based on local German experts' advice, NDR estimated that the original sixty-minute shows would have to be cut down to thirty minutes, and of those, about 30 percent would have to be produced by NDR. The show's permanent advisory board would be made up of psychologists, sociologists, pedagogues, education specialists, and kindergarten teachers, all of whom had met with Lesser on his trip to Hamburg in June. In addition to the new German version, the English version was planned to be shown from 6 to 7 p.m. as part of adult second-language education. This would give *Sesame Street* exposure that no other preschool program would ever match.

Klamroth was careful to explain that NDR had the financial and technical means to produce a high-quality show. She explained that three of the ARD's regional broadcasters secured the two million dollars for the project and that the ministry for education and science financed the research. The NDR team was responsible for the production, but the report shows that they would co-produce with the team at Westdeutscher Rundfunk (WDR), the local ARD boradcaster in Cologne. The fact that ARD as a network would cover the 1972 Olympics made NDR very confident that they had the technical capacity needed for the complicated co-production that involved playback and synchronization. This technical advantage, Klamroth insisted, allowed the German producers to take the lead rather than just follow the American directions, as was necessary with the Latin American production.

Klamroth's report emphasized an evaluation of the pilot made by the German Ministry of Science and Education and local experts on preschool education. This evaluation had shown a general satisfaction with the new German segments that NDR/WDR had produced. These included a multilingual segment about a ball especially targeted at children of "foreign workers," and a much-praised segment on the difference between left and

right. The left-right segment, however, was not limited to practical information, but presented an adult acting foolish when trying to understand the
concepts of left and right and encouraged children not to blindly trust adults.
The ministry and the advisers wanted to see more segments on cooperation
and possibly a new Muppet.

Upon receiving the report and viewing the pilot, the Workshop and
NDR negotiated the final contract needed to start the production of the
German version. The contract was signed at the beginning of 1972.[63] The
Workshop did not like the German-produced segments about the ball and
the left and right. It did not raise its disagreement with these segments before the contract was signed, however, but instead insisted on a clause that
if the German programs were "not in furtherance of and damaging to the
Workshop's established educational goals," then the license granted would
be terminated within ten days.[64] The Germans found this criterion too sub-
jective and wanted it replaced with license termination only if the program
failed to meet the educational goals set down by the German advisory board.
The Workshop agreed, if they could approve the board's members. In addition, the Workshop also wanted to ensure that the program was popular
with German children and suggested that the contract would hinge on a rea-
sonable proportion of German children watching the show regularly. Thus,
the program should not just live up to the Workshop's educational standards
but also have high viewership: a driving issue from the American perspective. The emphasis on viewer numbers was not explained in detail, but it was
surely a way for the Workshop to make the Germans focus on this aspect
of their local production. Another way the Workshop ensured control of its
brand was by inserting a clause that allowed the Workshop to withdraw the
right to use the *Sesame Street* name if "the Workshop is not satisfied or that
the children are not learning as well as children in the United States."[65] All of
this suggests a fundamental distrust of German educational ideas that did not
correspond with the Workshop's original philosophy. Even if the Workshop
said that the program could be adjusted to local educational requirements, it
still expected its own goals and measurements of outcomes to prevail.

The Workshop also tried to influence development of a second pilot
by "suggesting" ideas for the German content. In fact, the Workshop's
suggestions were a thorough critique of the content the Germans had
produced for the first pilot.[66] The Workshop disliked the multilingual ball
segment, which they found confusing as well as unattractive. But what
posed the biggest problem to the Workshop was the left-and-right segment

that the German advisers had received most positively. The Workshop staff thoroughly rejected that anything could be gained from presenting an adult acting foolishly. Even though German government officials and their expert advisers had praised this segment, the Workshop either from ignorance or disbelief still asked NDR to reevaluate its merits. The Workshop was worried that children would be confused if they saw an adult making mistakes and asked the Germans whether they indeed understood that they were projecting a negative image of adults. The Workshop instead suggested that mistakes should be made by a "fantastic animal character" as Big Bird, because he could be repeatedly corrected without undermining children's confidence in adults as the source of knowledge—the exact opposite of the German intent.

This disagreement on the role that adults could play on children's television shows one of the key differences in how the Workshop and the German team behind *Sesamstraße* wanted children to relate to them. The Germans were keen to show that adults could also make mistakes and it was all right for children to question their judgment. The Workshop, on the other hand, was afraid that showing adults making mistakes would damage children's interest in learning. To guide the German team toward content that was more acceptable to the Workshop, it offered to assist the German team in the early stages of production and research.[67] The guidance was presented as a way for the Germans to avoid unnecessary work, but it seems to a greater extent to have been an assertion of the CTW model's superiority and the Workshop's idea of education and the child-adult relationship.

How to Define Social Learning?

At the beginning of 1972, the work on defining the learning goals for *Sesamstraße* began in earnest.[68] The now official—and Workshop-approved—advisory board for *Sesamstraße* composed a long, detailed report outlining the basis for the production. This had two parts: a checklist of goals and a narrative summarizing the newest German literature on preschool children and socialization. The latter section made it clear that the program and the accompanying research were to explore whether it was possible to improve the educational opportunities of all preschool children with a general program that would also compensate for any learning deficit of underprivileged children. Thus, what was taken for granted in the American approach to the show—that a special target group could be served particularly well by a show built on a general model aimed at all children—was posed as a question still to be answered by the German advisers.

One aspect of the German report that was very different from the American discussions of preschool television's compensatory possibilities was the educational system's role in this process. Instead of addressing education as the key to helping underprivileged children fare better in life, the Germans focused on socialization more broadly. They pointed to social and other structural conditions as the reasons for differences in children's lives, including the difference in their individual educational achievements. Preschool children's educational needs and possible educational failures were not conceptualized within the framework of the child as a pupil, but a much larger one that looked at the child as a citizen. The structural approach also meant that the document discussed broader issues, such as class differences:

> As understandable as the demand for a "compensatory socialization" is, it collides with the insight that the socialization conditions of the socially weak classes are conditioned and determined by their social and economic situation. [A] "better" socialization of the children from [these classes] can only be expected if the social and economic conditions of their parents change.[69]

Because the problem of inequality among children was viewed from this broad perspective, social learning that would help children question the roots and fairness of existing social norms was presented as an important goal for *Sesamstraße*. The German experts warned that the "compensatory" learning that the Workshop promised could easily lead to further gaps between poor and affluent children by adhering to the ideals of middle-class socialization and education, as *Sesame Street* was accused of. To avoid this, the German experts urged the producers of the local version to consider two questions. The first was to ask if forms of nonlinguistic intelligence and expression existing among lower-class children were being undervalued and suppressed. The second was to question whether unfair pressure was put on lower-class children to adapt to social norms, thus drawing a wedge between them and the social and cultural values of their family environment. Bridging gaps between children of different classes was seen as a crucial task for *Sesamstraße*. All children needed to understand their social situation and be provided with the means to improve it, no matter their background, as middle-class children were also seen as being suppressed by social structures and cultural norms that made them abide by adult authority.

The problems that preschool children might face in German society were not seen as problems for the individual to solve alone, but structural problems that might be reproduced in the program if left unaddressed. Consequently, cognitive and creative learning should, the advisers said, collectively contribute to an offering for all preschool children that above all should support social learning. In fact, the most important thing in the program was knowing oneself and others; being self-aware, critical, and curious; and learning how to solve social problems and collaborate. The experts wanted these goals incorporated in every episode as an overarching framework so that all other goals, such as school-type and creative skills, would always work to support the more important goal of social learning.

When the goals for *Sesamstraße* were presented to the Workshop in April 1972, Lesser questioned Germans' ideas for social learning. He claimed he understood the reason for wanting to teach social learning, but like other members of the Workshop, he was worried that a substantial risk was involved in taking on this area, which he believed might be "arousing in the child emotions which he cannot yet understand or with which he cannot cope." Topics such as "questioning authority or deal[ing] with anger, jealousy, frustration, etc."[70] therefore had to be avoided, the Workshop advised. One issue that could present concerns from an American point of view was that some parents could see social learning as too liberal when the Workshop wanted to win over the broader public with a consensus idea of equality of opportunity based on a US context.

To help the Germans develop goals that the Workshop saw as more appropriate, Lesser offered to be a consultant and help define very specific goals and subgoals for the area of social learning that did not question authority but focused on softer targets such as tolerance and collaboration. He wanted to steer the Germans away from encouraging what the Workshop saw as unsafe and unproductive behavior that arose when authority was questioned or challenged.[71] The Workshop suggested that rather than seeing social learning as the overall goal, specific checklists with other goals and subgoals should be established. These outcomes would be easier to evaluate but also ensure that the program conformed more closely to the American learning goals and the CTW model. Though this might seem like a simple task of breaking down lengthier passages into a checklist, it was rooted in a bigger difference related to pedagogical disagreements. The Germans were stating the overall policy's moral and broader educational value in a narrative structure, whereas the Americans attempted to have educational value broken down into seemingly "objective" bite-size goals, without being explicit about the moral and overall educational choices behind the program's design.

The NDR production team was not interested in the Workshop's suggestions for articulating the goals for *Sesamstraße* and therefore did not send the newly produced showcase episodes to New York for screening.[72] In internal correspondence, the Workshop talked of this as a major failing and was worried that there would be more of what they called "bizarre" and "weird films," most likely referencing the pilots' German-produced inserts on social learning.[73] Workshop staff showed little understanding of German aims when they called the German-produced segments of "hazy curriculum value."[74] They had hoped that the Germans would abandon their ideas about social learning and understand that the Workshop wanted them to make disciplined films relating to man-made and natural environments and German literacy. Finally seeing the films NDR produced, the Workshop was alarmed.[75] The treatment of the topic "questioning authority" that encouraged children to defy regulations and restrictions imposed by adults in segments such as "Don't Walk on the Bridge, on Grass" and "Finish Your Soup and We'll Have Good Weather" was deeply troubling to the Workshop. Again, in its correspondence with NDR, Workshop staff claimed to understand the reasoning behind these segments and that the educational advisers might support them, but still they "wonder[ed] if German parents and teachers share your position or if indeed they will not be strongly opposed to it."[76] They strongly advised that NDR survey the attitude of teachers and parents toward these segments, as a lack of support would "seriously jeopardize" *Sesamstraße*'s acceptance.

I have been unable to find any source that indicate NDR's response to this letter. However, the minutes from the German advisory board meeting that took place about a month later might have made it easier for the *Sesamstraße* team to prove that the German public did not widely oppose their social learning goals. The advisers had found that the Hans-Bredow-Institute's first research report on the first five *Sesamstraße* pilot episodes was generally positive.[77] There was a mixed reception of the German-produced segments and how well integrated they were with the American ones, but educators and parents accepted as important the content and social learning goals, and children liked the segments too. Individual members of the advisory board also commented on the five shows. They were mainly concerned that some segments reproduced negative gender and racial stereotypes, that some of the German segments were too boring and had irrational storylines, and that in one story "the important learning object that the children may be right vis-a-vis adults" was reduced to something silly and unclear.[78] Lastly, the advisers stressed that the German production team should not follow the "Catalogue of Social Learning" it had received from the Workshop but adhere to its own recommendations. When the first official status report from NDR to the Workshop on *Sesamstraße* was submitted in January 1973, the German advisers' own social learning goals were still included.[79]

Sesamstraße I and *II*: A Threat to the *Sesame Street* Brand?

When *Sesamstraße*'s first season premiered, it was broadcast twice a day in three regions and once a day by two other regional broadcasters on ARD's Channel 3. The remaining four regional broadcasters had decided not to carry it, preferring German alternatives that had been developed parallel to *Sesamstraße* but that focused even more on social learning, self- and critical awareness, arts and crafts, and everyday life. These German shows were *Die Sendung mit der Maus* (The one with the mouse) and a later development of *Die Spielschule* called *Das feuerrote Spielmobil* (The fiery-red playmobile), as well as a few others.

Sesamstraße's premiere was accompanied by a range of activities that were not directly related to the production of the broadcast, but which certainly helped fuel its success and generate both revenue and publicity for the Workshop as well as the publishers involved. There was a range of nonbroadcast items in the form of booklets, games, puppets, and magazines for parents that the German producers and advisory board had agreed to with the Workshop.

A four-volume series paid for by the German Ministry of Education was to accompany the broadcasts and scaffold their learning goals. Surprisingly, the Workshop's Edward Palmer found the booklets to be well planned and suitable for persons who were not professional educators, even if they to a large extent supported the social learning goals that the Workshop so disliked.[80] However, the Workshop does not seems to have picked up on how different they actually were from the guides produced in the States, possibly because of the language barrier. The German guides were preoccupied with the social

00:04:31:00

Figure 4.1 Girl being helped to pee by her dad, lady walking by with her dog scolding them as she passes. *Sesamstraße*, airdate 9 April 1974.

goals of this specific adaptation and were oriented toward extending the concepts beyond the one-way communication of television. For instance, the German guides taught readers about the body and were explicit about their stance on social issues. Unlike the Workshop's products, they made no effort to avoid potential controversy by appearing objective.[81] Thus, the books actively discussed and rejected traditional gender roles and emphasized how society depended on collaboration, including workers' unions. The booklets also pointed to specific scenes in *Sesamstraße* and encouraged readings that enforced their messages regarding questioning authority—including, for instance, a scene from *Sesamstraße* that showed an adult woman as a hypocrite for wrongly scolding a small girl for urinating in the gutter because there are no public toilets, but afterward letting her own dog relieve itself on the sidewalk (see Figures 4.1 and 4.2).

By March 1973, two months into the show's first run, the booklets had sold more than 20,000 copies.[82] In addition to the booklets, there was a magazine for parents, which had sold more than 230,000 copies around the same time.

00:05:52:10

Figure 4.2 Dog relieving itself in the street after being asked to do so by the owner. *Sesamstraße*, airdate 9 April 1974.

To promote the show, 36,000 posters had been printed, a promotional film had been produced and Phylis Feinstein's very positive book about *Sesame Street*'s first year in the United States, *All about Sesame Street*, had been translated into German.

The general reception in the West German press was positive and aided by the vast amount of nonbroadcast material, the show attracted massive attention. An extensive article in the influential *Der Spiegel* suggested in jest that children should perhaps be forced to watch the series.[83] This article sums up the preliminary reception as mainly positive, but also reported, with a slight tone of disbelief and mockery, on the substantial criticism of the show. Disapproving educationalists were ridiculed for complicating matters with their long-winded discussions, and so was Bavarian broadcasting for their outspoken refusal to carry the show.

In July 1973 *Sesamstraße* garnered renewed attention when an independent preliminary survey of *Sesamstraße*, funded by the government, reported on its positive public reception.[84] The survey was based on

960 interviews with families who had television and children ages three to ten, as well as observations of families in Hamburg. There was still a mixture of praise and criticism for the series, but the survey found that the series was very popular with children. The fact that the contract between the Workshop and the German producers had stated popularity as a success criteria meant that viewer ratings featured prominently in the study. The survey reported that children liked *Sesamstraße*, but found *The Porky Pig Show, Stan and Ollie*, and *Lassie* more enjoyable. However, the report found that children enjoyed *Sesamstraße* slightly more than other preschool shows like *Unser Sandmännchen, Die Sendung mit der Maus, Maxifant und Minifant* and *Das Feuerrote Spielmobil*. Children enjoyed the Muppets best, and the segments with numbers and letters the least, in contrast to parents.

The popularity of *Sesamstraße* was the part of the research that received the most attention, which was very fortunate for the Workshop. This finding was reported in numbers and rankings that were easy for the news media to report. What received a lot less attention was discussion of the question that the group had first and foremost been charged to investigate on behalf of the Ministry for Education: to what degree television could be used as part of preschool education praxis. This was deemed too complex a question to be answered from the research carried out to that time. In the final report from 1975 published at the end of the Hans-Bredow-Institute's vast two-year project, the conclusion was equally ambiguous.[85] When the question of preschool television as compensatory education was measured not only by bite-size checklist goals as in the United States but broadened to include the social education goals of challenging structural inequalities, the effects of a single show were hard to measure. In 1975, as in 1973, this far more complex research would not receive as much attention in the press as simple measurements of the program's success in terms of viewer numbers and satisfaction.

As in the case of US coverage of the UK reception of *Sesame Street*, the American press had a hard time understanding the German resistance to *Sesamstraße*. An article in the *Baltimore Sun* described West German children's television as so backward that whatever its producers made would never compare favorably with the abridged version of *Sesame Street*—even if the German version was rigorously educational, slow, and without any fun.[86] The *Sun*'s perspective was echoed in a story about *Sesamstraße* in a morning show on CBS.[87] The segment played on negative stereotypes of Germany, claiming that laughter and learning could not coexist there without meeting criticism. In what was doubtless an attempt to be humorous, the CBS story reported how different *Sesamstraße* was from the English version—teaching children to question parental authority and disobey their parents, and suggesting that it was false modesty when parents would cover their bodies while dressing or taking a bath. The American entertainment industry magazine *Variety* reported that popular demand from parents and kids forced backward West German broadcasters to show *Sesamstraße* when they at first were reluctant.[88] As in the case of the UK reception, these news reports from the US press confirmed the Workshop's success and did nothing to challenge its careless attitude toward cultural differences.

An American perspective on *Sesamstraße* that perhaps more surprisingly ended up confirming the Workshop's skepticism of the German version's appropriateness came from an American mother living in Germany. Coinciding with the talks of contract renewal at the end of 1973 for a second season, the Workshop had received a letter from the mother accusing *Sesamstraße* of condoning nudism and of keyhole voyeurism.[89] The much more relaxed relationship to naked bodies in German culture, and consequently *Sesamstraße*, had clearly upset her and was now worrying the Workshop to the point where it considered if it should insist on restoring the precensorship right that had been removed from the first contract signed in 1972. Perhaps the Workshop found the complaint so worrying because it was not the first of this kind and it knew the German producers did not share its views regarding appropriate content.

Correspondence from March and April 1973 between the Workshop and NDR shows the Americans' displeasure about the use of slang in the German version, in particular the phrase "alles im Arsch" (literally: all in the ass).[90] The Workshop was offended that the NDR producers had allowed this kind of language. The disagreements show how preoccupied the Workshop was with protecting its brand and projecting it in a very specific way, and once again illustrates differences in how children's behavior and language could and should be presented on television. Where the Workshop found this language "offensive" and "obscene," the West German producers replied that slang should not be censored, as it was important that television mirrored children's reality.[91] They did not want to prevent children from using this kind of language because they believed this could create artificial taboos. They reassured the Workshop that slang was rarely used, but that in this case it had been approved by *Sesamstraße*'s board of advisers in Germany. Not satisfied with this explanation, the Workshop at the point of contract renewal considered whether to reserve the right to censor *Sesamstraße II* episodes to weed out issues that the Workshop deemed "flagrantly out of character with the CTW-produced Sesame Street."[92] This would mean that it could object to any content in the social learning films that approved of behavior that questioned adult authority, use of slang, a display of nudity, or any other content it did not find appropriate.

Interestingly, the disagreements about the content of *Sesamstraße* did not make the Workshop reevaluate its understanding of the goals of West German broadcasters and educational experts or that they might legitimately be different from American values. Rather, in internal memos, the Workshop was not shy about the possibility that they might want to move to ZDF if NDR proved too troublesome, blind to the fact that these views about mild disobedience, profanity, and nudity were embraced broadly in German culture rather than promoted by a single broadcaster.[93]

Despite the problems the Workshop had with NDR, the deal was so lucrative in terms of license fees that the Workshop wanted it to continue.[94] In addition, the *Sesamstraße* production team assumed the cost of the extremely expensive tape conversion of the English-language version that was necessary for the European market, meaning that the tapes used in West Germany could be reused in Britain and Ireland without any additional cost for the Workshop.

To gain more control of the German version, the Workshop suggested that NDR use the Open Sesame format for the second season, *Sesamstraße II*. Open Sesame had been developed by the Workshop in 1973 and was now used in France. The Open Sesame concept (covered in chapter 2) was produced in blocks of either thirteen minutes and thirty seconds or twenty-seven minutes that were combined with short, locally produced opening and closing segments. There were no studio street scenes included in the format. The NDR team had previously objected to the studio street scenes, probably because they had attracted criticism in Germany as being phony for displaying a false and romanticized version of inner-city slums and race relations in the United States.[95] Open Sesame blocks included all the learning goals advanced by the Workshop with no effort to accommodate the wishes of local broadcasters such as they had been for *Sesamstraße I*. This would give the Workshop total control over transmissions under their brand and eliminate the contested social learning goals from the German-language production.

Not surprisingly, the *Sesamstraße* production team and its German advisory board were not interested in the generic Open Sesame model. They liked the existing arrangement where about half of the content was produced by a West German team, mixed with dubbed sequences from the original English-language version. Instead of migrating to the Open Sesame format, the Germans proposed to collaborate further on an integration between *Sesamstraße* and the preschool program *Die Sendung mit der Maus* (The one with the mouse, *Die Maus*). The production of *Die Maus* was headed by WDR in Cologne but had contributions from a larger group of other ARD regional broadcasters.

The Workshop objected to this idea.[96] It did not want a program with anything but its own material and claimed that if a program had less than an unabridged block of thirteen minutes, thirty seconds of material based on the *Sesame Street* format it became educationally ineffective. Clearly, the Workshop's personnel did not fully understand how collaboration between the stations in West Germany worked. In reference to a document written around this time titled "The Uses of CTW Material," the Workshop assumed, wrongly, that it was

> generally accepted practice that when foreign broadcasters buy a series they are not permitted to dilute it by incorporating it into other programs. One buys Hanna-Barbera or Disney, but not both of them to make a hybrid cartoon series. Hence one buys CTW or not; but if so, then what one buys should bear the distinct CTW mark.[97]

However, this mixing and matching were exactly what happened in West German and other European children's television at the time. When broadcasters collaborated or exchanged segments, they were incorporated in collage-like formats. This was possible because branding and income from sales were not as big an issue. There were very few long series or program concepts. Broadcasters were not companies committed basically to one idea, like the Workshop with *Sesame Street*, but produced new formats and programs all the time.

For the Workshop, however, brand protection was essential for its survival.[98] As it stated in an internal policy memo on this issue,

> Both the broadcast and non-broadcast markets depend upon a broadcast vehicle universally known as Sesame Street. To allow the name to be used

by foreign broadcasters for a program which does not have the "essence" of Sesame Street is to invite a gradual audience transition to a vehicle over which we have increasingly diminished control, and which may eventually destroy our market base.[99]

As we see from this quotation, worries over possible damage to the Workshop's brand were clearly intertwined with nonbroadcast rights and brand recognition, and these issues were becoming more and more important, not only on the domestic market of the particular co-production, but also in relation to other potential international partners:

> Once the decision is made to allow one country to do it [mix Sesame Street material into their own show], all the stops are pulled, and our negotiating position has no base other than the financial. . . . The CTW has a reputation to maintain, at home as well as abroad, and the value of all its products is greatly determined by that reputation.[100]

The Workshop was convinced that if it allowed one country to mix *Sesame Street* material with their own under a new title, others would request to do the same to "enhance the attractiveness of their own programs with our materials."[101] One suggestion the Workshop made was to include *Die Maus* material but still preserve its own brand integrity by including the main character of *Die Maus* as a Muppet and have segments with locally produced street scenes or animation built around this character.

Despite the fact that the advisory board had been against the idea of Open Sesame material for *Sesamstraße II*, NDR tried change to this decision to get out of its impasse with the Workshop. It made a preliminary agreement about the Open Sesame material, but that was turned down by the German advisory board because the educational concept in Open Sesame was seen as "a remarkable backlash" when measured against the educational standards developed in *Sesamstraße I*, and was "neither transferable to German situations nor wanted."[102] The board had decided, in its first unanimous decision ever, that it would discontinue all corporations with NDR on *Sesamstraße II* if the Open Sesame format was bought.

This opposition from the advisory board and NDR made the Workshop realize that it would have to concede by allowing NDR to make 180 *Sesamstraße* programs of thirty minutes with 50 percent of the material coming from *Sesame Street* Seasons 1, 3, and 5 (paying $365,000, about $2 million in 2022 dollars), but also permitting the editing (i.e., deleting) of segments that were not consistent with "German cultural and educational standards."[103] The NDR also received the rights to dub segments into German and to include German-produced material, as it had done in *Sesamstraße I*. The material produced for *Sesamstraße II* could not be used in other programs such as *Die Maus*, except for a limited number of segments produced by WDR. The Germans substantially won.

When the three pilot episodes for *Sesamstraße II* were done, they were screened by the Workshop. This season had no street scenes from the English-language version and a substantial amount of live-action films were made by NDR to cover their social curriculum goals. After the screening of the shows in New York, Lutrelle Horne, the head of international productions, went to Hamburg to discuss them and other segments for the season with the German production team.[104] These informal but substantial talks about the production were the primary means for the Workshop to influence the design and content of *Sesamstraße*. It had no contractual rights to be involved in the production but felt it better to steer NDR's production team in what it saw as the right direction rather than later having to enforce its breach-of-contract rights. These meetings were also a way for the Workshop to gain substantial influence over the ways in which the goals for the program should be interpreted in the production.

It is clear from its internal correspondence about these German pilot episodes that the Workshop again did not like their content. First, in its view, the Germans used too little of the Workshop's original material. The Workshop also did not like the longer documentary segments the Germans had produced, showing activities like coal mining and the operation of trains to expose children to the wider society they were part of and make them take an interest in it. The Workshop preferred segments that focused on their immediate social sphere. It still disagreed with the social learning goals for *Sesamstraße*, even if it conceded that these social goals were now, from a Workshop point of view, better expressed in individual, bite-size goals on a list—and in principle, the Workshop accepted them. However, the Workshop did not like the way those goals were interpreted in the production. Children were, the Workshop said, "often portrayed as defiant and unnecessarily rebellious," and the segments were produced in a "heavy-handed" way.[105] It believed these kinds of segments to be dangerous and only tolerated them because they were "indeed valid in terms of the past experiences of German social thought," hinting that they understood the motivation for German emancipatory education, but not how it actually played out as a pedagogical strategy. However, the Workshop liked two social learning segments that directly tried to tackle the issue of prejudice against guest workers in West Germany, who were minorities in that nation.

While *Sesamstraße II* was being broadcast in 1976, an agreement for a different kind of production model for *Sesamstraße III* was made. Apparently, the German audience had missed the street scenes that NDR had left out in its second season, and the NDR production team wanted to have them back but produced in Germany to meet specific German requirements. The street scenes would have a German cast, and the Workshop would develop two new Muppets. These became the Big Bird–like character bear, Samson, and a smaller Oscar-like Muppet named Tiffy. With this production model, the Workshop's involvement in production planning would be higher than it had been previously, allowing for a greater degree of direct monitoring from New York. This made the production model for *Sesamstraße III* look more like the ones that had been produced for Latin America and in the Netherlands (which would start in 1976), and were closer to the original *Sesame Street* than any of the two first seasons of *Sesamstraße* had been. Unlike in Latin America, the German production team would carry the entire financial burden. Much of the Workshop's experience in West Germany had thus been an exercise in finding out how it wanted its partnerships to work, especially if it were to keep the *Sesame Street* brand intact while still allowing foreign broadcasters to produce new material locally. The new form of co-production aired in 1978 and is still running today.

Conclusion: What Made For an Ideal Co-production?

The experiences of the Workshop in West Germany significantly affected their business model for overseas sales and production. In contrast to the co-productions in Latin America and the initial attempt to make a French version—where small, independent production teams were highly dependent on the Workshop for funding—the German co-production team at NDR was technically and financially independent. The NDR team was also part of a collaboration with ARD broadcasters located in Cologne (WDR) and Hessen (HR), and had the support of the ARD network for policy discussions. The Germans used this strength to independently produce segments for the first two seasons of *Sesamstraße* with which the Workshop strongly disagreed but could not alter because of the way the collaboration was established. Had it wanted to stop these shows from airing, the Workshop would have had to end the contract entirely. The Workshop did not find this degree of independence in a partner desirable because it could not control the output on the detailed level it wanted. Consequently, co-productions more in the style of the Spanish version for Latin America, where the production resembled the American version to a greater degree, became the end goal for co-production partnerships. However, unlike in Latin America, the workshop wanted the financial burden placed solely on the overseas partner.

Two things were key in the conceptualization of co-production designs. One was the belief that a worldwide preschool audience would be best served with shows based on the CTW model and its inherent assumptions about education, childhood, and television. The other was brand integrity. Brand control was seen as the way to ensure not only the highest profit from nonbroadcast products underpinning the Workshop's survival, but also the best way to showcase a coherent *Sesame Street* concept to other potential buyers. Control over the *Sesame Street* concept was therefore crucial not only in the domestic market of the specific co-production but also served an important role in relation to other potential international buyers. The global marketplace in which the Workshop operated had a big influence on its local activities. The global outlook left limited room for adapting the concept if the end result had to please the Workshop. Demonstrating the combined influence of the Workshop's universalistic conceptual frameworks and global branding strategies on its conduct in West Germany, this chapter has shown how these matters directly affected local negotiations and outcomes.

In West Germany, the Workshop especially had problems overcoming the very different views of child-adult relationships and the needs German educators expressed for a particular kind of social education. It sometimes tried to ignore these conflicts or accommodate them within the strict limits that they believed were necessary to preserve brand control and its production design. The Germans on the other hand experienced pressure to conform to a foreign brand and production model, something they were not used to. In the case of West Germany, the desire for democratic, emancipatory education that stressed children's freedom and ability to question adult conduct was a particular problem for the Workshop. The Workshop's narrow and individualistic understanding of children's capabilities and needs did not include nuanced emotional behavior or morally complex issues that concern society more broadly. This clashed with the German view of children as in need of a whole range of social competencies to navigate their world independently, not only for their own benefit but as a way to improve society as a whole and avoid a repeat of the blind obedience that was seen to have led to the Holocaust. The explicit moral dimensions of preschool education especially affected the view of the child-adult relationship, making it oppositional to the ideal of the adult as a perfect role model upon which *Sesame Street* rested. In the German version, the child viewer was conceptualized as more independent and emotionally competent than in the American series, capable of interacting with adults who did not get everything right and dealing with difficult, complex feelings. As in the British *Play School*, *Sesamstraße* also emphasized children's creative abilities by highlighting child-created arts and craft projects in the intro and outro.

The German public service broadcasting system also contributed to *Sesamstraße*'s differences from *Sesame Street*. The German advisory board acted as engaged and critical interlocutors who were not automatically invested in the *Sesame Street* brand, as the US advisers were. This independence supported a strong stance on social learning goals. The separation of research from the broadcasting institution meant that *Sesamstraße* had a much broader scope than the American show, but also that research was not used as systematically in the production and evaluation of the program as in *Sesame Street*, a fact that seems to have given day-to-day producers rather than educational experts more influence on the actual production of *Sesamstraße*. However, as there was only limited experience with preschool production in West Germany at the point when the Workshop first promoted the *Sesame Street* concept, its American experts' ideas of what appropriate preschool programs were and their educational potential had a significant influence on the German debates about the potential role of television in preschoolers' lives. This made a difference in the German debates about *Sesame Street* compared to Britain and Scandinavia. In those areas, *Sesame Street* was an alternative to existing, locally produced preschool programs. In West Germany, only the regional broadcaster in Bavaria had experience in the area in 1970, and therefore, when it was first promoted, *Sesame Street* came as an offering without immediate local alternatives against which to measure its suitability. As we shall see in the next chapter, the existence of a tradition for producing television for young children made a difference in the Scandinavian reception of *Sesame Street*—also internally in the Nordic region. Furthermore, the ideological ties that solidified somewhat utopian progressive views of childhood in the Scandinavian children's departments were very strong because of the Nordic countries' collaboration within the Nordic Broadcasting Union.

5

Other Childhoods

Sesame Street in Scandinavia

Imagine an animated cartoon about a little elf in a red, dotted dress and her friend, a mouse in sweater and trousers. It's 1971 and the plot takes the two of them on vacation to Spain, where they meet a friendly mouse from the Basque country. Who else do they meet? Two cats, one who wears long black boots and one a little golden crown (see Figures 5.1 to 5.4). The one in the long black boots loves to torture mice, so when the Basque mouse is captured, the little elf needs to help free him from the torture chamber (a mousetrap). The target group of this animated cartoon was Danish children ages three to six. No themes seemed off limits in children's media culture at this point in Denmark, even torture or foreign politics. The children's department at the Danish Broadcasting Corporation caught a little backlash for this episode in the right-wing press because the names of the cats were first announced to be Franco and Don Carlos. However, nothing much was made of it because the broadcaster became unsure of what the implications might be of making fun of foreign heads of state, and changed the names at the last minute.[1] Because of the criticism it was, nevertheless, decided not to air the subsequent episode where the elf and her friend traveled to the United States and met a Black Panther mouse who was discriminated against by US police and eventually shot dead.[2] These stories about the elf and her friends encouraged children to consider themes like political discrimination, police brutality, and racism, albeit in a nondomestic context.

The animated series, named *Cirkeline* after the main character (the elf), was one of the period's most explicit examples of how television for very young children had content that at the beginning of the 1960s would have been unimaginable. Even as an outlier, it serves as an indicator of just how different young children and their needs were conceptualized by Scandinavia television producers in the late 1960s and early 1970s when compared to the key ideas of a program like *Sesame Street*. While the Children's Television Workshop believed that preschoolers' needs could be determined based

Sesame Street. Helle Strandgaard Jensen, Oxford University Press. © Oxford University Press 2023.
DOI: 10.1093/oso/9780197554159.003.0006

Figure 5.1 Cirkeline, Frederik and Basque mouse (Pedro). *Cirkeline on Vacation,* 1971. © Jannik Hastrup.

on seemingly apolitical, universal measures and served with television that taught facts and school-type skills, the Scandinavian television producers were deeply wedded to the countercultural idea that "everything is political," and children's media products had to show this to children, even very young children. As a report from a Nordic symposium on children's culture in 1969 clearly stated, "Many people believe that 'children's culture' represents an area of interest that is positive, free of conflict and a topic on which people can work together no matter their political views. They could not be more wrong."[3]

This profound difference in understandings of children's needs, childhood, and the role of television in preschoolers' lives shaped the Scandinavian ambivalence toward *Sesame Street* and the Workshop's production setup throughout the 1970s. There was deep admiration for the Workshop's budget, the size of its research team, the agreement to a fixed set of production rules, *Sesame Street*'s high aesthetic value, and the Muppets' popularity among children. However, *Sesame Street*'s strong focus on the supposedly universal need for television to teach a specific set of skills contrasted sharply

Figure 5.2 Fascist cat (Franco) and his royal friend (Don Carlos) hunting for mice. *Cirkeline on Vacation*, 1971. © Jannik Hastrup.

with Scandinavian ideas about appropriate television for a young audience. In line with broad trends within children's media culture across Scandinavia, the national broadcasters in the Nordic countries had begun to experiment with ways in which their programs could be used to empower children by supporting their sense of self, their understanding of the world around them, and their confidence in challenging adult authority.[4] These currents shared a likeness with child-centered trends in the United Kingdom and West Germany at the time, but comparative studies suggest that the Scandinavian ideas were somewhat more radical in the inclusion of children's voices, promoting a utopian form of progressivism where children were adult's equals.[5] In a broadcasting context, for instance, this outlook meant that older children were invited to write and produce films for television broadcast, and policies explicitly conceptualized television as children's spokesperson.[6]

Children's media culture and consumption had been at the center of intense public debates in the Nordic countries since the late 1960s, attracting attention from a wide range of political and professional groups. This attention to children's needs had roots in the progressive children's movement from

Figure 5.3 Fascist cat (Franco) holding Basque mouse (Pedro) captured in his torture chamber. *Cirkeline on Vacation*, 1971. © Jannik Hastrup.

the early twentieth century that had influenced the formation of the welfare states and educational reforms.[7] Heightened public awareness around the quality and content of media products for children meant that children's media attracted funding for research of many different kinds (sociological, aesthetic, and psychological) and that production and distribution were increasingly institutionalized on a national level. This research also bolstered the confidence of producers in the importance of their work, and although the child-centered, antiauthoritarian approach was attacked by both left- and right-wing political groups that wanted children to stay obedient subjects of adult control in schools and at home, it converged with developments of the welfare states in a way that strengthened and consolidated this progressive perspective.[8]

This chapter explores the many sources of Scandinavian ambivalence toward *Sesame Street* and how these conflicting perspectives influenced the Workshop's chances of selling the show to the region's broadcasters. The enormous amount of preserved documentation concerning the production of and policy toward television for young children as well as children's

Figure 5.4 Cirkeline and Frederik in America. *The Escape from America,* 1971.
© Jannik Hastrup.

media culture in Scandinavia provides insight into the differences between Scandinavian children's media producers and the Workshop. Contrary to what happened in the United Kingdom and West Germany, only one Nordic nation bought broadcast products from the Workshop during the 1970s. The documentation helps to understand this cultural demarcation: in this case, the reasons why *Sesame Street* simply did not travel well. One explanation for why the Scandinavian reception was different is the sweeping changes in views of childhood that had taken root in many corners of children's media production, including broadcasting, in Scandinavia just a few years before *Sesame Street*'s premiere.

Coinciding with the 1968 youth rebellions, a profound progressive view of children's media culture that had emerged in Sweden after the Second World War spread and strengthened in all of Scandinavia.[9] It emphasized children's culture as something different from adults' culture. Television productions for children should, in this view, therefore refrain from addressing children as subjects of their family or the educational system.

On the contrary, television programs should empower and emancipate children, as a policy paper from Nordvision, the Nordic broadcasting union, written in 1974 clearly stated:

> A shared cultural background has meant that the Nordic children and youth departments for the most part have a similar aim with their programmes. This aim is, primarily, to support children's emotional and cognitive development in order for them to become active and independent humans. To fulfil these intentions it is important to show children the world in a manner that is as truthful as possible, to demonstrate all humans' equal worth, but unequal living conditions, and to show how all humans depend on others.[10]

Thus, despite years-long attempts to make a Nordic version of *Sesame Street*, co-production would fail because of different opinions about whether children's television should be used for school-type educational purposes or aim at social and cultural enculturation and empowerment. Of the five Nordic countries, only Sweden would go on to collaborate with the Workshop in the 1970s, first on Open Sesame and later a full co-production.

Despite the failure to make a pan-Scandinavian version of *Sesame Street*, there was a parallel in the ways both the Workshop and the Nordic television producers wished to explore the empowering potential role of television in children's lives—but they saw the nature of that exploration very differently. In Scandinavia, broadcasters tried to distance their programs from the educational system. They wanted to stimulate children's sense of themselves, their everyday life, and society as a whole in order to support an "immediate" empowering effect, helping them to see and challenge social power structures that created inequalities in their lives, for instance, by granting adults a natural authority. The Workshop, on the other hand, wanted to use television for educational purposes that would help individual children fare better and be empowered later in life, creating equality of opportunity but without directly addressing the structural biases and power structures that affect children's lives. As a result, children were positioned very differently in terms of their needs and abilities in the policies of different broadcasters. The transformative role in which preschool television was cast was therefore also very different, as this chapter demonstrates.

The First Interest in *Sesame Street*

In the 1970s, all five Nordic countries (Sweden, Norway, Iceland, Finland, and Denmark) each had a single national broadcast corporation with a monopoly on radio and television broadcasting: Sveriges Radio (SR) in Sweden, Norsk rikskringkasting (NRK) in Norway, Yleisradio Oy (YLE) in Finland, Ríkísútvarpið (RÚV) in Iceland, and Danmarks Radio (DR) in Denmark. Modeled on the BBC's ideas of public service, all broadcasting in the region was at this point noncommercial. Public service broadcasting aimed to inform, educate, and entertain its viewers. The broadcasters were independent institutions funded by license fees and were subject to only limited oversight by boards of governors. All advertising (implicit and explicit) and sponsorships were banned. Norway, Iceland, and Denmark had one television channel each, and Sweden and Finland had two.[11] The broadcasters were part of the European Broadcasting Union, but also had their own broadcasting union, Nordvision (from Norden, another name for the region of Scandinavia).[12] The strong historical ties within Norden—the many shared cultural values and similarities in the countries' welfare models—led to a high level of cooperation between the national broadcasters in Nordvision. Since 1965, Nordvision had a subcommittee for producers of children's programs that gathered twice a year, and individual members often met between official meetings to exchange ideas or co-produce, or for technical training. This collaboration would greatly influence *Sesame Street*'s fate in Norden as Nordvision represented a united tradition of child-centered broadcasting that diverged greatly from that of the Workshop.[13]

Producers of children's television in Sweden were the first from the Nordic countries to take an interest in *Sesame Street*. Despite SR being a noncommercial public service broadcaster, its two television channels, Channel 1 (SVT1) and Channel 2 (SVT2), had a somewhat competitive relationship. *Sesame Street* was apparently so attractive that the channels competed over which of them had the right to buy the program.[14] The dispute was settled in favor of SVT2, whose employees would become the driving force in a joint Scandinavian attempt to co-produce a local version of *Sesame Street* called *Nordic Sesame*.[15] SVT2 was a very young channel, set up in 1969, and had not yet begun to produce preschool television. SVT1 already had a range of offerings for young viewers, including *Titta, leka, lära* (Look, play, learn), which began in 1965.[16]

The first screenings of *Sesame Street* in Sweden in early 1970 were a success, as many of those invited liked the program, but the Swedes wanted to see more episodes before deciding whether to buy it. Thus, immediately upon her return from Prix Jeunesse in the summer of 1970, the head of SVT2 children's department, Ingrid Edström, requested more tapes for screening sessions.[17] Simultaneously, the Workshop corresponded with the Danish Broadcasting Corporation (DR), which was also interested in the possibility of bringing *Sesame Street* to Scandinavia.

The Danes and the Swedes invited executive producer David Connell from the Workshop to visit in late 1970. With DR, there was no rivalry over who would have the right to air *Sesame Street*, there being only one channel. However, the organization already had its own program for preschoolers, *Legestue* (Play room), to which *Sesame Street* would be a competitor for the limited time for children's programs available in DR's television schedule.[18] Like other European preschool programs at the time, *Legestue* was very different from *Sesame Street*, both in its production and its content. Production was loose and experimental with few pedagogical consultants and driven mostly by its writers and production team. Also similar to other European children's productions, the small *Legestue* team was deeply embedded in the larger children's department, which had many other productions for children and youth of all ages. In this context, the vision for *Legestue* was part of department-wide policy discussions that were colored by a great mixture of political, professional, and technical viewpoints. The result was that the policy framework for a production like *Legestue* (and European productions for children in general) was very different from *Sesame Street*, because the ideas behind the program were not confined to fit one team's ambitions, but rested on ideas of television production and childhood that were intertwined with the broader frameworks of a department or institution.

The existence of *Legestue* largely influenced the ways in which DR prepared for Connell's visit and demonstrate how the presence of a local competitor could affect the decision of whether to buy *Sesame Street*. The discussions within the production team of *Legestue* that occurred both before and after the team had viewed *Sesame Street* show how it became a source of inspiration but also a perceived threat to the domestic Danish preschool production. These talks shaped DR's attitude toward the collaboration on *Nordic Sesame*, so digging a little deeper into their origins and context is important.

Legestue began in 1969 and was loosely inspired by SVT1's *Titta, leka, lära* and BBC's *Play School*.[19] The interest in making programs for Danish preschoolers was, like in the rest of Norden and Europe, rooted in a desire to use the television medium in a positive, structured manner to support a variety of goals, including greater social equality, a better-educated workforce, and ultimately higher living standards. The new wave of preschool programs was meant to provide stimulation to children at home in a similar way to what their peers in kindergartens and nurseries received from professionally trained teachers. However, as in the other European programs, school-type educational training was not part of *Legestue*. Similar to SVT1's *Titta, leka, lära* and BBC's *Play School*, the emphasis was on a semistructured introduction to social skills delivered in an engaging and entertaining manner that was supposed to motivate children to actively explore their surroundings and be creative.[20] Creativity was often encouraged by arts and crafts projects made by presenters on the screen, but also by having "participants" made out of everyday objects and toys, which presenters imagined were alive—just as children would with their own toys or other objects. Like other public service productions, much of DR's children's department programming came from trying things out in practice rather than the structured and regimented production modes in the Workshop.

The experimental approach of *Legestue* was reflected in the description that the children's department provided to DR's management for the allocation of funds for the first season. The application plainly said, "a program for 'the little ones' based on new and [yet] unknown pedagogical and artistic methods, which will make children learn through play."[21] There were budgets and some loose descriptions of the production setup attached to the application form, but this was radically different from *Sesame Street*, which was developed as a cohesive concept thoroughly documented in policy papers and grant proposals (as expected by American funding agencies). *Legestue* was a loosely formulated experiment. What it would be on screen was as much a day-to-day decision of the editorial staff of four people, a few external pedagogical consultants, six producers, and a group of writers and hosts. A road map for the show's authors outlined its basic principles. The emphasis was on entertainment because children were expected to learn through play. The show's producers wished for children to be inspired by the actions and activities presented by the hosts and the films they showed or stories they read, sang, or drew during the program. Fixed educational goals were not only deemed impossible, given the viewers' different developmental stages, but they were also ruled out because the primary aim was to inspire children to do a range of activities away from the screen, giving them a sense of themselves and their surroundings that would enable them to explore the world on their own. The show's themes related to hobbies (animals, games), daily life (meals, routines), emotions (sibling rivalry, friendships), and society at large (life in other countries, pollution, energy, food production). It comprised a mixture of studio recordings, live-action films, animated cartoons, and puppet sketches lasting in total about twenty-five minutes, with eight to ten different segments per program.[22] Arts and crafts featured heavily in the program, meant to inspire children to be creative at home. Compared to *Sesame Street* it was thus a much slower-paced program, made on a shoestring budget and with very different aims and content.

The differences between *Legestue* and *Sesame Street* showed clearly in the preparations that DR's children's department made in late 1970 before Connell's visit.[23] In general, *Sesame Street* was believed to be too long and therefore pacifying rather than activating children. The pace of the show was also seen to be too fast and therefore not suitable for narratives used to demonstrate complex issues. Some staff members liked that the hosts (Susan and Gordon) were married, as it indicated a story and stable fictional environment beyond the program itself; in *Legestue*, in contrast, the setting would change from week to week because of its experimental nature. The staff generally agreed that the quality of the films was very high, and the use of music was impressive. Most believed the show's success was due to teamwork: They were impressed that everyone at the Workshop seemed to have a designated role matching a specific part of the show. The show's popularity was attributed to its set decoration and the fixed set of humans and Muppets, which children would recognize and become attached to. The Danes clearly saw *Sesame Street* as primarily an educational show, focusing on school-type skills, in contrast to Danish children's programs that were mainly meant for entertainment and non-school-related activities, not for formal teaching. A few years prior, in 1968, the DR children's department had been separated from the school department based on the idea that the children's department's programs should serve children's interests beyond the educational system and other adult ideals, making television children's spokesperson.[24]

Despite the Danish producers' goodwill toward *Sesame Street*'s entertainment appeal, some of the questions the department prepared for Connell were very tough and reveal how the 1968 counterculture's ideological criticism of contemporary schooling had influenced thinking within the Danish department. Education was seen as essentially political, and orthodox views and research about children and education were questioned. The Danish producers prepared to ask Connell about the show's promotional material that claimed its research was done by "top educators."[25] Being wary of such definitive labels, seeing no research as unbiased, they were curious as to what "top educators" actually meant, and who had decided that the researchers the Workshop favored belonged in this category. In line with some of *Sesame Street*'s American, British, and German critics, the Danish producers doubted that it was possible to address social problems such as poverty and racism if the show portrayed a "nice and cozy" world, thus indirectly glorifying the existing culture and society. This approach, the Danish producers thought, would foster ignorance of existing social inequalities rather than teach children how to deal with them.

Other questions related to how the program's success was measured. The Danish producers wanted to know how information about viewers was collected and if success was mainly based on audience ratings. One of the reasons for this specific interest might have been the children's department's own struggles to find formats that were attractive to children, but at the same time conveyed the content they believed their audience needed. This, the Danes seem to have realized, was a problem the Workshop had been successful in solving even if its conception of children's needs was very different from the Scandinavians'. The Danish producers thus prepared questions for Connell about ratings and whether other measurements of success were used, such as collecting children's statements and reactions in the way they did, using more qualitative methods inspired by ethnography and sociology with which they were more familiar.

Ready to present the Workshop's ideas to a Scandinavian audience, Connell visited first Copenhagen and next Stockholm in early December 1970.[26] Unfortunately, no documents are preserved from this meeting that can tell us how Connell answered the questions the Danes had prepared. However, the head of SVT2's children's department, in a letter sent to a friend after the meeting, clearly expressed her admiration for *Sesame Street*. Still, like DR's staff, she saw the program as a reflection of American culture and conditions and was uncertain whether its focus on the US problem of underprivileged children in urban areas was relevant to a Swedish audience.[27] This was a big challenge for the Workshop. However, despite ideological differences and concerns about *Sesame Street* as a very American program, there was still interest in *Sesame Street* in Scandinavia after Connell's visit. Given the shared interest in *Sesame Street* in the children's departments of SVT2, DR, and NRK, a logical next step was to bring up the question of a co-production on a Nordic level in their broadcasting union, Nordvision.[28]

At a meeting in Copenhagen in February 1971, the five Nordvision partners discussed whether they should try to co-produce a Nordic version of *Sesame Street*.[29] Everyone agreed that *Sesame Street* was a great source of inspiration because of its impressive production values and wanted to explore the possibility of adopting the program to a Nordic context. The Finnish broadcaster's representative was the most reluctant, deeming the format as one that tried to imitate advertising and thus would be inappropriate because of its similarity to commercial television. The Finns had for some time aired *Romper Room*, which might also be the reason they did not want another preschool program from the States.[30] To explore the possibilities for a common Nordic version of *Sesame Street*, the Nordvision committee agreed on a joint expedition to the Workshop in New York to find out more about the show and the organization behind it.

Culturally Compatible? A US Trip Reveals Big Differences

The Nordvision representatives' visit to the Workshop in the summer of 1971 became part of a larger field trip to the United States. The heads of the children's departments at DR and SVT2, Ingrid Edström and Mogens Vemmer, respectively, as well as representatives from the Norwegian NRK, participated in an international television conference at the New England Center for Continuing Education, University of New Hampshire, prior to going to New York.[31] The conference revealed the Scandinavians' different, and at times controversial, approach to children's television when compared to a US context.

The conference was in essence a screening of American children's television not produced by the big US commercial networks (ABC, CBS, and NBC), mixed with a range of programs made by public service broadcasters from other parts of the world.[32] As a noncommercial entity, famous for its stance against the commercial US system, the Workshop was of course also present at the conference.

Children's programs from the BBC, DR, and SVT dominated the conference's international sessions, including an episode of *Cirkeline*. Vemmer, the head of DR's children's department, even delivered the keynote address. The interest in Scandinavian children's television and its policies demonstrate the curious nature of US noncommercial broadcasting at the time. However, if we take a closer look at Vemmer's keynote, we might see why a Norwegian participant would later write in his account of the conference that it was too controversial for the Americans.[33] In his speech, Vemmer focused on why a key policy decision for his department was to make television act as a spokesperson for children.[34] He talked about why programs for children and young people had to

> deal with *all* facets of life—child life as well as adult life, and not excluding the unpleasant aspects which our generation has involved our children in! Children's programs must participate in questioning the established generation's "solutions" of the problems of the world. Not in order to turn our children against us—not in order to widen the generational gap—but to stimulate a discussion *across* the generational gap—and to motivate children to make up their own minds and express their ideas.[35]

To ensure children's genuine empowerment, Vemmer strongly argued for handing over the "means of production" to children, just as DR had done in buying cameras for children and broadcasting their films.[36] Vemmer criticized what he called "authoritarian forms of television" in "the East," referring to the Soviet Union, and the capitalist commercialism of "the West," referring to the United States.[37] Directly addressing *Sesame Street*, he said that the program had effectively used the commercial form, but he did not like that it had to adapt to existing structures in this way to be a success. He instead wanted to help children and young people develop new formats and content. He believed that this aim might be viewed as partial, biased, and seen as too "left-wing" in the West and "right-wing" in the East, but that these criticisms were

> misdirected: the viability of a society, a school or a family pattern is in fact proven by its ability to question itself. It is the children, the young people, who are asking the relevant questions. Let them do it on television, so that several generations will be forced to reflect—and search for answers. Let television for children and young people be something *different!*[38]

The experimental approach in DR's *Legestue* can be seen as a result of this policy. Constantly looking to represent children's wishes and needs and supporting their empowerment meant chasing a moving target, which could not be done with a fixed format. Its producers also attempted to abide by this policy by having producers watch *Legestue* together with children at nursery schools and kindergartens, asking the children to give feedback on programs, surveying the responses of children and their co-watching parents, and having researchers do sociological analyses of preschool children's lives. The Workshop's lack of interest in breaking the one-way communication of television—using it to teach simple answers rather than pose questions—was one of the concerns raised about *Sesame Street* at Nordvision's meetings.[39] Just as the BBC's Monica Sims accused the show of being authoritarian, the Scandinavians questioned whether the strong didactic style, form, and content of the show would be desirable in a Nordic context.

In the report from the New Hampshire conference, information about work done at SVT2 demonstrated very clearly how the Swedes tried to adapt their programs to the interests of children. SVT2 described a survey with interviews of more than nine hundred children in which they were asked what kinds of questions they would like television to address.[40] These were questions representative of their preschool respondents:

For three- to five-year-olds:

- How does one make snakes, actually?
- Why does one get a temperature?
- Who decides that there is going to be a war?
- Why do all women put on makeup?
- What does the inside of a prison look like?
- How does one become Chinese?
- How does the sun rise?
- How is glass made?
- How are airplanes made?
- Why can birds fly?

For five- to seven-year-olds:

- How big is the earth?
- How did the earth come into existence?
- How are newspapers made?
- Why are some people poor and others rich?
- Why aren't all people equal?
- What does a person look like inside?

SVT2 was supposed to start producing preschool television before 1972 but had begun earlier, as they found it pertinent to start answering some of the questions their young viewers had posed. They did so in a program series on Sundays called *Vill du veta?* (Do you want to know?). Shows like this one, and the survey that inspired it, demonstrate a widespread commitment in Scandinavia to finding ways of representing preschoolers' voices on the screen.

After the conference, the Scandinavians went to New York to visit the Workshop, where Vice President Michael Dann was eager to close a deal. In a memo circulated to Workshop leadership before the meeting, Dann reminded the rest of management that while the purpose of the seminar was to acquaint the Scandinavians with the "*Sesame Street* operation," they had to keep in mind that the "immediate, primary objective [was] to sell them the English program," and the long-term strategy was to "eventually hav[e] Scandinavian versions."[41] Anxious not to seem like this was just business (even if it was), Dann also reminded his colleagues that they should not attempt "to suggest that they buy the English version. If they would like to buy, we will simply tell them under what conditions it is available." As we saw in chapter 2, this kind of playing coy was a deliberate strategy the Workshop used to distance itself from the hard sell of other production companies.

During their two days in New York, the Scandinavians got the grand tour of the Workshop, and the team clearly went a long way to dazzle them with a display of marvelous hospitality.[42] The Workshop screened for them Latin America's Spanish-language version, *Plazá Sesamo*, to show how the *Sesame Street* concept could be adapted to local cultural preferences. Also, even if collaboration with German and British partners was not exactly on track at this point, the Workshop told how interested these partners were and that it was almost certain that local productions would be made there very soon.[43]

The Workshop succeeded in convincing the Scandinavians that the research behind *Sesame Street* had proven that television could be a highly efficient medium for teaching children.[44] Even if they did not agree with what should be taught, the Scandinavian producers liked the idea that television's value for children could be documented, confirming their work's importance to others. They were also clearly impressed by how well produced the show was and its popularity among children. Still, the Scandinavians were not entirely convinced. Vemmer of DR and the Finnish and Norwegian representatives (who had just begun to air a local Norwegian version of BBC's *Play School*) were reluctant, seeing *Sesame Street* as being too different from their own productions and policies. However, Edström from SVT2, who had been very impressed with *Sesame Street* already from the beginning and did not have a daily preschool show at her channel, was most eager.[45] Upon her return to Stockholm she wrote the Workshop about how she felt convinced that the "group behind Sesame Street is the most honest and skillful team dealing with Children's Television in the world today."[46]

The different attitudes toward *Sesame Street* among the Scandinavians were a source of worry in the group, at least to the Norwegians. In a report to NRK's management, the Norwegian representative revealed his fears about the pressure it might put them under if Sweden decided to air it. In his opinion, "No country in the world will escape contact with *Sesame Street*," either in the form of research that derived from it or as a program.[47] Therefore, should any of their neighboring Nordic countries decide to transmit it, broadcasters not doing so would have to argue very strongly for why they did not. Who would press them for answers was left unspecified, but looking at the United Kingdom, we can see that this was not an unfounded worry. The Workshop was good at using the local press, networks in the broadcasting industry, and connections with national authorities to create pressure on broadcasters that decided against *Sesame Street*, and the Scandinavian press had already taken an interest in the program at this point.[48]

The situation in West Germany and Italy regarding the commercial aspects of the Workshop's operation—where they tried to maximize their revenue from merchandise and international sales—was a particular worry to all of the Scandinavians.[49] No matter the Workshop's status as a nonprofit entity, the commercial aspects of their operation damaged its reputation in the eyes of the Scandinavians, and they were suspicious of the fact that it needed to make money from selling the program to broadcasters abroad and had to have its own sales division. Dann's efforts to have the Workshop keep a low profile about their intentions to sell the show might not have worked as well as he had hoped.

Accelerating Collaborative Efforts

Despite some reluctance and undecidedness on the part of the Scandinavians, they continued to explore a possible collaboration with the Workshop. In the fall of 1971, the Workshop was again invited to Scandinavia. Notes from a planning meeting prior to its trip show how it saw the Scandinavian market and the possible challenges it posed. Broadcasting in the Nordic countries was (quite accurately) viewed as done in a "totally non-commercial environment, ergo they are relaxed, experimental, etc."[50] While the Workshop might have seen here a point of agreement insofar as it viewed itself also as a nonprofit, anticommercial group (at least in the States), it did not. It was worried that the financial freedom these countries had to experiment would be a problem, as it might make them less prone to stick to a fixed concept for long, a problem from an economic point of view, as Workshop wanted a stable source of income.[51] The Scandinavians were anticipated to want locally produced elements mixed with *Sesame Street* segments, which meant that the Workshop might lose control over the content. The Workshop preferred that a Nordic version would include a relatively high proportion of US-produced material and studio scenes for wraparounds, like in Latin America. This solution was favored as it meant a high level of content control, which would ensure consistency in their branding as well as income because the Workshop was continually involved in such solutions as consultants and technical co-producers.

Worried over losing control in the co-production, at the upcoming seminar in Stockholm the Workshop was prepared to demand that the Nordic countries set up curriculum seminars to fine-tune the original *Sesame Street* goals for a Scandinavian version with help from the Workshop. Second, it wanted full details about how research-related fieldwork would be conducted. Third, it wanted a curriculum statement along with the pilot. Internal notes show that Workshop staff was not sure how far they dared press this issue, probably out of fear of pushing away the Scandinavians, so they discussed to what extent they could demand a full prospectus including the planned facilities, resources, organization, curriculum, and so on. These anticipated problems were not just phantoms of the Workshop's collective fear for their brand. As time would show, it was not easy to agree with the Scandinavians over who would control which parts of the production.[52]

On the other side of the Atlantic, the Nordvision members also prepared for the upcoming meeting. The Scandinavians focused on what Nordic psychologists and pedagogical experts thought of *Sesame Street* and the possibilities for implementing it in a Nordic context. At a meeting in Stockholm, these experts concluded that a Nordic version of *Sesame Street* had to be adjusted to a Nordic cultural pattern and include "topics where the Nordic countries have advanced further than the US."[53] What these topics were was not specified, but as the seminar in the United States in August 1971 had clearly shown, the Scandinavians understood that *Sesame Street* was meant to teach children what they needed to do well at school, whereas the focus in Nordic countries expected television to reflect children's interests and concerns. In other policy papers from Nordvision, the Nordic producers argued that exactly this child-centered approach was what had brought them ahead of other countries.[54]

The meeting must have gone well because the collaboration continued—or at least the Nordic partners continued their work and started planning a pilot.[55] As would be clear in the summer of 1972, and a source of much dismay, the Workshop had not understood that after this November meeting the Scandinavians would begin making a pilot. Evidently, the Workshop thought they would be involved, whereas the Scandinavians did not, believing that adaptations to a Nordic context would be their responsibility alone because only they knew the cultural needs of Nordic children. The exclusive local control was probably expected because that was what the Nordvision partners were used to, based on their internal collaboration, and it was the arrangement when NRK adapted BBC's *Play School* to a Norwegian context. This misinterpretation of the Workshop's method of operation and their view of what a pilot production should be complicated the collaboration immensely. However, as none of the parties were aware of the other's intentions for some time, the Scandinavians began producing a pilot of a Nordic version of *Sesame Street* titled *Nordic Sesame*.[56]

Representatives from the children's departments in Denmark, Norway, and Sweden met in Oslo in May 1972 to discuss the goals for the pilot of *Nordic Sesame* based on the goals of *Sesame Street* season two.[57] At this point, the Finnish YLE decided not to take part in the production of the pilots that were subsequently produced in Danish, Swedish, and Norwegian. The inserts from *Sesame Street* would be the same, but also be dubbed into Danish, Swedish, and Norwegian. The Danes would create the Nordic animation, and the Norwegians would produce the music for all three versions. The Scandinavians saw it as their task to select inserts from two hours of *Sesame Street* they had obtained and then make Nordic items that would match it so that it all added up to a program lasting about twenty to twenty-five minutes. As we know from the collaboration the Workshop had initiated in West Germany, this bits-and-pieces approach, where local material (over which the Workshop had no control) and *Sesame Street* material were matched was exactly where the Workshop would have strong objections.

The Scandinavian writing group met for a week to flesh out goals for the program.[58] The group decided to include the following five goals in their program: (1) symbols (letters, numbers, and geometric shapes); (2) concepts (relational); (3) understanding of the self (sense of self), including the body and its functions as well as emotions; (4) understanding of social surroundings (sense of others), social roles and collaboration, and milieu/environment; and (5) reasoning and problem-solving. Just as the Scandinavian impression had been right from the outset, the group concluded that *Sesame Street* was mostly focused on the two first goals. For this reason, they determined that the program was of limited value in a Nordic context.[59] They thought also that *Sesame Street* had an overly fast-paced collage format. To them, this format was only good for teaching cognitive skills and not at all suited for teaching children about social interaction and empowering them socially and emotionally, as "the collage format was too limited to tell the kinds of complex stories needed to describe the social relations between individuals."[60] Therefore, the Scandinavians believed that a potential Nordic version of *Sesame Street* should only take up a limited part of the children's television schedule, if any.

Despite the many limitations, the Scandinavians saw in the American material some parts that profoundly captured their interest.[61] Their favorites were items with Bert and Ernie and some of the other Muppet segments because these, in their opinion, allowed for interpretation and involvement on the part of the viewer. Some of the animations also impressed them with their advanced technical standards. Overall, they looked for items that were deemed the least culturally biased and that best fit the tall order of honing children's social skills and interaction. The preference for Muppet sketches clearly aligned with the opinion of the BBC staff and producers in West Germany, all of whom admired how popular they were with both kids and adults and the funny ways in which they interacted. At the end of their writing retreat, the Scandinavian group still was not sure that the Nordic and American goals could work together when the show came to life.

SVT2's Edström wrote to the Workshop in the summer of 1972 to inform it about the progress of the Scandinavian pilot.[62] Because the Scandinavians thought the pilot was exclusively a Nordic affair, this was the first time that they informed the Workshop about their work, eight months after their last meeting. However, as the Workshop had been closely involved in the attempts to localize the shows elsewhere—even to the point where the Workshop was in charge, as in Latin America—it came as quite a shock that the Scandinavians had started making a pilot without involving them. Correspondence between the Workshop and the Scandinavians throughout August 1972 shows that they were miles apart in how they viewed the route to a possible collaboration. The Scandinavians believed they should be free to explore if *Sesame Street* as a concept was suited for the Nordic countries, whereas the Workshop could not accept that they were not involved in this process.

Prompted by Edström's letter, the Workshop's Peter Orton quickly phoned SVT2.[63] He wanted to know exactly why Nordvision had started making a pilot without the Workshop's involvement. To make sure he was understood correctly, Orton followed up the call with a letter detailing all the information that the Workshop considered essential to evaluate a pilot production.[64] With this letter, the Workshop tried to gain control over the situation by making several detailed demands, including those it had been reluctant to push for earlier in the process. It stressed how the Scandinavians needed to carefully follow all of its instructions to make a production both they and the Workshop could be "proud of."[65] In other words, the Scandinavians had to show they could produce a "quality pilot reflecting Sesame Street's basic approach to research, curriculum content and production."[66] The pilot production should prove to the Workshop that it was feasible when it came to a curriculum statement, a program concept, the budget, and scheduling. The Workshop also wanted detailed outlines of seminars with Scandinavian educators' recommendations for *Nordic Sesame*, and a plan for research to ensure the production's accountability. Attached to the letter was a standard template, originally made for Latin America and remodeled for West Germany, for a production proposal to be sent to the Workshop. Before they made any further arrangements, the Workshop told the Scandinavians to get in touch with its legal counsel to make sure everything was done properly. There was no doubt that the Workshop wanted to be in charge and hardly trusted the Scandinavians to produce something that would make the Workshop proud.

The Workshop not only was angry for not being informed about the Scandinavians' efforts to produce a pilot but now wanted them to roll their progress back to a point they had long passed. Shocked by these demands for scrutiny and oversight, the Scandinavians immediately scheduled a three-way phone call with the heads of departments and people involved in the production of *Nordic Sesame* at DR, SVT2, and NRK. Minutes from the call reveal that the Scandinavians saw the Workshop's demands as grossly out of place and "controlling beyond everything" they had ever encountered.[67]

Though very seasoned in international collaboration, they had not at all anticipated this reaction. Apparently, they still did not believe that the Workshop should be involved in making the test pilot at all, convinced that they alone were capable of adapting the show to their own cultural context. They quickly decided not even to send the Workshop their response and considered instead initiating a collaboration with the BBC on *Play School* or *Kli-Kla-Klawitter* from ARD/BR in Germany. However, because of the resources they had already poured into the pilot, they decided to keep working on *Nordic Sesame*, even if this meant that they knowingly were not abiding with the terms the Workshop had outlined.

The Scandinavians clearly felt they were doing the Workshop a favor, in a way exploring their own market's potential for an adapted version of *Sesame Street*.[68] They were not interested in a co-production effort that would end up in a partnership but rather wanted to explore how they could do an adaptation, as the Norwegians had done with manuscripts from BBC's *Play School*.[69] In Nordvision they were already used to working in this way: developing a shared concept that they then pursued in each country in the way that country's producers thought best. In their response to the Workshop the Scandinavians threatened to terminate their work on *Nordic Sesame*. They stressed the point that the Workshop should be very thankful to them, for the pilot was a kind of "marketing research, whereby the Scandinavian countries—at [their] own expense—investigate a possible commercial market for the CTW."[70] To press their points, the Scandinavians had made it very clear that if the pilot could not be produced, they had other options.[71]

The Workshop promptly replied in a way that left no doubt that the Workshop thought the Scandinavians had overstepped a boundary and needed to understand their conditions for collaboration about *Nordic Sesame*. The Workshop told how this was a business arrangement that had to legally be sketched out before any further agreements could be made. To reach an understanding, the Workshop invited a Scandinavian representative to come to New York where that person would be taught everything about the production of *Sesame Street* from a technical, economic, and conceptual point of view. The Workshop believed that after such schooling in its methods, the Scandinavians would be able to make a production based on the CTW model with curriculum assignment sheets that could govern the production process (all with help from the Workshop's staff). This, of course, meant that the Workshop expected the Scandinavians to comply with all the demands it had made earlier, and which the Scandinavians had already refused once. At this point, the Workshop seems to have lost its patience and played hardball. Things should be rolled back to the beginning, the Scandinavians starting all over again in the way the Workshop wanted.

Despite this virtual ultimatum, no one came to New York; it was instead the Workshop's financial representatives who went to Scandinavia in September 1972.[72] Before the meeting, the Scandinavians calculated the cost of the Nordic side of the production, which would be about 50 percent of the program— inserts from *Sesame Street* making up the other half. Excluding what they had to pay for American material, they calculated that *Nordic Sesame* would cost about five times more than an episode of *Legestue*. On top of this, they would also have to pay for dubbing, translation of manuscripts, and conversion of tapes for each of the American inserts. In Denmark and Norway, this meant that if they chose to produce *Nordic Sesame*, they would have to stop producing their current offerings for preschoolers to have enough room in their budgets.[73] On a positive note, however, was the fact that the *Sesame Street* production cost so much that the Scandinavians could use it as an example to demonstrate how much could actually be spent on preschool programs and the high-quality production outcome.[74] The high price and the limited use for *Sesame Street* in the Scandinavian schedules meant that no business arrangement was arrived at in the end. However, as the pilots were already made, they were sent to a full Nordvision committee for evaluation as a screening had already been arranged and because it might be possible to draw up some lessons for future Nordic collaboration in this area.[75]

The group that had produced the pilots offered a set of recommendations to the Nordvision committee concerning the pros and cons of a *Nordic Sesame* series made in collaboration with the Workshop.[76] It had found it refreshing to work with the collage format and produce from a fixed set of goals, but its work had confirmed that it was difficult to get the American inserts to work in a Nordic program. Possible gains were listed against the disadvantages. The group warned that *Nordic Sesame* would be far more expensive than locally produced programs, which would suffer if it was bought. Once again, they saw the *Sesame Street* material as best suited for intellectual stimulation— something they long ago had concluded was a secondary need for Scandinavian preschoolers who would get this when they attended school. Television had to be a space that focused on empowering preschoolers socially and culturally beyond the family and educational sphere. Based on their experiments with the pilot, they did not believe it possible to steer a *Nordic Sesame* away from this overall direction, even if they had tried. They concluded that the collage format hindered substantial exploration of social skills, and on top of that, they did not think the inserts the Workshop offered them were very attractive (too few of the Bert and Ernie sketches they wanted). *Nordic Sesame* would end up looking a lot like a watered-down version of *Sesame Street* in both format and content. While they acknowledged *Sesame Street*'s format as attractive entertainment that had proven effective and attractive in the United States and even beneficial to American children in need of cognitive stimulation, they argued for a format more appropriate for a Scandinavian context without the American inserts that looked out of place in the Nordic pilot. Working on *Nordic Sesame* had demonstrated a fundamental difference between the Nordic broadcasters and the Workshop not only when it came to formal educational skills training but to the nature of preschool ideals.

When the pilot was screened at the official Nordvision meeting, the representatives present agreed that these were relatively well-produced versions of the American original and they had shown interesting solutions in adapting the content to fit local preferences.[77] Despite this positive assessment, they also listened to the recommendations of the group and determined that there were too many drawbacks to the production. Thus, they decided not to make *Nordic Sesame*, but instead to further develop a purely Nordic collaboration, based on their combined practical experience and recommendations from Nordic experts.

In spring 1973, Nordvision informed the Workshop of its final decision not to make *Nordic Sesame*.[78] However, the Workshop did not give up; they had set their eyes on the affluent Scandinavian market and wanted a piece of it, even if the Scandinavians had made it clear that they saw the *Sesame Street* concept as incompatible with their own policies for preschool television.[79] The Workshop therefore devised a new strategy. Building on their positive results with the Open Sesame concept in France, they now wanted to offer the Scandinavians this half-hour economy version with dubbing to each of the countries separately. The question was if this would work now that the Scandinavians had decided to pursue their own path.

Sesame Street's Influence on National Preschool Productions in Denmark and Sweden

With the relations between the Workshop and Scandinavian broadcasters on pause for most of 1973, the influence of *Sesame Street* on Nordic production of preschool programs showed. As *Play School* had sparked the first interest in making preschool programs in Scandinavia in the mid-1960s, *Sesame Street*'s ambitious setup and its reliance on research and re-sourceful production pushed the broadcasters to reflect on their aims for their own offerings.

First, Nordic collaboration on a joint preschool "collage" show con-tinued with a focus on a mixture of introducing cognitive and social skills. This was a small project, but its production included panels and talks with Nordic experts from preschool education, sociology, mass media re-search, and psychology.[80] Instead of ending up with a fixed set of produc-tion goals and concrete guidelines as the expert seminars the Workshop had done for *Sesame Street*, these seminars exposed "disagreement, uncer-tainty, and indecisiveness," as key characteristics of the present discussions about preschoolers among leading experts.[81] Focusing on spectrums of possibilities, these seminars were viewed as providing everyone involved in television production with new ideas and therefore leading to better programs.

Second, the Scandinavians' collaboration on *Nordic Sesame* had also made the producers question what they might do to be more inclusive of children from less resourceful homes, something that fit the Scandinavian child-centered empowerment agenda extremely well. In Norway, working with *Nordic Sesame*, for instance, inspired a discussion of whether there was a need for a program that targeted the children of immigrants in Norway as a special group.[82] As this group was found to be very small (a total of ten thousand out of a population of four million), this idea was dismissed. Instead, they considered stepping up efforts to produce televi-sion for Sámi children.[83]

The most direct influence of the work with *Nordic Sesame* could be seen in Sweden. SVT2 began making the program *Fem myror är fler än fyra elefanter* (Five ants are more than four elephants) in 1973. The program description from May 1973 explicitly says that the program "builds on ex-perience from working with the pilot [Nordic] *Sesame Street*. The intention is in a clear and goal-oriented form to develop and adapt the ideas behind the American program to a Swedish context."[84] The program had clips ar-ranged as a collage with animations and sketches, just like *Sesame Street*, though the pace was slower. It also had the same kind of dual address as the Muppets, where jokes would target both adult and child viewers, making it more likely that parents and other adults would co-watch. Swedish parents were impressed with their children learning numbers and letters from a television program.[85] Thus, despite the broadcaster's own researchers having questioned the value of this ability, this was a way to get parents to sympathize with the show, just as it had been with *Sesame Street*.[86] The description of goals for the Swedish program was brief compared to the Americans', but focused on the same areas.[87] The American model had clearly been influential.

The Danes also adopted the Workshop's practice of articulating fixed outcomes for the production of *Legestue*. On his trip to the Workshop in 1972, the head of DR's section for preschool programming, Jimmy Stahr, had been very impressed with the ways in which everyone working on the show, from writers to producers to research, collaborated to reach shared goals. He, therefore, commenced the work of writing a policy statement for *Legestue* hoping they would have a similar unifying effect on his own staff, whose collaboration did not always go as smoothly as he wished.[88] The outcomes for the Danish program were, however, very different from *Sesame Street*'s narrowly defined skills. Rather than specific learning goals, it was more a statement of intent. The one-page policy paper for *Legestue* stated that its overall aim was to "encourage children's development of positive social attitudes."[89] The programs should aim to stimulate and support the "social, linguistic, emotional, intellectual and physical movement and expressive development of the child."[90] All this would help children "know and understand itself, the social interplay between people, its surroundings, everyday concepts"; support their ability to express themselves; face problems in a "questioning, analytical, constructive and flexible way"; as well as stimulate the imagination.[91] Compared to *Sesame Street*'s detailed curriculum, the policy statement for *Legestue*'s was very brief and open-ended; there were no boxes to be ticked.[92] Working toward a shared outcome was inspired by the Workshop's production methods, but as in other Nordic programs, the focus was on social competencies. The Muppets inspired a new character on *Legestue*. The parrot puppet Andrea had been a viewer favorite since the programs began in 1969, but Stahr insisted that she get a friend—a little green frog named Kaj and inspired by Kermit.[93] Thus, even if a Nordic version of *Sesame Street* was never made, the American program had clearly stimulated producers of children's television in the Nordic countries to consider their own policies and how they differed from it, inspiring them to adapt details from the program and production setup that they liked.

Open Sesame—A New Way of Selling *Sesame Street*

At the end of 1973, the Workshop still believed Scandinavia was a good market, despite the fact that all Nordic countries by then had regular, well-researched, and locally produced programs for preschoolers. Promoting preschool television around the world was not about aiding local producers in doing preschool television on their own terms—it was business, and that required the Workshop to sell its product as the best fit for preschoolers' needs, no matter that it might destroy local preschool productions along the way. It clearly saw its own preschool offering as the absolute best on the market and was prepared to convince the rest of the world to buy it.

In October 1973, the Workshop offered to make Open Sesame available to Nordvision. The Nordic representatives, still interested in some of the Workshop's research activities and the Muppets, decided that a group from the Nordic preschool departments would fly to New York and evaluate the material.

The assessment of the Open Sesame items was not particularly favorable. This is obvious in a report written by the Swedish representatives, who viewed the items not only as a possible contribution to the Nordic co-production but also as possible inserts to *Fem myror är fler än fyra elefanter*.[94] From a total of 1,200 items from Open Sesame they believed that only 149 suited SVT2's pedagogical and ideological outlook. Examples of inappropriate items were Muppet sketches that displayed aggressive behavior, animations dominated by what they called "a technocratic view of society," films with "ingratiating and tacky American hit songs [schlagermusik]," and puppets singing about nuclear family patterns. Perhaps these were all expected reactions of a Nordic programmer to the particularities of American culture and society. What they wanted, however, was what had interested them the entire time: puppet and animation items that in terms of quality were much better than what they could produce with the money and personnel then available in Sweden.

As with *Sesame Street*, Open Sesame was overall seen as too far removed from what was desirable in a Scandinavian broadcasting context. The Swedes noted that Open Sesame eliminated the "Sesame Street framework," meaning that the street scenes had gone. This rearrangement was interpreted as "the CTW's attempt to obtain higher international diffusion and maximize profit from *Sesame Street* while keeping control over the format and content."[95] The opposition toward American commercialism had definitely not faded.

The popularity of *Sesame Street* elsewhere, however, seems to have made the Scandinavians wonder if they would miss out on something if they turned it down completely. The "fame over gain" strategy developed by the Workshop and its international sales agents in Television International Enterprises in late 1970 and 1971, explained in chapter 2, paid off once again: giving the show away almost for free had created worldwide brand recognition and fear of missing out among broadcasters. Thus, despite the rather damning review of the Workshop's Open Sesame, Nordvision wanted to know if the few items they liked could be bought separately.[96]

While waiting for Nordvision's reply regarding Open Sesame, things took a positive turn for the Workshop. Even though Swedish Channel 2, SVT2, had been the Workshop's main contact point in Norden, the head of purchase from Swedish Channel 1, SVT1, had been invited to a screening of Open Sesame at the same time Nordvision considered Open Sesame.[97] The Channel 1 representative told the Workshop on the spot that they were willing to buy the show. As in Britain where the Workshop had used the competition between the BBC and ITV, it again used competition between two channels to pressure both parties, and it worked even if in Sweden the two competitors were part of the same broadcaster: as soon as the Workshop had an offer from Channel 1, Channel 2 capitulated to the Workshop's demands and decided to go solo in buying blocks from Open Sesame.[98] An internal memo shows that Channel 2 was afraid that if the competing channel bought it, their own *Fem myror är fler än fyra elefanter* might be outcompeted.[99] Thus, even if they feared Open Sesame would drain the resources from their local production, they figured that having both shows would minimize the risk of Open Sesame being used against them by their competitor at Channel 1. The result was that Open Sesame was sold to Sweden in 1975, but not as part of a Nordvision project.[100]

The promotional material describing the Swedish show based on the Open Sesame concept, *Sesam*, was the same as the other versions made from the format for Italy and France. *Sesam* was defined in the information kits' press release as a show that would teach valuable cognitive skills that were "universally accepted" and "culture free," but somehow at the same time delivered in an "entertaining and educationally balanced format culturally applicable to Sweden."[101] What had been developed for the particular needs of a group of children in the United States was again lifted up as the universal norm, claimed to be "culture free" and applicable in all local contexts. The claim to have localized the show was grounded in the fact that the soundtrack (of a maximum total of two minutes) was made in Stockholm and the block segments picked from the Workshop's international library by Swedish producers. Returning to their fame-over-gain strategy for branding and commercial effect, the press release boasted about the Brazilian, Spanish, German, and French versions (Canada and France) as well as the more than forty nations where the English-language version was broadcast. The Muppets Bert, Ernie, Grover, Kermit, Count van Count, and Cookie Monster were heavily featured in the promotional pictures and the accompanying the text, weaving them into the claim that despite their American origins, they were now universally charged with the aim of providing all of the world's TV sets with an American-*cum*-universal idea of what children needed from preschool television.

Danish and Norwegian Weariness

In contrast to SVT2, DR and NRK rejected the offer to buy Open Sesame.[102] The heads of the respective broadcasters' children's departments, Mogens Vemmer and Rolf Riktor, had been in New York in the summer of 1975 to visit the Workshop again, but it had not persuaded either of them. The reason Vemmer gave the Workshop for DR's refusal was purely financial. Having calculated the costs of preparing a Danish soundtrack for the twenty-six programs, the demands of the actors' union and license cost meant that the Danes would pay more than $270,000 (about $1.5 million in 2022). There was, however, much more to the Danish refusal than financial considerations. The *Legestue* team's unfavorable assessment of Open Sesame weighed heavily on the Danish decision.[103] Because of the pressure DR had experienced from the Workshop after the Swedish broadcaster had bought Open Sesame in 1975 and feared from the press and the public once SVT2 began broadcasting the show in 1976, the team produced a very long report laying out their arguments in minute detail.[104]

DR's assessment of Open Sesame shared many points with that of SVT2's representatives who had been in New York on behalf of Nordvision to evaluate the concept in 1974.[105] It emphasized how this spin-off of *Sesame Street* was as an outcome of the Workshop's economic interest. DR feared that no money would be left for *Legestue* should it buy Open Sesame, and with no money left for Danish preschool productions and experiments in this area, local expertise would dwindle. Nevertheless, the competition from Open

Sesame was not only seen as a financial problem. Because the production values of the Workshop were so high, the team argued that the Danish attempts to produce something different would be outshined, and DR's productions would risk losing their high esteem among viewers—adults and children alike—even though the Danish programming was in their opinion better suited for their child audience than US programs.[106] Similarly to what Vemmer had argued in 1971, the team argued that television had to create dialogue, not be a one-way communication of adults' idealized version of reality. Children's television had to empower children and support them, and this could only happen if there was room to experiment with the medium and make relationships and dialogue the center of productions and policies. *Sesame Street*, they argued, did not do this because it offered traditional, conformist one-way communication. *Sesame Street*'s "sterile" universe was seen as working against the aims of DR's productions, in which children learned about their social environment and the world in general. Taking children seriously entailed teaching them about things they encountered in their everyday life and helping them understand themselves and their environment. This was the only way to address children as "whole" individuals who needed emotional, social, and physical stimulation, the team argued.

In the case of Norway, the Workshop's Peter Orton used the Swedish decision to buy Open Sesame to put the proposal to NRK once more.[107] The reply from NRK's Riktor was cordial but suggested some irritation with the Workshop's persistence. He clearly felt a need to reassure Orton that he did appreciate the quality of *Sesame Street* and was interested in their material and research, but noted, "We want at all times to be the decision-makers as to what we shall present to Norwegian children and in what context."[108] He made it plain that he did not think NRK could keep control over these things with the formats that the Workshop offered.

Having no breakthrough in 1975 or 1976, Orton again approached Ada Haug, the deputy head of the children's department at NRK, in 1977.[109] She turned him down. She had seen the Swedish version, and it had not changed her mind; the pacing of *Sesame Street* was too fast, and she insisted—in line with previous Scandinavian producers—that slower, more complex, and more contextualized learning was better than fast repetition. Not taking no for an answer, the Workshop's new man, Frank Blackwell, tried to use his personal connection with Riktor, Haug's boss, to circumvent Haug's very firm refusal.[110] In a letter from March 1978, Blackwell—perhaps deliberately—misinterpreted Haug's answer as an implication that Haug thought

Norwegian children were slower than other children because she disliked the fast pace and cognitive skills training. Cheekily, Blackwell wrote to Riktor,

> I just can't accept that Norwegian children are less alert or slower than Swedish, or French, or Italian, or Portuguese, or Spanish kids—or children of many other places around the world where the programs have been found useful and effective.[111]

Again, Blackwell pushed for NRK to consider Open Sesame, but if it still though the tempo was not right, to go again for a "full-scale Nordic co-production of Sesame Street" similar to the West German and Dutch, Latin American, and pan-Arabic versions. These were, he emphasized, "genuine, full-blooded *national* programs, reflecting the cultures and the habits of the producing areas."[112] Blackwell ended by proposing that the heads of the children's departments in Denmark, Sweden, and Norway should get together at the International Market for Content Development and Distribution (MIP) in Cannes or Prix Jeunesse in Munich and explore the idea. The outcome of this tireless pursuit was that Haug, who became head of NRK's children's department, visited the Workshop in New York in 1981. After the visit, she signaled interest in co-production.[113] However, not until 1991 did Norway begin airing a co-production, *Sesam Stasjon*, that ran for eight years with a total of 198 episodes. In Denmark, a version of a *Sesame Street* spin-off, *Elmo's Corner*, ran for three seasons—from 2009 to 2013 with the title *Sesamgade*—on the commercial TV2 network.

New Attempt at Co-production in Sweden

With a foot in the door in Sweden in 1976, the Workshop worked hard to secure a co-production with SVT2. Internal memos show how it hoped that the relative success of *Sesam* would lead to reruns and ultimately a co-production.[114] Just as everywhere else, a full-blown co-production was apparently the end goal: the one that would mean the highest commitment to their product and vision for preschool television and the greatest profit in the end. To achieve this goal, the Workshop stepped up and used its personal connections with SVT2's parent organization, SR, and other high-level Swedish officials. Thus, in 1976, an exchange of visits took place between the Swedish minister of education and cultural affairs and Gerald Lesser, head

of the Workshop's board of advisers.[115] Not only Lesser but also Cooney visited SVT in March 1976, increasing the pressure from the Workshop's side.[116]
On a lower organizational level, an assistant to Peter Orton also developed
a friendship with a Swedish producer from SVT2 who often attended international events on the department's behalf. She repeatedly used this
friendship to survey the opportunities to (re)open negotiations about a
co-production.[117]

Eying a new opportunity with SVT2, the Workshop was understand-
ably very disappointed when the network did not schedule reruns or new
seasons of *Sesam* for the autumn of 1976.[118] Edström explained that Sweden
did not run long series as in the United States; television was simply planned
in another way. Once again, based on the experiment with *Nordic Sesame*,
Edström proposed a replacement in a mixed format where a presenter was
brought in between the inserts from *Sesame Street*, as there was a sense at
SVT2 that the Open Sesame format was not working.[119] Also, they now had
had great success with their own program *Fem myror är fler än fyra elefanter*,
which had been very well received in the press.[120]

The Workshop once more expressed a keen interest in developing a preschool series for SVT2 based on its co-production model, promising that
they would "put all of our resources at your disposal in order to create the
'perfect' series for Swedish children."[121] The presumption that Sweden did
not yet have a "perfect" series for preschool television seems to be based on
the sole fact that the Workshop was not included in Swedish preschool production, as the Workshop was well aware of the positive reception of the
domestic *Fem myror är fler än fyra elefanter*. Despite this snub, apparently
aware of past negative encounters with the Scandinavians, the Workshop assured SVT2 that the Workshop had matured over the past few years partly
due to a change in staff. A Workshop representative informed SVT that it
was much more open now: "so much has changed since we first dreamed
of a co-production with you, including personalities and policies," hoping
this would make SVT2 consider a co-production.[122] There was no interest
in 1977.

Never giving up, the Workshop had a meeting with the head of international relations at SVT2 in March 1978.[123] This persistence eventually
bore fruit, and after the Workshop had charmed SVT2's staff with drinks at
Orton's family yacht at the MIP in Cannes in 1979, Edström signed on for another twenty-six episodes of *Open Sesame* and initiated talks about a Swedish
co-production.[124] A contributing factor seems to have been that SVT2

representatives had attended a conference of the European Broadcasting Union (EBU) in 1977 where they had been impressed with various adaptations of *Sesame Street*.[125] Horne and Orton went to Stockholm in May to discuss the project, and in early 1979 SVT2 producers went to New York to see if they could agree on a Swedish version of *Sesame Street* that emphasized "social and emotional development" over cognitive goals.[126]

In the end, SVT2 committed to produce thirty half-hour episodes of a Swedish version of *Sesame Street*. The co-production model was different from the West German, as the Swedish version contained two-thirds material from the Workshop's international library and one-third new Swedish-originated material, and was in essence a mixture of an individual co-production and Open Sesame. The overwhelming majority of the clips that SVT selected were Muppet sketches—the result being that, in the end, SVT2 produced a series that alternated between Swedish-produced studio scenes (the fictional universe was a theater, not on a street), and items from the Workshop, many with Bert and Ernie. This format was not far from the original vision for *Nordic Sesame*, but it left the Workshop with oversight and control. The series ran only in 1980 and as a rerun in 1981.

Conclusion: The Workshop's Perseverance and the Stubborn Scandinavians

The history of *Sesame Street* in the Nordic countries shows the perseverance of the Workshop in selling its product as well as its commitment to the *Sesame Street* brand and the CTW Model. Their insistence on controlling what happened to their show as it was adapted was incompatible with the Nordic approach, because the Scandinavians felt entitled to experiment with the format on their own and decide for themselves whether it matched their visions for preschool television. The exploratory nature of television in the noncommercial broadcasting environment—where producers, writers, and all other staff were used to a great deal of freedom—was not a good match for the Workshop's fixed concept.

Despite their admiration for *Sesame Street*'s entertaining and attractive format, the Scandinavians could not make it encompass the Nordic ideas of television that had to engage children profoundly in social and emotional issues. Even with the freedom that the Scandinavians had had in producing the pilot without the Workshop's knowledge, the idea of using television for child-centered empowerment was seemingly incompatible with the Workshop's idea of teaching school-type skills. Thus, even if *Sesame Street* was viewed as a "game-changer," in the words of Danish Stahr from 1974, it should not play a dominant role in children's programs.[127] For the Scandinavians, dazzling children with smooth production values did not work, because the main thing was to teach children that television itself was "nothing mysterious, that it is human, that it may be mistaken, and that [children] should have a critical attitude towards it."[128] The key notion underlying such a policy was not to make a "masterpiece within children's TV" like *Sesame Street*, nor to create uncertainty toward the work of broadcasters, but to help viewers have "a more relaxed and confident relationship" with the medium.[129] With a strong Nordic sense of entitlement, tradition, and uniqueness, the broadcasters at Nordvision kept to the child-centered policies that they believed would help their viewers to question the world around them—including how television portrayed it.

The existence of a strong local network in Nordvision based on the public service ideals of collaboration, not competition, helped consolidate a strong local front. The Nordic broadcasters confirmed each other in their claims about *Sesame Street*'s unsuitability for Nordic children to the point at which, when SVT2 bought Open Sesame, other countries' view of the *Sesame Street* concept did not change. From a broader cultural transfer perspective, this dynamic demonstrates how a tightly knit local network can strengthen local ideas of exceptionalism, leading to forceful cultural resistance. The Scandinavians clearly felt superiority over the Workshop, not in their program's production values, but in their understanding of what children needed from television—which made them reluctant to offer *Sesame Street* even if they liked parts of it.

As in West Germany and Britain, collaboration with researchers and educational experts was not incorporated into the production model in Scandinavia to anywhere near the extent it was in the Workshop. Research results, literature, and the advice of experts were seen as sources of inspiration rather than guidelines or diktat to follow strictly. A program's writers and production teams pursued policies that had been loosely formulated and gave a lot of room for experiments with content and formats. Thus, even if the Workshop's rigid setup was admired, it was not copied.

The wider cultural influence of the youth rebellion and counterculture on children's broadcasting meant that children's departments were inspired to work toward types of programs that would help empower children. This made way for a more utopian form of progressivism in Scandinavia than in West Germany and Britain, where the child-adult relationship was influenced by a stride toward equality, meaning that television was to serve the interests of children as they expressed those interests—at least this was a stated ideal. The belief in children's ability to understand complex social, emotional, and cultural problems resulted in rejection of the ideal of television-as-preschool-teacher on which *Sesame Street* staked its existence.

Conclusion

Narrow Vision: Looking Back at a Global Success

"*Sesame Street* literally circles the globe," wrote Jeffery Dunn, president of Sesame Workshop, in a celebratory publication when the show turned fifty in 2019.[1] In the introduction to this brief historical overview, Dunn informed readers that the Workshop was the "world's largest informal educator, reaching more than 150 million children across more than 150 countries."[2] As Joan Ganz Cooney herself framed it in 2016, she believed *Sesame Street* to be " 'the longest street in the world,' benefiting more children in more countries across more cultures through more channels than any program in history."[3] Cooney's old dream of the sun never setting on *Sesame Street* had come true: the Workshop's global reach now rivaled that of the British Empire.[4]

Today the Workshop prides itself on its global impact and long history but is careful to frame its international success as something it has not actively pursued. Its historical narratives about *Sesame Street* are used to promote its image as a nonprofit interested not in money but in helping kids around the world. In the fiftieth-anniversary publication, the first global expansion is explained both as something that came as a shock to the Workshop and as something that grew out of its popularity in the States: "As our popularity grew, people around the world saw that this new way of reaching preschoolers—mixing education with a healthy dose of fun—could help children in their countries, too. Soon, they were approaching us for help in creating local versions of the show."[5] This explanation for the sudden interest in *Sesame Street* clearly frames the Workshop's first international experiences as accidental rather than a planned business adventure—a rather different view of its early international history than what this book has presented.

Not only in its own publicity material does the Workshop use its history to support a certain image of its brand. The organization's early history is also highlighted as significant for its development and activities today in scholarly

Sesame Street. Helle Strandgaard Jensen, Oxford University Press. © Oxford University Press 2023.
DOI: 10.1093/oso/9780197554159.003.0007

writings such as *The Sesame Effect: The Global Impact of the Longest Street in the World*. Edited in 2016 by Charlotte Cole and June Lee, two associates of the Sesame Workshop, the volume took stock of *Sesame Street*'s global impact from the Workshop's perspective. In the acknowledgments, Cole and Lee tell readers how Gerald Lesser, the first chair of its advisory board, and Edward Palmer, the first head of its research division, were instrumental in the company's international efforts: "their contribution to the first international co-productions still impacts the ways teams engage and move through the production process."[6] Evidently, the Workshop continues to attribute great importance today to key people from the early years. Furthermore, *Sesame Street*'s history is actively used to demonstrate to stakeholders in the United States and internationally the longevity and influence of the show and its many spin-offs—as was the case with the fiftieth-anniversary publication.

As the early international history of the Workshop is still used to frame its activities today, I devote this conclusion to an investigation of how *Sesame Street*'s global success has been interpreted in hindsight. I discuss how different uses of the show's past continue to underpin certain takes on children's needs and wants in relation to media. In doing so I consider how powerful a tool history has been in shaping *Sesame Street*'s and the Workshop's public images, nationally and internationally. By contrasting the findings of this book (and other research) with the rather narrow interpretation of the past made by the Workshop and its affiliates, I consider how a limited, instrumental use of history might hinder a critical outlook on *Sesame Street*'s international influence and the Workshop's activities going forward.

Early Stocktaking

From as early as the mid-1970s there was a fair amount of stocktaking of *Sesame Street* and its influence on the children's television market nationally and internationally. To demonstrate the role that research had played in making the show, the Workshop's research division published an annotated bibliography in 1976, the *CTW Research Bibliography*.[7] This was advertised as an overview of the research used to establish the Workshop's business between 1968 and 1976, intended for public distribution and sold from its office for $1 to scholars and others interested in the academic aspects of children's media. This bibliography of research papers relating to the Workshop and both of its TV series, *Sesame Street* and *The Electric Company*, also included comments about the entries. The bibliography's introduction promised a display of research from the Workshop and outside experts on domestic as well as international productions, and even additional research on topics broadly related to children and media.

The annotated bibliography reflects the Workshop's narrow orientation in terms of research interests. Most of the listed research came from its own staff or researchers with the same cognitive psychology background, who shared the Workshop's scientific viewpoints and methods, especially quantifiable effect measures related to predefined academic goals. The objectives that had defined the Workshop's agenda from the beginning were clearly reflected in all the kinds of research it conducted and showcased: this was strategic research that could be used to demonstrate to funders and other academics that the Workshop did what it promised. The focus on quantitative measures and audience reach was what it needed to get backing in the first place. Besides the Workshop's own publications and some that supported its approach, the bibliography listed only two critical pieces: Cook et al.'s *Sesame Street Revisited* and Herbert Springle's article, "Who Wants to Live on Sesame Street?" The Workshop had already expended much time and energy to contradict and refute this work, so including them in this bibliography presented little risk to the *Sesame Street* brand.

The annotated bibliography did not include any work that questioned the Workshop's international efforts, even though such work existed. In 1973 a group out of Columbia University called the Network Project released *Down Sesame Street*.[8] Reporting its research on *Sesame Street* and the Workshop, it posed some rather critical questions about the kind of education instruction the show offered. The report's critical conclusions regarding the international expansion of *Sesame Street* were based on primary sources from some of the countries that had broadcast the show. It should have been of interest to the Workshop—and the Workshop's intended readership—but was perhaps overlooked because it offered a less rosy picture of the transfer process than Workshop staff projected and the international research it had chosen to list in its bibliography.

The international research listed in the Workshop's 1976 bibliography was limited. In the section "Research on Sesame Street International," none of the substantial West German research from the Hans-Bredow-Institute commissioned by the Germany ministry for education in conjunction with *Sesamstraße* was on the list. Neither was the Swedish research on the test broadcast of *Nordic Sesame* that the Swedes had translated into English and sent to the Workshop years earlier. In the section "Other Reports on Media and Children," most literature came from the Workshop's own employees and associates and had its usual trademark of being strategic, quantitative, and oriented toward effects. None of the researchers whom Edward Palmer and Gerald Lesser had become familiar with when traveling in Europe to meet foreign broadcasters at Prix Jeunesse, the European Broadcasting Union, or the national broadcasting corporations were represented. Ignoring any research that was based on other research traditions and other views of education and childhood can only be seen as a deliberate choice on the Workshop's part. They certainly were aware that other traditions existed. The lack of all but two entries from researchers outside of the Workshop or its close allies made it look like the Workshop was a lone pioneer researching children's media, especially children's television. The pioneer spirit was also present in Gerald Lesser's 1974 book, *Children and Television: Lessons from Sesame Street*, which similarly positioned the Workshop's research as the first to break ground in the field of children's television.[9]

A contrast to the Workshop's narrow vision of educational television and representation of *Sesame Street*'s international reception can be found in a special 1976 issue of *Fernsehen und Bildung* about the show.[10] Some of the very pro–*Sesame Street* contributions were translations of the Workshop's own articles in the *Journal of Communication* from that same year (more later). Others took a much more critical stance.

The introduction to the special issue of *Fernsehen und Bildung* critically discussed *Sesame Street*'s success from the perspective of the journal's international community. The editor praised the show for contributing to the conversation between producers and researchers of children's television, an effort Prix Jeunesse had tried to encourage since the mid-1960s with its festivals, research center, and journal. But where the Workshop was devoted to one model only for the researcher-producer collaboration, there was diversity in the community affiliated with Prix Jeunesse. The editor concluded that no single answer existed to many questions about children's television, neither for researchers nor for producers.[11] In general, her editorial reflected the open-ended approach and international exchange that Prix Jeunesse tried to foster for research and production, rejecting the Workshop's one-size-fits-all approach. Of course, in contrast to the Workshop, the Prix Jeunesse organization had a completely different purpose and vision: Prix Jeunesse had nothing it needed to sell, other than its mission to foster a broad international community around children's television.

The special issue of *Fernsehen und Bildung* included a *Sesame Street* bibliography that demonstrates the broad interest of *Fernsehen und Bildung*'s research community in *Sesame Street* and the Workshop's transnational activities. A comparison with the Workshop's own bibliography shows the journal's much wider scope. It also offers a chance to see how much more research the Workshop could have surveyed for its own publications. Comparing the Workshop's bibliography with *Fernsehen und Bildung*'s shows the limit of the Workshop's engagement with academic research when there was no ultimate profit to be made in terms of sales, brand recognition, or positive press.

The bibliography in *Fernsehen und Bildung* listed research on *Sesame Street* and included works in English, Spanish, and German. It had 124 entries in total and included studies of *Sesame Street* in the United States, the United Kingdom, Sweden, Japan, West Germany, Latin America, Australia, Israel, Curaçao, Mexico, Canada, and Jamaica. In contrast, the Workshop's own bibliography's international section offered only twelve references for works on *Sesame Street* internationally, which dealt with the global efforts of the Workshop on a grand scale and included work done on the program in Mexico, Australia, Jamaica, and Japan. In contrast with the *Fernsehen und Bildung* bibliography, and the special issue more widely, the Workshop's narrow representation of literature in the international area contradicts the group's claim of interest in serving and understanding local needs and cultures more broadly. Ultimately it reveals the tension between the Workshop's interest in producing credible research and the use of that research for commercial purposes.

The same year that this special issue of *Fernsehen und Bildung* and the Workshop's annotated bibliography were published, the American-based *Journal of Communication* devoted a section of its spring issue to the show. The authors of the introduction to the section were unnamed, but they were clearly impressed with *Sesame Street* and saw it as the most "widely discussed, researched, evaluated—and successful—children's television program."[12] Oddly enough for a journal of communication, the measurement of success here was the fact that it had reached a worldwide audience in forty countries, rather than any qualitative measures; nor were there any discussions of what the criteria for a successful children's program might be. The lack of reflection in the editorial might be because this American journal's editors had not seen many critical discussions of *Sesame Street* based on alternative research methods.

For this special issue Workshop employees Edward Palmer and Milton Chen had written, together with Gerald Lesser, "an authoritative account of the history, economics, cultural politics and research directions of the international adaptations."[13] However, instead of offering an academic analysis, as one would expect from an academic journal, the article presents the narrowest interpretation possible of the Workshop's international activity. It contained nothing about the use of foreign agencies to advance *Sesame Street* around the world, nothing about its activities to stimulate demand, nor any of the serious problems it had had with broadcasters in the localization processes. On the contrary, the article claims that foreign countries contacted the Workshop out of the blue and to its big surprise. The importance of the revenue from foreign sales is heavily downplayed, thereby positioning the international activities more as a help to broadcasters who could not figure out how to make interesting, educational television on their own, rather than the result of massive sales efforts to raise revenues to cover the domestic production.

With a total of only eighteen references, the article had a rather short bibliography for being an allegedly authoritative history. Even stranger for something that claims to be a historical essay, virtually no primary sources appear. The article did, however, refer to one publication in Spanish and one in German, as well as a UK research report. But rather than discussing the complicated cultural issues that the British report raised or the German's discussion of research methods, problems with measuring effect, and using children's television to improve underprivileged children's lives, the Workshop writers cherry-picked facts that fit their success narrative. In this tale, all the Workshop wanted to do was "to encourage diversity to meet the needs and interests of children in different countries" and help with their lack of educational programming and research in children's television—all at a cost the various countries could meet.[14] What the Workshop did not want was to encourage the production of uniform content around the world, or so the authors claimed.

As we have seen repeatedly throughout this book, creating uniform content is exactly what the Workshop did and wanted done. But *Sesame Street*'s content was designed specifically for the American context, using a specific line of research (a narrow interpretation of cognitive psychology) to address an American problem (equality in education in a country divided by class and race), all while calling it culture free. To be sure, small steps were taken to accommodate local interests, but reluctantly and with much resistance.

Popular appeal and school-type skills were the Workshop's benchmarks for the program's success, and the Workshop did not acknowledge the very different way children's television programs were produced and assessed elsewhere or the reasons for doing so.

Looking back on its early transnational negotiations, the Workshop writers admitted that some difficulties and sensitive issues had arisen. One such difficulty had been "assuring high quality of local adaptations, both content and form," it claimed, putting the blame for any issues on the inability of foreign television officials to live up to standards that the Workshop had set, rather than the clash of norms regarding production or content.[15] The Workshop also believed that it had avoided imposing any of its own values on the programming of other countries because local committees of educational advisers had been established. As we know, such committees did not exist when the original English version was sold, nor in the countries that bought Open Sesame. Even in the cases when they were established, as in West Germany, their advice was not necessarily deemed relevant by the Workshop. It is clear from the "authoritative history" that these Workshop representatives believed that the Workshop had done the best possible job adapting to all the needs that local broadcasters and viewers might possibly have had. On the whole, the special issue of the *Journal of Communication* was another homage to *Sesame Street* and the Workshop, a brief entry from two Cornell sociologists representing the only exception.

The backing both from American research communities such as the *Journal of Communication* and the American press made it easy for the Workshop to ignore its critics, as did its close ties with many American political, commercial, and philanthropic organizations. As we saw when the BBC's Monica Sims criticized *Sesame Street* or when the West German *Sesamstraße* included a kind of social learning that the Workshop did not approve of, the American press backed the Workshop. When *Sesame Street*'s international expansion and influence on the world market met criticism, coverage followed the script that American businesses, foundations, and policymakers had rehearsed on a global scale for two decades: resistance toward US products and ideas must be rooted in misunderstandings, envy, or backwardness.[16] Clearly, for the Workshop and its backers, any dismissal of *Sesame Street* had to have its source in something other than a wish for different kinds of preschool television.

One of many examples of the Workshop's success in controlling the narrative of *Sesame Street*'s international success can be seen in a 1974 report from the Center for Educational Research and Innovation of the Organisation for Economic Co-operation and Development (OECD). At this point, the OECD was interested in how learning systems could be transferred cross-culturally, and, with the Workshop, saw *Sesame Street* as a case of fait accompli in this regard.[17] The report is an excellent illustration of how the program's international reputation of success reflects the Workshop's self-understanding. This document was mainly based on interviews with the Workshop staff and its official materials (official goal statements, newsletters, and research articles). In terms of why the program was popular, the OECD publication stated simply that *Sesame Street* appealed to children and adults, forgoing any explanation that had to do with intentional exposure and sales strategies.

Based on the Workshop's own material, the OECD report oversimplified and confused the question of localizations based on language or national cultures. On the one hand, the report foregrounded the foreign-language versions in Portuguese, Spanish, German, and French, adopting the Workshop's point of view that since its material was "culture free," it was not national educational cultures, but languages that mattered the most. In its main example of Latin America, it foregrounded how a Spanish version could easily cater to all Spanish-speaking countries in Latin America, ignoring national diversity and local dialects.[18] Still, the report stated that the educational goals were very flexible and varied from country to country and modifications should be made whenever possible (but apparently not in Latin America). This ambiguous conclusion left the questions unanswered of whether educational transfer could indeed be culture free, and to what extent *Sesame Street* could sufficiently adapt to national cultures.

The absence of a serious discussion of the complexity involved in questions of educational cultures meant that the OECD author also adopted the Workshop's view of foreign criticism, failing to recognize that the way *Sesame Street* tackled the question of preschool education was tied to American social questions, its broadcasting landscape, and specific academic traditions. In fact, the report stated that critics' arguments were "bordering on the ridiculous" when they saw *Sesame Street* as US propaganda or were skeptical of the program's didactic choices.[19] In effect, the OECD helped further the narrative that *Sesame Street* was simultaneously adaptable and also so culture free that it needed little or no substantial adaptation to fit into local cultures.

This uncritical understanding of the Workshop's triumphs continues today. The *New York Times* bestseller Michael Davis's *Street Gang: The Complete History of Sesame Street* from 2008, made into a documentary in

2021, was created mainly from interviews with the Workshop's staff. Again, this resulted in an unambiguously positive history. Just as in the OECD report, *Street Gang* not only mocked critics such as Monica Sims for her "thumbs-down" on *Sesame Street*, but also suggests that co-productions were weird, though tolerated by the Workshop because of its cultural sensitivity.[20]

As time has passed, *Sesame Street*'s early history has become a common topic in research articles and popular books. However, these accounts still are rarely based on unpublished primary sources. Much of what is written about the early international history is anecdotal, building on the Workshop's own accounts of the early transfer. As past and current employees and associates of the Workshop are active in publishing articles in scholarly journals that push the narrow vision of its history set out in the mid-1970s, almost-mythical accounts are entering academic research when other scholars cite them.

One such example of an influential article written by a Workshop employee is Gregory Gettas's "The Globalisation of Sesame Street," published in a scientific journal in 1990, which is frequently cited in research on the Workshop's international involvement in co-productions.[21] Gettas was a producer from the Workshop's International Production Group, and the account offers an inside narrative of the history that is similar to other accounts written by Workshop staff and associates over the years.[22] It lists four central principles for the Workshop's international co-productions that are said to have been in place since its beginning. These principles were (1) commercial-free financing and (2) the highest production standards, but also (3) that the Workshop would not let its values "slip unwanted, into another country's programming, [and consequently] CTW proposed that all foreign adaptations of *Sesame Street* be produced to reflect the values and traditions of the host country's culture."[23] The last principle was (4) that, in foreign productions, "any proposed alterations to the series would have to be approved, initiated, and supervised by a local committee of educational experts working in conjunction with the Workshop." The article features West Germany as an early success of *Sesame Street* adapting to another culture, never mentioning that much of this attempt happened in clear violation of the second two principles. The same omission is seen in the article's description of the Latin American co-production: it never mentions that the Workshop made a strategic decision to initiate this co-production itself and that the Workshop had control of it because it had secured funding from Xerox for the local production team. The article's lack of critical engagement with the actual processes of transfer once again contributes to the hegemony of the Workshop's own version of its international engagement.

A Particular "Solution"

The Workshop never wavered from the conviction that *Sesame Street* and the CTW model are in essence so culture free that, if slightly adapted, they represent the values of the adapting culture. Leaving aside the problem of ignoring cultural diversity within a language and geographical region, as in Latin America, the problem is that *Sesame Street* was made as a particular educational solution, based on particular ideas about research, production, children, and childhood from a select group of people in the 1960s' United States. More than fifty-year-old ideas of television production, education, and equality of opportunity are still woven into its very fabric, and so are ideas of developmental psychology and what it calls "objective standards of accountability."[24] The CTW model thus represents a specific solution made to fix a specific problem. While *Sesame Street*, and particularly the Muppets, have appealed to children and adults around the world, that doesn't make them culture free or timeless.

Thus, when the Workshop's former vice president for program research, Shalom Fisch, claims that the Workshop is careful "not to impose American culture or approaches," he shows that the Workshop's lack of critical engagement with its own international history hampers its self-awareness.[25] Myriad other production cultures, views of education, and views of childhood exist, meaning that preschool programs are created very differently elsewhere. However, these are not taken seriously. Fisch, for instance, brushes off any child-driven approaches as interesting but basically "impractical."[26] He also dismisses Heather Hendershot's thorough criticism of the program as a disseminator of American culture worldwide, saying that no research to date has addressed this question.[27] This dismissal is interesting for two reasons. First, it again simply disregards an undeniable fact that an American program is embedded in American culture; second, it raises the question of why the Workshop, which prides itself on being interested in how cultural transfer works and claims to avoid such Americanization, has never researched this question itself. Perhaps the reason is that then the Workshop would have to acknowledge that the neutral standpoint it has been maintaining does not exist.

That *Sesame Street* was a particular solution to an American problem is not the only fact that the Workshop overlooked. As we have seen throughout this book, the Workshop promoted *Sesame Street* as an educational program, downplaying the fact that it was a show that builds on a particular kind of education—namely, rote learning of school-type and simple social skills presented in an entertaining framework. This approach in turn also hid other choices, such as the fact that the program defined children's needs in terms of equality of opportunity rather than equity, a rather hierarchical relation between adults and children, and also focused on children as future pupils rather than on their lives as citizens here and now.

Since the 1990s the Workshop has moved on to co-productions that are less focused on the show's promotion of academic skills and more on cultural and social learning. Some of the newer co-productions were cheaper formats, much like Open Sesame—for example, the *Sesame Street* spin-off *Elmo's Corner* broadcast in Denmark. Other productions, particularly after 2000, have been co-productions focusing on so-called developing countries, many with financial support from USAID, the US Department of State, and the Bill and Melinda Gates Foundation.[28] The Workshop and a range of other scholars have pointed to its success in reaching its goal to make children "smarter, stronger and kinder."[29] Achieving and measuring these goals are still based on the CTW model that was developed more than fifty years ago, but is now said to be adjusted to fit these new, less easily quantifiable targets. However, as Naomi Moland has shown in her excellent book on the Nigerian co-production *Sesame Square* (2011–), the Workshop still aims to stay culturally unbiased in its application of a multicultural approach. It apparently still operates as if such a neutral position does exist even if the program's production model originates in the United States and many parts of the co-productions are made in cooperation with the Workshop. Moland suggests that "international organizations should recognize that localization does not solve all problems; complex power dynamics will always be at play whenever different groups work together."[30] To me, the Workshop's many attempts to localize their content and take a nonimperialist approach to such collaborations are undercut by their lack of openness about the particular educational and cultural position from which they speak. This blindness reaches back to its early history, but is also engrained in much American soft power, of which *Sesame Street* has been a part.

Naturally, the Workshop's seemingly unwavering efforts to help children dealing with difficult problems around the world, like living with HIV/AIDS and coping with armed conflicts, can only be applauded. But failure to consider the fact that its production model builds on a set of choices that are historically and culturally bound to particular views of childhood, education, and media production makes it more difficult to address the complex power dynamics at play in such productions. In her PhD thesis about the Palestinian/Israeli co-production *Shara'a Simsim*, first aired in 1998, and the never-realized Palestinian story in the Panwapa project from 2007, Faryal Awan analyzed how often unacknowledged differences between local (Arab/Palestinian) views of childhood and international (Israeli/Western) views, together with the political nature of aid, created a situation where the local television community in Palestine saw the Workshop as "naïve and culturally insensitive."[31] This does not seem far from how the Workshop behaved when it first entered the international market.

The seemingly neutral position that the Workshop tries to inhabit when it evokes ideas of childhood from cognitive psychology and narrow concepts of education fits as well with its business model now as when it was constructed. A more sociological, historically informed idea of childhood as bound by time and space would not necessarily prevent the Workshop from operating on a global scale. However, it would make the task harder because acknowledging the limits of its previous approach might compromise the Workshop's access to foundation funding. A less universalistic approach would also force the Workshop to limit its practice of using research to promote its business, with the risk of reducing the power of its brand. It would ultimately mean moving away from what has been one of its strongest claims to success: the universal benefits of using television to teach school-type skills, which would undermine its claim that its version of educational content is the best that a television program can offer children.

Despite broadening its mission since the 1990s, the Workshop's focus continues to be school readiness.[32] In a recent interview, its current senior vice president said that the Workshop has moved on from the main focus on academic skills to so-called executive functions like flexible thinking and self-regulation, as these are the mental skills that cognitive psychologists today say are the most important when it comes to school readiness. Though this has resulted in a slightly different focus for the Workshop on the so-called whole child, cognitive psychology and the conceptualization of children and childhood embedded in this academic discipline remain central to its work. The Workshop knows that measuring the new cultural learning outcomes they outline (making children more creative, healthy, and resilient) is more difficult than doing so for facts and simpler school-type skills.[33] The whole-child strategy has added some extra semantic elasticity to its educational goals, but it recognizes the difficulty of measuring these with its current research models. Still, the Workshop does not appear to have yet developed other lines of research, such as critical childhood studies, that might help it evaluate its strategy in other ways.[34] The Workshop's core research is still heavily influenced by psychology: an academic field with a particular understanding of children and childhood and their relationship to media.[35]

The Workshop's disinterest in engaging with its critics and honestly with its own history has prevented the organization from acknowledging its narrow research outlook and the complexities of its international conduct. This disregard has been possible for two reasons: first, funders throughout its fifty years of activity have been satisfied with the relatively narrow research approach of the Workshop. Second, the press and researchers outside of the Workshop have failed to challenge its work. As already mentioned, it has long been a darling in the American press because it presented an alternative to commercial television. The avoidance of critical scrutiny has in part been possible because preschool education and children's television are not areas of critical interest in either the American or the foreign press; stories of children and media might appeal to readers but are rarely the stuff of serious in-depth investigations. Thus, when the Workshop has presented its well-narrated idea, its research, and its cute Muppets, not many journalists have had the background knowledge that would have prompted critical questions. Because the Workshop was such a professionally run entity outsiders could be easily convinced that the alternatives were old-fashioned, silly, or pure entertainment and no match for *Sesame Street*. The dominance of US liberalism in geopolitics after the Cold War along with the influence of international organizations such as the OECD and UNICEF gave the Workshop easy access to power centers that all shared its core values.[36] The Workshop also won almost uncritical acceptance in scholarly communities. Few people have questioned that its own accounts were based on anecdotes or personal experience rather than primary sources. The lack of critical engagement with the Workshop's fundamental ideas and practices has been a missed opportunity for the Workshop to revise its production practices and ideas about childhood and education. Unfortunately, the need to survive in an ever more commercialized, globalized, and competitive broadcasting landscape seems to have fortified the Workshop's beliefs and practices. Today, it holds to its claim of universality, with the key lessons that might have come from its experience in the first years to have all the world's children walk down *Sesame Street* long forgotten.

Even at Prix Jeunesse the discussions that *Sesame Street* caused when it was first aired are no longer part of the show's legacy. In 2014 the Prix Jeunesse festival celebrated its fiftieth anniversary. That year the festival presented *Sesame Street* with an award for the TV program that had the greatest impact on children's television. The former general secretary of Prix Jeunesse, Ursula von Zallinger, who had been a part of Prix Jeunesse since its foundation, declared that *Sesame Street* has been "a great concept, a concept which has traveled around the world and which is still going strong, and which has catered to kids of a minor social class, and which was extremely well researched."[37] Just as in the vast majority of popular histories about the show, Zallinger highlighted the features of *Sesame Street* that the Workshop worked relentlessly to promote for fifty years: the research, the ability to reach international audiences, and a desire to help underprivileged children in particular.

It is an enormous achievement of the Workshop to have been able to create a brand as strong and positive as that of *Sesame Street*. However, the at-times rather contradictory claim for its international success—that of universal appeal and vigorous efforts to localize the content—is only half the story. In this book, I have shown how the Workshop developed the global *Sesame Street* brand through tough international sales, promotion campaigns and a strong, professionally crafted business model. Though centered on *Sesame Street*, the book also tells the history of other alternative preschool programs that the Workshop tried to outcompete. These two narratives need to be recognized if we are to understand the history of children's television and the possibilities of this medium for improving children's lives.

In a world where much children's media production operates on an international scale, often with global ambitions like the Workshop's, the critical reflection that a transnational history offers is crucial. Historicizing pathways of the rise and decline of different views of childhood, education, and the role of media in children's lives—and their intertwined nature with products such as *Sesame Street*—provides a backdrop that lets us imagine alternatives to exciting ideas and modes of production. Everyone with an interest in the media products offered to children today can learn from knowing why we got to where we are and the cultural, sociopolitical, and economic powers that made this happen—globally and locally. History is an interpretation of the past, but with a little courage, it can be used to reflect on the present.

Consulted Archival Material

Bayerischer Rundfunk, Internal Archive of Prix Jeunesse International (BR/IPJ)

Prix Jeunesse, Binders 1964–1965, 1969–1973

BBC Written Archives Centre, Caversham Park, Reading, UK (BBC WA)

European Broadcasting Union

> T10/57/8–10, 12
> T10/160

Children's

> R78/2560/1
> T2/275/1–2
> T2/298/1
> T2/315/1-318/1
> T2/327/1, 2
> T47/113/1

Danish National Archives, Rigsarkivet, Danmarks Radio, Børne- og ungdomsafdelingen, (RA(dk)/DR/B&U)

Børne og Ungdomsafdelingen, Udsendelser 21, 27
Småbørnsafdelingen, Diverse 1
Børne og Ungdomsafdelingen, Internationalt 1, 2

Dokumentarkivet, Sveriges Radio, Stockholm (SRD/ TV2Barn/C90)

Sveriges Radios Dokumentarkiv, TV2 Barn C90, Series C
Sveriges Radios Dokumentarkiv, TV2 Barn C90, Series E1
Sveriges Radios Dokumentarkiv, TV2 Barn C90, Series F

Hornbake Library, University of Maryland, The Children's Television Workshop (UM/HL/CTW)

Series 1, boxes 1, 2, 28, 31, 32
Series 2, boxes 33, 37, 38, 40–42, 47, 49
Series 12, boxes 346, 349, 359–62, 365, 366, 369–72

Please note that the material I have consulted for this book from the Children's Television Workshop held by the Hornbake Library's Special Collections was gathered on two trips in 2014 and 2015. In 2017–2018, the archive's staff reorganized the collection, with some boxes renumbered, and some folders moved to new boxes. The reorganization was wide-ranging and pervasive. For instance, the new catalog only contains boxes numbered up to 168, meaning that most of the records I used for chapters 3–5, which were previously in boxes 359 to 372, have been rearranged into other boxes (nothing has been removed, the archivists assured me). What this means is that the references in this book to boxes and folder numbers in this collection refer to the old catalog and will thus be hard to find using the digital catalog made after the reorganization (this, of course, also applies to all other previous work published using this collection). I consulted the staff at the archive about this problem and, following their advice, I decided to keep the references to the old catalog. It would be impossible to reconcile the two catalogs when not being able to revisit the collection on-site and double-check everything (I had scheduled a research trip in the summer of 2020 to investigate this possibility, but the pandemic got in the way). Readers who want to look at the material I am referencing are advised to contact the staff directly for help. My references are very specific and include the titles, dates, authors, and, in the case of letters and memos, the names of people involved in the correspondence. This level of detail should make it possible, with the help of the staff, to find the exact documents without looking through too much material.

National Archives, Norway, Norsk rikskringkasting (RA(n)/NRK)

RA/S-4162/F/Fe/L0004, 5–7
RA/S-4162/F/Ff/L0004, 5–9
RA/S-4888/D/L0001, 2

Norddeutscher Rundfunk (NDR)

NDR/Sesamstraße/Binders 1970–1974

Norsk rikskringkasting, internal archives, Oslo (IA/NRK)

Various documents preselected by staff on the European Broadcasting
Union and Nordvision, 1969–1976

Rai Teche, Roma

"Verbale della Seduta del Comitato Direttivo RAI," 1969

Rare Book and Manuscript Library, Columbia University (CU/RBM)

Children's Television Workshop project: oral history, 1972, call number
NXCP87-A584
Carnegie Corporation, New York, Series III.A, boxes 487–89
Carnegie Corporation, New York, Series III.B, box 33

Staatsarchiv Hamburg

- Unterlagen und Schriftwechsel zur Begleituntersuchung zur Fernsehserie Sesamstraße (Vorschule im Fernsehen) im Hans-Bredow-Institut, 621-1/144_3452
- Staatliche Zuschüsse an die Rundfunkanstalten für das Vorschulerziehungsprogramm "Sesamstraße," 131-1 II_6191
- Rechtsabteilung—Fernsehreihe "Sesamstraße": Provisionsforderungen I-V (Rechtsstreit United Film Enterprises Inc/Munio Podhorzer gegen Studio Hamburg) 621-1/144_3953
- Stellvertretender Intendant (Hammerstein-Equord) und Intendant (Hilpert)—Schriftwechsel mit Hans-Bredow-Institut, 621-1/144_3445

Notes

Preface

1. See, for instance, Sophie Brickman, *Baby, Unplugged: One Mother's Search for Balance, Reason, and Sanity in the Digital Age* (New York: HarperOne, 2021), 207–12; *John Dillermand: Last Week Tonight with John Oliver* (Web exclusive), 2021, https://www.youtube.com/watch?v=A51mJjFyG_w; Elsa Keslassy, "Danish Broadcaster Defends Kids Show about Man with Superhuman Penis," *Variety* (blog), January 8, 2021, https://variety.com/2021/tv/global/denmark-children-john-dillermand-dr-1234881201/; Thomas Erdbrink and Martin Selsoe Sorensen, "A Danish Children's TV Show Has This Message," *New York Times*, September 18, 2020, https://www.nytimes.com/2020/09/18/world/europe/denmark-children-nudity-sex-education.html.
2. Jill Lepore, "How We Got to Sesame Street," *New Yorker*, May 11, 2020; Jeffrey D. Dunn "Sesame Street Responds," *New Yorker*, May 25, 2020, https://www.newyorker.com/magazine/2020/05/11/how-we-got-to-sesame-street.

Introduction

1. "RAI introduces 'Sesamo Apriti,' an Italian Language adaptation," July 1977, 1, University of Maryland (UM) / Hornbake Library Special Collections (HL) / Children's Television Workshop (CTW) / Series 12 / subseries 3 / box 369 / folder 12. Please see the list of consulted material for an important note on the reorganization of the CTW collection that affects references to records in this collection throughout the book.
2. Joan Ganz Cooney, "Der Children's Television Workshop," *Fernsehen Und Bildung* 2, no. 3/4 (1968): 156–58.
3. Sam Healy to Al Dwyer, October 26, 1972, UM/HL/CTW/362/3. Dating of sales to the year 1970 was deduced from the airdates in this document.
4. Bob Feldman, "Entertaining Australians to be Americans," *The Bulletin* (Sydney), September 26, 1970, 42.
5. Survey referenced in Cooney, "Der Children's Television Workshop," 156.
6. J. D. Halloran and P. R. C. Elliott, Center for Mass Communication Research, University of Leicester, England, unpublished manuscript for EBU Monograph, *Television for Children and Young People*, June 1968, Riksarkivet Norge (RA) / Norsk rikskringkastning (NRK), RA/S-4162/F/Fe/L0007. Average calculated on basis of Table 4 in the Halloran and Elliott paper.

7. On the makeup of the American schedule, see Gary Cross, *Kids' Stuff: Toys and the Changing World of American Childhood* (Cambridge, MA: Harvard University Press, 2009). For an English-language example of schedules for children, see David Buckingham, Hannah Davies, Ken Jones, and Peter Kelley, *Children's Television in Britain: History, Discourse, and Policy* (London: BFI, 1999), 78–116. In the United Kingdom there was a commercial broadcaster, the ITV, but it was nothing like the American networks; see chapter 3.

8. Helle Strandgaard Jensen, "TV as Children's Spokesman: Conflicting Notions of Children and Childhood in Danish Children's Television around 1968," *Journal of the History of Childhood and Youth* 6, no. 1 (2013): 105–28. https://doi.org/10.1353/hcy.2013.0010. An example of an American show that resembled the Scandinavian approach to children's television in the United States was *Zoom* (1972–1978). Leslie Paris, "'Send It to ZOOM!': American Children's Television and Intergenerational Cultural Creation in the 1970s," in *Literary Cultures and Twentieth-Century Childhoods*, ed. Rachel Conrad and L. Brown Kennedy (Cham: Springer International, 2020), 237–54, https://doi.org/10.1007/978-3-030-35392-6_14. And in terms of a wider American cultural product, *Free to Be . . . You and Me* might serve as good example; see Lori Rotskoff and Laura L. Lovett, eds., *When We Were Free to Be: Looking Back at a Children's Classic and the Difference It Made* (Chapel Hill: University of North Carolina Press, 2012).

9. On public debates about children's media culture as places where cultural and social norms are defined, see David Buckingham and Helle Strandgaard Jensen, "Beyond 'Media Panics,'" *Journal of Children and Media* 6, no. 4 (2012): 413–29, DOI: 10.1080/17482798.2012.740415; Helle Strandgaard Jensen, *From Superman to Social Realism* (Amsterdam: John Benjamins, 2017).

10. Michael Davis, *Street Gang: The Complete History of Sesame Street* (New York: Viking, 2008); Shalom M. Fisch and Rosemarie T. Truglio, eds., *G Is for Growing: Thirty Years of Research on Children and Sesame Street* (Hoboken, NJ: Taylor and Francis, 2000); David Kamp, *Sunny Days: The Children's Television Revolution That Changed America* (New York: Simon & Schuster, 2020); Robert Morrow, *Sesame Street and the Reform of Children's Television* (Baltimore: Johns Hopkins University Press, 2006).

11. See, for instance, Gregory J. Gettas, "The Globalization of Sesame Street: A Producer's Perspective," *Educational Technology Research and Development* 38, no. 4 (December 1, 1990): 55–63, https://doi.org/10.1007/BF02314645; Edward L. Palmer, Milton Chen, and Gerald S. Lesser, "Sesame Street: Patterns of International Adaptation," *Journal of Communication* 26, no. 2 (June 1976): 108–23; Charlotte F. Cole and June H. Lee, eds., *The Sesame Effect: The Global Impact of the Longest Street in the World* (New York: Routledge, 2016), https://doi.org/10.4324/9781315751399; Fisch and Truglio, *G Is for Growing*; Gerald S. Lesser, *Children and Television: Lessons from Sesame Street* (New York: Random House, 1974).

12. For examples of critical analyses of the Workshop's conduct abroad, see Naomi Sakr, "'Smarter, Stronger, Kinder,'" *Middle East Journal of Culture and Communication* 11, no. 1 (March 19, 2018): 9–28, https://doi.org/10.1163/18739865-01101002; Naomi A. Moland, *Can Big Bird Fight Terrorism?: Children's Television and Globalized*

Multicultural Education (New York: Oxford University Press, 2019); Heather Hendershot, "Sesame Street: Cognition and Communications Imperialism," in *Kids' Media Culture*, ed. Marsha Kinder (Durham, NC: Duke University Press, 1999), 139–76; David Buckingham, "Bridging the Gaps? Sesame Street, 'Race' and Educational Disadvantage," https://davidbuckingham.net/growing-up-modern/, https://ddbuc kingham.files.wordpress.com/2019/12/sesame-street.pdf; Helle Strandgaard Jensen and Katalin Lustyik, "Negotiating 'Non-Profit': The Survival Strategies of the Sesame Workshop," *Media International Australia Incorporating Culture and Policy* 163, no. 1 (2017): 97–106, https://journals.sagepub.com/doi/10.1177/1329878X17693930; Barbara Selznick, *Global Television: Co-Producing Culture* (Philadelphia: Temple University Press, 2008), 132–46.

13. My use of television culture builds on the notion of media cultures as defined by Nick Couldry and Andreas Hepp in "Comparing Media Cultures," in *The Handbook of Comparative Communication Research*, ed. Frank Esser and Thomas Hanitzsch (New York: Routledge, 2012), 249–60.

14. On Americanization in relation to media and children, see Ib Bondebjerg, Helle Strandgaard Jensen, Michele Hilmes, Isabelle Veyrat-Masson, Susanne Vollberg, and Tomasz Goban-Klas, "American Television: Point of Reference or European Nightmare?," in *A European Television History*, ed. Jonathan Bignell and Andreas Fickers (Malden, MA: Wiley-Blackwell, 2008), 154–83; Liesbeth De Block and David Buckingham, *Global Children, Global Media: Migration, Media and Childhood* (New York: Palgrave Macmillan, 2010). On wider aspects of Americanization, see Victoria De Grazia, *Irresistible Empire: America's Advance through Twentieth-Century Europe* (Cambridge, MA: Harvard University Press, 2009); Louis Menand, *The Free World: Art and Thought in the Cold War* (New York: Farrar, Straus and Giroux, 2021); Inderjeet Parmar, *Foundations of the American Century* (New York: Columbia University Press, 2014).

15. On transnational and entangled history as ways to challenge methodolog- ical nationalism, see Michael Werner and Bénédicte Zimmermann, "Beyond Comparison: Historie Crosée and the Challenge of Reflexivity," *History and Theory* 45, no. 1 (2006): 30–50, https://doi.org/10.1111/j.1468-2303.2006.00347.x; Magnus Qvistgaard, "Cultural Transfers in the Shadow of Methodological Nationalism," in *Cultural Transfer Reconsidered*, ed. Steen Bille Jørgensen and Hans-Jürgen Lüsebrink (Leiden: Brill, 2021), 44–63.

16. De Grazia, *Irresistible Empire*, 4–5.

17. Steen Bille Jørgensen and Hans-Jürgen Lüsebrink, "Introduction: Reframing the Cultural Transfer Approach," in *Cultural Transfer Reconsidered*, ed. Steen Bille Jørgensen and Hans-Jürgen Lüsebrink (Leiden: Brill, 2021), 3.

18. Transnational approaches: Jurgen Kocka and Heinz-Gerhard Haupt, *Comparative Transnational History: Central European Approaches and New Perspectives* (New York: Berghahn Books, 2009); Ann Taylor Allan, *The Transatlantic Kindergarten: Education and Women's Movements in Germany and the United States* (Oxford: Oxford University Press, 2017) 5–6; Michele Hilmes, *Network Nations: A Transnational History of British and American Broadcasting*

(London: Routledge, 2012); Andreas Fickers and Catherine Johnson, eds., *Transnational Television History: A Comparative Approach* (London: Routledge, 2013). Cultural transfer approaches: Jørgensen and Lüsebrink, "Introduction"; Qvistgaard, "Cultural Transfers." The study of entanglement: Marie Cronqvist and Christoph Hilgert, "Entangled Media Histories: The Value of Transnational and Transmedial Approaches in Media Historiography," *Media History* 23, no. 1 (January 2, 2017): 130–41. The study of glocalization: De Block and Buckingham, *Global Children, Global Media*.

19. Sebastian Conrad, *What Is Global History?* (Princeton, NJ: Princeton University Press, 2016); Lynn Hunt, *Writing History in the Global Era* (New York: W. W. Norton & Company, 2015).

20. For this move from a particular US (Western) concern to universalistic notions of childhood, see also Daniel Thomas Cook, *The Moral Project of Childhood: Motherhood, Material Life, and Early Children's Consumer Culture* (New York: NYU Press, 2020), 166–67, and Sarada Balagopalan, "Childhood, Culture, History: Redeploying 'Multiple Childhoods,'" in *Reimagining Childhood Studies*, ed. Spyros Spyrou, Rachel Rosen, and Daniel Thomas Cook (London: Bloomsbury, 2019), 23–39.

21. Inderjeet Parmar, "The US-Led Liberal Order: Imperialism by Another Name?," *International Affairs* 94, no. 1 (January 1, 2018): 151–72, https://doi.org/10.1093/ia/iix240.

22. Meredith A. Bak, *Playful Visions: Optical Toys and the Emergence of Children's Media Culture* (Cambridge, MA: MIT Press, 2020); David Buckingham and Margaret Scanlon, "Selling Learning: Towards a Political Economy of Edutainment Media," *Media, Culture & Society* 27, no. 1 (2016): 41–58, https://doi.org/10.1177/016344370 5049057; David Buckingham and Margaret Scanlon, *Education, Entertainment, and Learning in the Home* (Buckingham: Open University Press, 2003). Cross, *Kids' Stuff*.

23. Elizabeth Rose, *The Promise of Preschool: From Head Start to Universal Pre-Kindergarten* (Oxford: Oxford University Press, 2010), 15; Nikolas Rose, *Governing the Soul: The Shaping of the Private Self*. (London: Routledge, 1990), 196.

24. In the book, I build on Laura Tisdall's categories of utopian progressivism and nonutopian progressivism to distinguish between different progressive educational approaches and especially their view of the child-adult relationship. Laura Tisdall, *A Progressive Education?: How Childhood Changed in Mid-twentieth-century English and Welsh Schools* (Manchester: Manchester University Press, 2019), 1–10.

25. See special issue of *Strenæ*, May 2018, on the Children's '68, introduced by Sophie Heywood: "Children's 68: Introduction," *Strenæ: Recherches Sur Les Livres et Objets Culturels de l'enfance*, no. 13 (May 15, 2018), https://doi.org/10.4000/strenae.1998; Jensen, *From Superman to Social Realism*.

26. Karin Aronson and Bengt Sandin, "The Sun Match Boy and Plant Metaphors," in *Images of Childhood*, ed. Philip Hwang, Michael Lamb, and Irving Sigel (New York: Psychology Press, 1996); Anne Katrine Gjerløff, Anette Faye Jacobsen, Ellen Nørgaard, and Christian Ydesen, *Da skolen blev sin egen. 1920–1970*, vol. 6, Dansk skolehistorie, ed. Charlotte Appel and Ning de Coninck-Smith (Aarhus: Aarhus Universitetsforlag, 2014); Ning de Coninck-Smith, *Skolen, Lærerne,*

Eleverne Og Forældrene: 10 Kapitler Af Den Danske Skoles Historie (Århus: Klim, 2002); Paula Fass, *The End of American Childhood: A History of Parenting from Life on the Frontier to the Managed Child* (Princeton, NJ: Princeton University Press, 2017), 185–202; Ann Hulbert, *Raising America: Experts, Parents, and a Century of Advice about Children* (New York: Vintage, 2011); Tora Korsvold, *Barn og barndom i velferdsstatens småbarnspolitikk: En sammenlignende studie av Norge, Sverige og Tyskland 1945–2000* (Oslo: Universitetsforlaget, 2008); Steven Mintz, *Huck's Raft: A History of American Childhood* (Cambridge, MA: Belknap Press, 2006); Tisdall, *A Progressive Education*; Ellen Condliffe Lagemann, *An Elusive Science: The Troubling History of Education Research* (Chicago: University of Chicago Press, 2002).

27. Buckingham et al., *Children's Television in Britain*; Maya Götz, "Kinderfernsehen," in *Handbuch Kinder- und Jugendliteratur*, ed. Tobias Kurwinkel and Philipp Schmerheim (Stuttgart: J. B. Metzler, 2020), 251–57; Jensen, *From Superman to Social Realism*; Anne Li Lindgren, *Från små människor till lärande individer. Föreställningar om barn och barndom i förskoleprogram 1970–2000* (Stockholm: Stiftenseln Etermedierna i Sverige, 2006); Ingegerd Rydin, *Barnens röster: Program för barn i Sveriges radio och television 1925–1999* (Stockholm: Prisma, 2000).

28. The roots of such new theories of learning and their relation to views of childhood are, for instance, described in Gary McCulloch, "Learners and Learning," in *A Cultural History of Education in the Modern Age*, ed. Judith Harford and Tom O'Donoghue (London: Bloomsbury Academic, 2020), 100–101.

29. Joan Ganz Cooney, for the Carnegie Corporation of New York, "The Potential Uses of Television in Preschool Education," December 1966, 4, UM/HL/CTW/s1/ss1/b1/f1.

30. Helle Strandgaard Jensen, "Scandinavian Children's Television in the 1970s: An Institutionalisation of '68'?" *Strenae*, no. 13 (2018), https://doi.org/10.4000/stre nae.1998; Mathew Thomson, *Lost Freedom: The Landscape of the Child and the British Post-war Settlement* (Oxford: Oxford University Press, 2013).

31. Wilson P. Dizard, *Television: A World View* (New York: Syracuse University Press, 1966).

32. On production ecology and preschool television, see Jeanette Steemers, *Creating Preschool Television: A Story of Commerce, Creativity and Curriculum* (Houndmills, UK: Palgrave Macmillan, 2010), 7–8.

33. Bondebjerg et al., "American Television."

34. See Laura Lee Downs, *Childhood in the Promised Land* (Durham, NC: Duke University Press, 2002); Sophie Heywood, "Pippi Longstocking, Juvenile Delinquent? Hachette, Self-Censorship and the Moral Reconstruction of Postwar France," *Itinéraires. Littérature, Textes, Cultures*, no. 2015-2 (January 19, 2016), https://doi. org/10.4000/itineraires.2903; Sophie Heywood, "Adapting Jules Verne for the Baby-Boom Generation: Hachette and the Bibliothèque Verte, c. 1956–1966," *Modern & Contemporary France* 21, no. 1 (February 1, 2013): 55–71, https://doi.org/10.1080/ 09639489.2012.722613; Jensen, *From Superman to Social Realism*.

35. On the "schedule approach," see, e.g., Buckingham et al., *Children's Television in Britain*, 76–98.

36. See, e.g., Davis, *Street Gang*; Fisch and Truglio, *G Is for Growing*; Kamp, *Sunny Days*; Morrow, *Sesame Street*.

Chapter 1

1. Joan Ganz Cooney, interview with Richard Polsky, Columbia University (CU) / Rare Books and Manuscripts (RBM) / Children's Television Workshop project (CTW), oral history, 1972, call number NXCP87-A584.
2. Ibid., 14.
3. "Television and the Public Interest" speech delivered by Newton N. Minow May 9, 1961 to National Association of Broadcasters, Washington, DC. Transcript and audio recording retrieved from *American Rhetoric Online Speech Bank*, accessed January 3, 2023, https://www.americanrhetoric.com/speeches/newtonminow.htm.
4. On *Sesame Street*'s transfer from NET to PBS, see Morrow, *Sesame Street*, chapter 3.
5. American historians of childhood have often been focused on the cultural differences between the 1950s and the (late) 1960s, but that difference does not apply in this case. See Berit Brink, "Between Imagination and Reality: Tracing the Legacy of Childhood as a Utopian Space in the Free Schooling and Unschooling Movements," *Strenæ. Recherches Sur Les Livres et Objets Culturels de l'enfance*, no. 13 (May 15, 2018), https://doi.org/10.4000/strenae.1795; Fass, *The End of American Childhood,* chapter 5; Mintz, *Huck's Raft,* 327–28.
6. *Report of Second EBU Workshop for Producers and Directors of Television Programmes for Young People, Stockholm, 22–27 February 1970,* ed. Doreen Stephens and European Broadcasting Union (Geneva: European Broadcasting Union, 1970).
7. See, e.g., Kamp, *Sunny Days*; Davis, *Street Gang*; Morrow, *Sesame Street*.
8. On the conservative result of adherence to traditional educational ideas, see Zeus Leonardo, *Race, Whiteness, and Education* (New York: Routledge, 2009), see esp. chapter 2.
9. On Carnegie's interest in cognitive psychology, see Ellen Condliffe Lagemann, *Politics of Knowledge: Carnegie Corporation, Philanthropy and Public Policy* (Chicago: University of Chicago Press, 1992), 209.
10. Ibid., 231.
11. Lloyd Morrisett, interview with Richard Polsky, CU/RBM/CTW project, oral history, 1972, call number NXCP87-A584. See also Richard Polsky, *Getting to Sesame Street: Origins of the Children's Television Workshop* (New York: Praeger, 1974), 18–19.
12. On "ages and stages" in developmental psychology, see, e.g., Erica Burman, *Deconstructing Developmental Psychology*, 2nd ed. (London: Routledge, 2008), 68–70.
13. For an interesting parallel behind the development of teaching machines in American education, see Daniel Tröhler, "The Technocratic Momentum after 1945, the Development of Teaching Machines, and Sobering Results," *Journal of Educational Media, Memory, and Society* 5, no. 2 (2013): 1–19.

14. David Connell's comments at the Educational Media Laboratory of Cincinnati in April 1970, printed in the pamphlet *The Itty-Bitty Nitty-Gritty Farm and City Little Kiddies Show and How It Grew* ... (Cincinnati: University of Cincinnati, 1970).

15. Notes from French curriculum seminar, May 11, 1972, 3, UM/HL/CTW/s12/ss3/ b366/f9.

16. Heywood, "Children's 68: Introduction"; Jensen, *From Superman to Social Realism*; Helle Strandgaard Jensen, "Prix Jeunesse and the Negotiation of Citizenship in Children's Television." *Journal of the History of Childhood and Youth* 11, no. 1 (2018): 101–7.

17. On progressive views of childhood in the United States, see, for example, Hulbert, *Raising America*; Fass, *The End of American Childhood*; Mintz, *Huck's Raft*; Lagemann, *An Elusive Science*.

18. Tisdall, *A Progressive Education?*, 9.

19. Tröhler, "The Technocratic Momentum," 5; Lagemann, *An Elusive Science*, 159–64.

20. Joan Cooney, "The Potential Uses of Television in Preschool Education," Carnegie Corporation of New York, December 1966, UM/HL/CTW/s1/ss1/b1/f1.

21. Daniel Tröhler, "Knowledge, Media and Communication," in *A Cultural History of Education in the Modern Age*, ed. S. Judith Harford and Tom O'Donoghue (London: Bloomsbury Academic, 2020), 47; Tröhler, "The Technocratic Momentum," 5; Lagemann, *An Elusive Science*, 159–64; Tisdall, *A Progressive Education?* 9.

22. Lagemann, *An Elusive Science*, 161.

23. This framing is used in Lagemann, *An Elusive Science*, 182, to characterize what happened in the field of educational administration, but it certainly can be applied more widely to the scientific contexts in which the Workshop was operating.

24. Tröhler, "Knowledge, Media and Communication," 47.

25. Lagemann, *An Elusive Science*, 161.

26. On the individualization of American society in relation to psychology, see Michell Ash, "Psychology," in *The Cambridge History of Science*, ed. Roy Porter and Dorothy Ross (Cambridge: Cambridge University Press, 2003), 270, doi:10.1017/ CHOL9780521594424.016.

27. Cooney, "The Potential Uses of Television in Preschool Education," 17.

28. Cooney, interview with Polsky, 9.

29. Morrow, *Sesame Street*, 44–45; Buckingham, "Bridging the Gaps?"

30. Joan Ganz Cooney, "The Potential Uses of Television in Preschool Education," in *Teaching Disadvantaged Children in the Preschool*, ed. Carl Bereiter and Siegfried Engelmann (Englewood Cliffs, NJ: Prentice Hall, 1966).

31. Deutsch, Martin, *The Disadvantaged Child* (New York: Basic Books, 1967). For an analysis of Deutsch's work see also, Rose, *The Promise of Preschool*, 19–20.

32. Joan Ganz Cooney, *The First Year of Sesame Street: A History and Overview, Final Report*, vol. 1 (New York: Children's Television Workshop, December 1970). Digitized report at *ERIC*, accessed January 3, 2023, https://eric.ed.gov/?id=ED047821, p. 2.

33. For an elaborate discussion of this problem, see Buckingham, "Bridging the Gaps?"

34. Buckingham, "Bridging the Gaps?" makes a convincing argument as to why the Workshop saw urban Black children as their particular target group, and his analysis

is confirmed by documents from the Workshop's 1968 summer seminars, in particular, by Ogilvie, "A Partial History of Sesame Street: Summer 1968," January 1970, UM/HL/CTW/s1/ss3/b2/f22, as well as from letters participants sent to Lesser after the seminars had concluded. See UM/HL/Papers of Keith W. Mielke, Special Series 1, Box 1, Folder 1.

35. Hendershot, "Sesame Street"; Buckingham, "Bridging the Gaps?"

36. Leslie Alexander and Michelle Alexander, "Fear," in *The 1619 Project: A New American Origen Story*, ed. Nikole Hannah-Jones, Caitlin Roper, Ilena Silverman and Jake Silverstein (London: W. H. Allen, 2021), 119.

37. The emphasis that it was not the educational system that needed fixing but the families of the children who did not fare well was reinforced by the publication of first the controversial report by Daniel Patrick Moynihan for the Johnson government in 1965 and later the so-called Coleman Report and a joined report by the two. Lagemann, *An Elusive Science*, 193–200; Daniel Patrick Moynihan, *The Negro Family: The Case for National Action.* (The Department of Labor, 1965), https://www.dol.gov/general/aboutdol/history/webid-moynihan; James S. Coleman, *Equality of Educational Opportunity* (Inter-university Consortium for Political and Social Research, 1966), https://doi.org/10.3886/ICPSR06389.v3

38. Robert Davidson, interview with Richard Polsky, 6–7, CU/RBM/CTW project, oral history, 1972, call number NXCP87-A584.

39. Cooney, "The Potential Uses of Television in Preschool Education," 9–10.

40. For a detailed study of how commercials inspired *Sesame Street*'s style, see Steven Holiday, "How They Got to Sesame Street: Children's Television Workshop's Appropriation of Advertising Tactics for Effective Childhood Literacy Education," *Journal of Early Childhood Literacy* (April 1, 2021), https://doi.org/10.1177/146879 84211003245.

41. See also Polsky, *Getting to Sesame Street*, 11.

42. Ogilvie, "A Partial History of Sesame Street."

43. Ibid., 3, and Davidson, interview with Polsky, 16.

44. Ogilvie, "A Partial History of Sesame Street," 21–24.

45. Ibid., 25.

46. Ibid., 25.

47. Ibid., 13. For further discussion of the way a focus on cognition can blind researchers to structural inequality, see Heather Hendershot, *Saturday Morning Censors: Television Regulation before the V-Chip* (Durham, NC: Duke University Press, 1998), 143, https://hdl-handle-net.ez.statsbiblioteket.dk:12048/2027/heb.08296.

48. Davidson, interview with Polsky, 5; but see also Ogilvie, "A Partial History of Sesame Street."

49. Polsky, *Getting to Sesame Street*, 18.

50. This problem is also discussed in Buckingham, "Bridging the Gaps?," as well as in Morrow, *Sesame Street and the Reform of Children's Television.*

51. There has been considerable debate about what children learn from *Sesame Street* and how it can be tested. These questions, even if very interesting, are beyond the scope of this book. What matters here is how the Workshop used the claim of being

able to help underprivileged children in particular and their tests of educational efficiency to market the program overseas. For the discussion of *Sesame Street*'s educational efficiency, see Buckingham, "Bridging the Gaps?"; Thomas Cook, Hilary Appelton, Ross Conner, Ann Shaffer, Gary Tamkin, and Stephen Weber, *Sesame Street Revisited* (New York: Russell Sage Foundation, 1975); Morrow, *Sesame Street*, 146–49; Lagemann, *The Politics of Knowledge*, 236–37.

52. Cooney, letter to Ogilvie, February 27, 1970, UM/HL/CTW/s1/ss3/b2/f22.
53. See, for instance, how Lesser repeated the point of *Sesame Street* being able to close the achievement gap in France: notes from Curriculum Seminar, May 11, 1972, 1–2, UM/HL/CTW/s12/ss3/b366/f9. The possibility of helping disadvantaged children, in particular was also mentioned on page 1 in the proposal for Latin America, see "The Spanish Edition of Sesame Street: A Proposal," December 2, 1970, 1, UM/HL/CTW/s12/ss1/b173/folder entitled "The Spanish Edition of Sesame Street a Proposal."
54. Polsky, *Getting to Sesame Street*, 14.
55. Ogilvie, "A Partial History of Sesame Street," 12.
56. Wraparounds were a coherent set of scenes that would appear between the other sketches and bind an episode together.
57. Morrow, *Sesame Street*, 69.
58. David Connell, interview with Richard Polsky, 25, CU/RBM/CTW project, oral history, 1972, call number NXCP87-A584.
59. Davidson, interview with Polsky, 5.
60. Lesser's idea as described in Morrow, *Sesame Street*, 99.
61. Ibid., 87, 103.
62. Cooney, interview with Polsky, 29.
63. Davidson, interview with Polsky, 23.
64. Ibid., 11.
65. For an insightful and rich analysis of the role of Maria on the show, played by Puerto Rican actress Sonia Manzano, see Marilisa Jiménez García, *Side by Side: US Empire, Puerto Rico, and the Roots of American Youth Literature and Culture* (Jackson: University Press of Mississippi, 2021), chapter 4.
66. Sarah Banet-Weiser, *Kids Rule!: Nickelodeon and Consumer Citizenship* (Durham, NC: Duke University Press, 2007), 149.
67. For critical discussions of how urban neighborhoods are depicted on *Sesame Street*, see Pamela Robertson Wojcik, *Fantasies of Neglect: Imagining the Urban Child in American Film and Fiction* (New Brunswick, NJ: Rutgers University Press, 2016), chapter 5, and Benjamin Looker, *A Nation of Neighborhoods: Imagining Cities, Communities and Democracy in Postwar America* (Chicago: University of Chicago Press, 2015), chapter 7.
68. Feldman, "Entertaining Australians to Be Americans," 42.
69. Morrow, *Sesame Street*.
70. Cooney, interview with Polsky, 11.
71. Ibid., 17.
72. Herman W. Land, "Children's Television Workshop, How and Why It Works," 202, UM/HL/CTW/s1/ss3/b2/f27.

73. Lloyd Morrisett, interview with Richard Polsky, 9, CU/RBM/CTW project, oral history, 1972, call number NXCP87-A584.

74. Davidson, interview with Polsky, 32.

75. See also Morrow, *Sesame Street*, 99, and Hendershot, *Saturday Morning Censors*.

76. Statement of the Instructional Goals for Children's Television Workshop. December 31, 1968, UM/HL/CTW/s2/ss1/b33/f3.

77. Polsky, *Getting to Sesame Street*, 22.

78. Hendershot, *Saturday Morning Censors*, 138. On the environment of children's television at the time viewed through the prism of *Mr. Rogers' Neighborhood*, see David Newell, Mark Collins, and Margret Kimmel, eds., *Mister Rogers' Neighborhood: Children, Television, and Fred Rogers*, 2nd ed. (Pittsburgh: University of Pittsburgh Press, 2019).

79. The five volumes were Joan Ganz Cooney, *The First Year of Sesame Street: A History and Overview. Report I*; Barbara Frengal Reeves, *The First Year of Sesame Street: The Formative Research. Report II*; Samuel Bell, *The First Year on Sesame Street: An Evaluation. Report III*; Bruce Samuel, *The First Year of Sesame Street. Report IV*; Samuel Gibbon and Edward Palmer, *Pre-reading on Sesame Street. Report V*. All reports were published by the Children's Television Workshop in 1970 and sponsored by the National Center for Educational Research and Development, the Office of Education, or both. For an overview, see, e.g., Bill Blanton, "How Effective Is Sesame Street?," *The Reading Teacher* 25, no. 8 (1972): 804–5, 807.

80. On the history of the federal government and the ineffective financing and regulation of children's television in the United States, see Colin Ackerman, "Public or Private Interest? The History and Impacts of Children's Television Public Policy in the United States, 1934 to Present," *Journal of the History of Childhood and Youth* 12, no. 2 (2019): 285–304, https://doi.org/10.1353/hcy.2019.0024.

81. Notes from meeting with Commissioner Sidney Marland, April 6, 1971, CU/RBM/Carnegie NY Box III.A. 488, folder 5.

82. Ibid.

83. Palmer to Cooney et al., April 10, 1973, UM/HL/CTW/s1/ss2/b2/f29. The arguments made in the memo from Palmer were eventually expanded in a study by Robert K. Yin sponsored by the Markle Foundation titled *The Workshop and the World: Toward an Assessment of the Children's Television Workshop* (Santa Monica, CA: RAND, 1973). Budgets from the analysis show that nonbroadcast products brought in around $2 million in 1973, and was expected at $4.2 million in 1974, as the Workshop expanded its activities with more educational materials. Foreign language activities brought in a total of $3.7 million, which was 20 percent of CTW's income in 1973 (see table 4).

84. Palmer to Cooney et al., April 10, 1973, UM/HL/CTW/s1/ss2/b2/f29.

85. Victoria De Grazia, *Irresistible Empire: America's Advance through Twentieth-Century Europe* (Cambridge, MA: Harvard University Press, 2009); Louis Menand, *The Free World: Art and Thought in the Cold War* (New York: Farrar, Straus and Giroux, 2021); Alan Osgood, *Total Cold War: Eisenhower's Secret Propaganda Battle at Home and Abroad* (Lawrence: University of Kansas, 2006).

86. Palmer to Cooney et al., April 10, 1973, 4.

87. "The Spanish Edition of Sesame Street: A Proposal," 2.

88. Ibid.

89. Advisory board meeting, May 27, 1971 (note dated June 7, 1971), CU/RBM/ Carnegie NY/bIII.A.488/f5.

90. De Block and Buckingham, *Global Children, Global Media*; Jensen, *From Superman to Social Realism*; Janet Wasko, Mark Phillips, and Eileen R Meehan. *Dazzled by Disney?: The Global Disney Audiences Project* (London: Continuum, 2005).

91. Advisory board meeting May 27, 1971 (note dated June 7, 1971).

92. Smith to Cooney, September 21, 1970, UM/HL/CTW/37/52. This letter was written the day after Roger Jellinek's "Is Sesame Street One Way to Reading?" had appeared in the New *York Times*, September 20, 1970, https://www.nytimes.com/1970/09/20/ archives/is-sesame-street-one-way-to-reading.html.

93. Smith to Cooney, September 21, 1970.

94. Cross, *Kids' Stuff*, chapter 5.

95. Bak, *Playful Visions*; Buckingham and Scanlon, *Education, Entertainment, and Learning in the Home.*

96. Horner and Haynes to Cooney, March 13, 1973, memo entitled "Need for Marriage Counselling," UM/HL/CTW/s2/ss2/b37/f52.

97. Ibid.

98. David Buckingham *After the Death of Childhood: Growing Up in the Age of Electronic Media* (Cambridge, UK: Polity Press, 2000), 162.

99. This is evident from the very large amount of publicity material produced in its first years, but public relations was also a focus in the cost-benefit analysis it wanted to be made in 1973, see Plamer to Morrisett et al., May 30, 1973, UM/HL/CTW/s1/ss2/ b2/f29, as well as the actual analysis by Yin, *The Workshop and the World.*

100. Cross, *Kids' Stuff*, 184–85.

101. Cooney's, "Financing Children's Television," speech to Action for Children's Television conference at Yale University Child Study Center, New Haven, Connecticut, October 17, 1972, UM/HL/CTW/s1/ss15/b32/f17.

102. John Holt, "Big Bird, Meet Dick and Jane," *The Atlantic*, May 1, 1971, https://www. theatlantic.com/magazine/archive/1971/05/big-bird-meet-dick-and-jane/305125/.

103. Ibid.

104. Lesser, *Children and Television*, 175.

105. Morrow, *Sesame Street*, 150.

Chapter 2

1. Joan Ganz Cooney, quoted in Linda Francke, "The Games People Play on Sesame Street," *New York*, April 5, 1971, 29.

2. Feldman "Entertaining Australians to Be Americans," 42.

3. See, e.g., Michael Dann, "Television," *New York Times*, August 6, 1972; Harry Lasker, "Sesame Street among the Mountains of Jamaica," *Harvard Graduate School of Education Bulletin* 17 (Spring 1973): 18–22; Jeffery Dunn, "Introduction," in *Sesame Street: 50 Years and Counting* (New York: Sesame Workshop, 2019), https://www.ses ameworkshop.org/who-we-are/our-history/sesame-street-history-50-years-impact; Gettas, "The Globalization of Sesame Street"; Palmer et al., "Sesame Street"; Cole and Lee, *The Sesame Effect*.

4. Conrad, *What Is Global History?*

5. De Grazia, *Irresistible Empire*, 4–5.

6. On the history of Prix Jeunesse, see Monika Hohlmeier, *A Market of Good Ideas: 40 Years of Prix Jeunesse International* (Münich: Prix Jeunesse International, 2004); Jensen, "Prix Jeunesse and the Negotiation of Citizenship in Children's Television"; David Kleeman, "Prix Jeunesse as a Force for Cultural Diversity," in *Handbook of Children and the Media*, ed. Dorothy G. Singer and Jerome L. Singer (Thousand Oaks, CA: SAGE, 2001), 521–32.

7. Cooney, *Der Children's Television Workshop*; Edward Palmer, "Begleitunterscushungen zu der Sendreihe Sesame Street," *Fernsehen und Bildung* 3 (1970): 258–62.

8. "List of participants, Prix Jeunesse International 1970," Bayerischer Rundfunk (BR) / Internal Archive (IA) / Prix Jeunesse International (PJI), binder 1970.

9. This Norwegian program was a folktale brought to life by filming real mice in actual situations. It was praised for being entertaining, simple, and straightforward with outstanding camerawork and film direction.

10. "Motivation of the Jury, Category I (Children's Programmes up to 7 Years), Prix Jeunesse International 1970," BR/IA/PJI, binder 1970.

11. Though not as well documented, a similar gain in terms of publicity could have been a potential outcome when *Sesame Street* won the Japan Prize in 1970. Toru Yamamoto, "The Japanese Experience," *Journal of Communication* 126, no 2 (June 1976): 136–37, https://doi.org/10.1111/j.1460-2466.1976.tb01392.x.

12. Interestingly, no one at the festival questioned Paul Taff's role in chairing the committee that chose *Sesame Street* the winning program. Taff was at this point working for NET, the American network that had broadcast the first season of *Sesame Street* and thus, aside from the positive exposure of a program broadcast on his own network, stood to gain half the prize money.

13. For the screening schedule of Prix Jeunesse 1970, see "Time-Table and Order of the Showings," n.d., BR/IA/IPJ, Binder 1970,

14. See chapters 3, 4, and 5.

15. Jensen, "Prix Jeunesse and the Negotiation of Citizenship in Children's Television."

16. See BR/IA/IPJ, Prix Jeunesse archives, Munich, Germany. Binder "1963–64."

17. Palmer to Cooney, "Recommendations That 'The Electric Company' Not Be Entered in the Prix Jeunesse Competition," November 15, 1971, UM/HL/CTW/s1/ss14/b31/f48.

18. Palmer to Winkler, August 14, 1970, UM/HL/CTW/s12/ss3/b365/f2.

19. See chapter 5.

20. Palmer to Lewis, August 14, 1970, UM/HL/CTW/s12/ss3/b365/f2. See chapter 3 for more details.

21. See chapter 1, but also Fisch and Truglio, *"G" Is for Growing*. For a critical examination of the research and its function, see Buckingham, "Bridging the Gaps?"

22. On the innovative nature of research in children's television and the precedence it set here, see Anna J. Akerman, Alison Bryant, and Mariana Diaz-Wionczek, "Educational Preschool Programming in the US: An Ecological and Evolutionary Story," *Journal of Children and Media* 5, no. 2 (2011): 204–20, https://doi.org/10.1080/17482798.2011.558284.

23. This is evident from most of the research presented in *Fernsehen und Bildung*. A specific example in relation to preschool programming is James Halloan's proposal for the Prix Jeunesse Foundation to study preschool programming, which referred explicitly to its differences from what the Workshop did. "Workshop, producer-research, proposal II," February 1973, Sveriges Radios Dokumentarkiv (SR) / TV2 Barn C90.

24. On the specific study by Halloran, see J. D. Halloran and P. R. C. Elliott, Center for Mass Communication Research, University of Leicester, England, "Television for Children and Young People," EBU Monograph, June 1968, Riksarkivet Norway (RA)/Norsk Rikskringkastning (NRK), RA/S-4162/F/Fe/L0007. On Halloran's research agenda, see Vincent Mosco, *The Political Economy of Communication* 2nd ed. (London: SAGE, 2009), 89.

25. For the differences in these two research traditions, see Buckingham, *After the Death of Childhood*.

26. On the Workshop's views of Halloran's research, see Palmer to Sufferet, April 22, 1971, UM/HLSC/CTW/366/8.

27. Internationales Zentralinstitut für das Jugend- und Bildungsfernsehen, Report, "Findings and Cognition on the Television Perception of Children and Young People based on the prize-winning programme of Prix Jeunesse 1968 The Scarecrow," introduction, 1, UM/HLSC/CTW/s1/ss14/b31/f44.

28. Despite these studies being some of the first attempts to undertake transnational media research on children's television, historians have not given them much attention. They are even omitted in the special issue of the Prix Jeunesse Foundation Research Centers' own accounts of their research history; see special issue of *Televizion*, "50 Jahre IZI," no. 28 (Munich: Internationalesentralinstitut für das Jugend-und Bildungsfernschen, 2015).

29. Hayes to Magold, February 4, 1971, UM/HLSC/CTW/s1/ss14/b31/f48.

30. Ibid.

31. Ibid.

32. On Palmer's disagreement with Halloran, see Palmer to Suffert, April 22, 1971. See also Palmer to Emrich, March 16, 1972, UM/HLSC/CTW/s1/ss14/b31/f48. On the Workshop's engagement with critics in the US, see chapter 1.

33. Lee Polk and Rolf Riktor, eds., *Third EBU Workshop for Producers and Directors of Television Programmes for Children, Marseilles, 20–25 February 1972*, English ed. (Geneva: European Broadcasting Union, 1973).

34. Asa Briggs and Peter Burke, *A Social History of the Media: From Gutenberg to the Internet* (Cambridge, UK: Polity, 2009), 211–22; Dizard, *Television*, 155–79.

35. Alexander Stephan, ed. *The Americanization of Europe: Culture, Diplomacy, and Anti-Americanism after 1945* (New York: Berghahn Books, 2005).

36. Bondebjerg et al., "American Television."

37. Jensen, *From Superman to Social Realism.*

38. Office of Education, Progress Report, December 1, 1970, 7, CU/RBM/Carnegie NY/sIII/bIIIA488/4.

39. Trip described in TIE to CTW, "A Marketing Proposal for Sesame Street Series II," February 1971, UM/HLSC/CTW/s12/ss3/b361.

40. Ibid.

41. This is the first trip recorded in the archive. There might have been some earlier in 1970, as the recordkeeping in 1970 was rather sparse in some areas of the CTW's organization. Metcalfe to Dann, October 28, 1970, UM/HL/CTWs12/ss3/b362/f1.

42. Ibid.

43. Orton, Japan report, received February 23, 1971, UM/HLSC/CTW/s12/ss3/b362/f2.

44. "A Marketing Proposal for Sesame Street Series II."

45. Ibid.

46. Twenty is a conservative number and based on the report. The accuracy is called into question by statements elsewhere that list higher numbers—e.g., an interview from 1970 with Joan Ganz Cooney that says twenty-six countries. See Feldman, "Entertaining Australians to Be Americans."

47. "A Marketing Proposal for Sesame Street Series II."

48. Ibid.

49. On setup of the Workshop's International Division in 1969, see John K. Mayo, Joao Batista Araujo e Oloveira, Everett Rogers, Sonia Dantus Pinto Guimarães and Gerdinando Morett, "The Transfer of Sesame Street to Latin America," *Communication Research* 11, no 2 (1984), p. 264. Representatives from the Australian ABC were already invited for screenings before the program was entirely finished in the summer of 1969; see Allan Kendall, producer of the Play School unit at Australian Broadcasting Service, to Jo Anne Symons, BBC, "Report on Overseas Trip Children's Television Workshop," ref. 243:92, BBC WA T2/317/1.

50. Office of Education, Progress Report, December 1, 1970, 7–8.

51. Parmar, *Foundations of the American Century*, chapter 7.

52. The Brazilian version in Portuguese does not feature in discussions about foreign versions in the CTW's papers on international sales generally. The Brazilian version is covered in Adriana Maricato de Souza, *Programas Educativos de Televisão para Crianças Brasileiras: Critérios de Planejamento Proposto a partir das Análises de Vila Sésamo e Rá Tim Bum*, PhD diss., Universidade de São Paulo, 2000; see also Laura Cade Brown, "Building Vila Sésamo: Children's Television and the Race across the Nation," presentation given at "Brazilian Regionalism in a Global Context" conference, Alice Campbell Alumni Center, University of Illinois, April 26–27, 2019.

53. Jorge Baxter, "Building Relevance and Impact: Lessons of Sustainability from Plaza Sésamo in Mexico and Beyond," in *The Sesame Effect: The Global Impact of the Longest*

Street in the World, ed. Charlotte F. Cole and June H. Lee (New York: Routledge, 2016), 208.

54. Mayo et al., "The Transfer of Sesame Street to Latin America," 265.

55. "The Spanish Edition of Sesame Street: A Proposal."

56. Wright to Kennedy, "Guidelines for Foreign Language Production," April 29, 1971, UM/HL/CTW/s12/ss3/b365/f3. For a critique of the Workshop's approach to Latin America, see Rose K. Goldsen and Azriel Bibliowicz, "Plaza Sesamo: 'Neutral' Language or 'Cultural Assault'?," *Journal of Communication* 26, no. 2 (June 1976): 124–25.

57. Wright to Kennedy, "Guidelines for Foreign Language Production."

58. Undated handwritten note (possibly by Tom Kennedy): "Foreign Versions. Since the last meeting the workshop has been very active in exploring and developing the basis for Foreign Versions of Sesame Street. On Latin America *we* have developed a pilot and plan to produce the program under the direct control of the workshop—this will not be the case in other countries however." UM/HL/CTW/s12/ss3/b366/f5.

59. Rochat to Cooney, December 8, 1970, UM/HL/CTW/s12/ss3/b366/f5.

60. Ibid.

61. Contract between COFCI and CTW, February 5, 1971, UM/HLSC/CTW/s12/s3/b366/f5.

62. Dann, "Television"; Lasker, "Sesame Street among the Mountains of Jamaica"; Dunn, "Introduction"; Gettas, "The Globalization of Sesame Street"; Palmer et al., "Sesame Street"; Cole and Lee, *The Sesame Effect*; Charlotte Cole, Beth Richman, and Susan Brown, "The World of Sesame Street Research," in *G Stands for Growing*, ed. Shalom Fish and Rosemarie Tuglio (New York: Routledge, 2001).

63. Itinerary from Rochat and Giroux's visit to CTW in New York, February 23–24, 1971, UM/HL/CTW/s12/ss3/b366/f5.

64. Cooney to Wright, February 26, 1971, UM/HL/CTW/s12/ss3/b366/f5.

65. Claude Giroux and Eric Rochat to CTW, "Progress Report No. 1," March 1, 1971, UM/HL/CTW/s12/ss3/b366/f5.

66. Ibid.

67. Ibid.

68. Heather Hendershot considers similar questions in relation to the language of co-productions in the Middle East and Latin America; see Hendershot, "Sesame Street: Cognition and Communications Imperialism."

69. See also later COFCI, "Progress Report No. 3," UM/HL/CTW/s12/ss3/b366/f5.

70. On the French schedule and politics of French television at the time, see Christina Adamou, Isabelle Gaillard, and Dana Mustata, "Institutionalising European Television: The Shaping of European Television Institutions and Infrastructures," in *A European Television History*, ed. Jonathan Bignell and Andreas Fickers (Hoboken, NJ: Wiley, 2008), 79–101.

71. On the political and financial history of the Radiotelevisione Italiana (RAI), see Franco Chiarenza. *Il cavallo morente. Storia della Rai*, vol. 2 (Milan: FrancoAngeli, 2002).

72. Giroux and Rochat to CTW, "Progress Report No. 1."

73. Ibid.

74. Dann to Cooney, attached to draft of text in telex, saying, "sent on cable 3/9/71," UM/HL/CTW/s12/ss3/b366/f5.

75. His meeting was reported in COFCI, "Progress Report No. 3." Several copies of this report appear in the collection, some with only the French part of the visit, others reporting both the French and German.

76. Dann to Orton, May 8, 1971, UM/HL/CTW/s12/ss3/b366/f3.

77. On the importance of MIP to distribution, see Denise D. Bielby and C. Lee Harrington, *Global TV: Exporting Television and Culture in the World Market* (New York: NYU Press, 2008).

78. Dann to Orton, May 8, 1971.

79. Dann to Cooney, March 22, 1971, UM/HL/CTW/s12/ss3/b366/f5.

80. Ibid.

81. Dann to Cooney, attached to Rochat to Dann, April 16, 1971, UM/HL/CTW/s12/ss3/b366/f5 See also Rochat to Kennedy, May 12, 1971, UM/HL/CTW/s12/ss3/b366/f5.

82. Giroux to Kennedy, June 9, 1971, UM/HL/CTW/s12/ss3/b366/f5.

83. Contract between CTW and COFCI, February 15, 1972, UM/HL/CTW/s12/ss3/b366/f7.

84. Ibid.

85. Wright to Connell, February 7, 1972, UM/HL/CTW/s12/ss3/b366/f9.

86. For an analysis of the localization of the English version in Canada, see Matthew Hayday, "Brought to You by the Letters C, R, T, and C: Sesame Street and Canadian Nationalism," *Journal of the Canadian Historical Association / Revue de La Société Historique Du Canada* 27, no. 1 (2016): 95–137, https://doi.org/10.7202/1040526ar.

87. Overview of *Rendezvous Rue Sesame* pilot, June 15, 1972, UM/HL/CTW/s12/ss3/b366/f10.

88. Ibid.

89. Translation of *L'Express* article, October, in memo from Vaughn, December 14, 1972, UM/HL/CTW/s12/ss3/b366/f9.

90. Budget for *Rendezvous Rue Sesame*, June 1973, UM/HL/CTW/s12/ss3/b366/f9.

91. "Economy-Styled Production (France)," June 1973, UM/HL/CTW/s12/ss3/b366/f9. See also Wright to Cooney et al., June 5, 1973, UM/HL/CTW/s12/ss3/b366/f10.

92. Dann to Davis et al., December 10, 1973, UM/HL/CTW/s12/ss3/b366/f10.

93. Wright to Cooney et al., June 5, 1973.

94. Dann to Davis et al., December 10, 1973.

95. Ibid.

96. Wright to Dann et al., December 19, 1973. UM/HL/CTW/s12/ss3/b366/f10.

97. Vaughn to Kennedy, December 21, 1973, UM/HL/CTW/s12/ss3/b366/f10.

98. Vaughn to Kennedy December 7, 1973, UM/HL/CTW/s12/ss3/b366/f26.

99. Newsletter attached to note from Horne to Trish, dated September 11, 1974, UM/HL/CTW/s12/ss3/b366/f24 (emphasis added).

100. Ibid.

101. Clippings from various French newspapers and magazines, including *La Soir*, October 8, 1974, UM/HL/CTW/s12/ss3/b366/f30.

102. Irwin to Kennedy, February 18, 1975, UM/HL/CTW/s12/ss3/b366/f35.

103. Vaughn to Dwyer, "Memo on Italy," January 8, 1974, UM/HL/CTW/s12/ss3/b369/f1; but see also Vaughn to Kennedy, December 21, 1973.

104. Kennedy to Vaughn, "Memo on Italy," January 8, 1974, UM/HL/CTW/s12/ss3/b369/f1.

105. Ibid.

106. Ibid.

107. Cooney, "Financing Children's Television," speech to "Action for Children's Television" conference at Yale University Child Study Center, New Haven, Connecticut, October 17, 1972, UM/HL/CTW/s1/ss15/b32/f17.

108. CTW to Izard, telex, December 18, 1974, UM/HL/CTW/s12/ss3/b366/f37.

109. Lu Horne to Connell, May 16, 1975, UM/HL/CTW/s12/ss3/b366/f32.

110. Horne to Connell, March 4, 1975, UM/HL/CTW/s12/ss3/b366/f35.

111. This wish was granted in 1977 when TF1 signed a contract for a full co-production, *1 Rue Sesame*, for which half of the content was produced by TF1 and half by the Workshop. *1 Rue Sesame* aired in 1978 and included street scenes with French actors as well as the two new Muppets, the Big Bird–like character Toccata and the Oscar-like character Mordicus. A Muppet snail, Trépido, was introduced later. The production was terminated after two seasons.

112. Memorandum to Kennedy and Dwyer, first part dictated by Dann to Orton, and the second part written by Orton, May 8, 1971, UM/HL/CTW/s12/ss3/b362/f2.

113. Contract between the CTW and the TIE, dated August 4, 1971, UM/HLSC/CTW/s12/ss3/b362/f2.

Chapter 3

1. "B.B.C. Orders Ban on 'Sesame Street,'" *New York Times*, September 8, 1971, https://www.nytimes.com/1971/09/08/archives/bbc-orders-ban-on-sesame-street-sesame-street-barred-by-bbc.html.

2. BBC press release, September 3, 1971, British Broadcasting Corporation Written Archives (BBC WA) T2/327/2. Please note that all material from the BBC Written Archives is covered by the institution's copyright and reproduced with the courtesy of the British Broadcasting Corporation. All rights are reserved by the BBC.

3. Ibid.

4. See also Buckingham et al., *Children's Television in Britain*; Steemers, *Creating Preschool Television*, and Anna Home, *Into the Box of Delights: A History of Children's Television* (London: BBC Books, 1993), for accounts of this controversy between the Workshop and the BBC.

5. The previous writings on the rejection focus on the bilateral relations between BBC and the CTW and the differences between preschool television in the United Kingdom and what *Sesame Street* was seen to offer. See Home, *Into the Box of*

Delights; Steemers, *Creating Preschool Television*; Buckingham et al., *Children's Television in Britain*.

6. Gary Thomas, *Education: A Very Short Introduction* (Oxford: Oxford University Press, 2013), 50–55.

7. About utopian vs. nonutopian education in Britain see Tisdall, *A Progressive Education?*, 3.

8. For a brief introduction to the Plowden Report, see Thomas, *Education*, 53. See also Tisdall, *A Progressive Education?*, 3.

9. Dizard, Television, Table 1, 293; numbers from the United States Information Agency indicate that there were 45,931,600 TV sets in Western Europe in December 1964 and a total of 94,474,400 in the world outside the United States at the same time.

10. *A Marketing Proposal for Sesame Street Series II*, February 1971, UM/HLSC/CTW/s12/ss3/b361. The proposal estimated sales of the entire Season 2 to the British to be $870,000 (gross) with an expenditure of $152,392 for tape conversion from the US standard of 525-line color to the UK standard of 625 lines, plus another $1,000 for airfare. This would mean that sales of the full *Sesame Street* Season 2 would bring in a revenue of $716,605 to the CTW. (The price of one *Play School* episode at the time was 175£ [$212].)

11. Hilmes, *Network Nations*.

12. Tom O'Malley, "The BBC Adapts to Competition," in *The Television History Book*, ed. Michele Hilmes and Jason Jacobs (London: BFI, 2003), 86–87; Jeffrey Milland, "Courting Malvolio: The Background to the Pilkington Committee on Broadcasting, 1960–62," *Contemporary British History* 18, no. 2 (June 1, 2004): 76–102, https://doi.org/10.1080/1361946042000227742.

13. On limits of weekly broadcast per company, see Jeremy Potter, *Independent Television in Britain*, vol. 3, *Politics and Control, 1968–80* (Basingstoke, UK: Macmillan, 1989), 70.

14. Peter Orton to Gerald Lesser, explaining how UK television worked, June 8, 1971, UM/HL/CTW/s12/ss3/b361/f2.

15. ITA, "Reactions to Sesame Street in Britain, 1971. Part 1," 8, UM/HL/CTW/s12/ss3/b361/f26.

16. Monica Sims, head of children's programmes, to Poul Fox, BBC1 controller, General Advisory Council, unaltered policy paper, July 29, 1969, BBC WA T47/113/1.

17. David Buckingham, "Watching with (and without) Mother: Education and Entertainment in Television for Pre-school Children," *Growing Up Modern* (blog), accessed November 20, 2022, https://davidbuckingham.net/growing-up-modern/watching-with-and-without-mother-education-and-entertainment-in-television-for-pre-school-children/watch-with-mother/.

18. Sims to Fox, July 29, 1969. See also Play School, "Background Information about Play School," [likely November or December 1967], BBC WA, T2/275/2.

19. For this and the following paragraphs: Play School, "Background Information about Play School."

20. Su Holmes, "Revisiting Play School: A Historical Case Study of the BBC's Address to the Pre-school Audience," *Journal of Popular Television* 4, no. 1 (January 1, 2016): 29–47, https://doi.org/10.1386/jptv.4.1.29_1.
21. Molly Cox, producer of *Play School*, BBC, to Joan Ganz Cooney, October 9, 1967, UC/RBM/Carnegie NY/sIII Grants/bIII.A.487/f6.
22. David Hendy, *The BBC: A People's History* (London: Profile Books, 2022), 381.
23. Holmes, "Revisiting Play School"; Máire Messenger Davies, "Production Studies," *Critical Studies in Television* 1, no. 1 (2012): 21–30, https://doi.org/10.7227/cst.1.1.5.
24. The price to produce *Play School* per program in 1967 was £175. Comparing this with the price of *Sesame Street* is very difficult because the Workshop had to start from scratch, whereas *Play School* was an integrated part of the BBC production of children's programs.
25. There was one producer and four producer assistants who, as a team, directed and compiled the programs, wrote the scripts, and managed a film library. This small team was, however, part of a much larger children's department with whom they collaborated on schedules and policies.
26. Note on *Play School*, [likely 1966 or 1967], five pages, BBC WA T2/317/1.
27. Edward Barnes to assistant senior education officer, April 30, 1971, attachment to note, BBC WA T47/113/1.
28. Cox to Cooney, October 9, 1967.
29. Ironically, the BBC's idea of *Play School*'s superiority to other offers was not dissimilar to the Workshop's view of *Sesame Street*. See Sims to Fox, July 29, 1969.
30. Allan Kendall (producer, Play School Unite, Australian Broadcasting Service), to Jo Anne Symons (BBC), "Report on Overseas Trip Children's Television Workshop," 4. BBC WA T2/317/1.
31. Ibid.
32. Sims to Fox, July 29, 1969; Edward Barnes to assistant senior education officer, "BBC Provision for Children Aged Five and Under," April 30, 1971.
33. One of the examples of the rather loose adaptations is the local Italian version, *Giocagió*, based on scripts RAI had bought from the BBC in 1969 to carry out a policy from 1968 that had emphasized that RAI should do more for preschool children. See RAI Teche, "Verbale della Seduta del Comitato Direttivo RAI," Rome, May 17, 1969; see also Marina D'amato, *La TV Dei Ragazzi: Storie, Miti, Eroi* (Roma: Rai Libri, 2002).
34. Cox to Cooney, October 9, 1967.
35. Ibid.
36. Reference to trip in ibid.
37. Play School, "Background Information about Play School."
38. Kendall to Symons, "Report on Overseas Trip Children's Television Workshop."
39. Henry P. McNulty (at "Carl Byone Ass.") to David Connell, January 29, 1970, UM/HL/CTW/s12/ss3/b361/f13.
40. Sims to Connell, January 23, 1970, BBC WA T2/237/1.
41. Sims to Robin Still, March 3, 1970, BBC WA T2/327/1.

42. Robeck to Fellgate, telex, December 31, 1969, BBC WA T2/327/1; Cooney to Sims, January 27, 1970, BBC WA T2/327/1; Sims to Connell, August 17, 1970, BBC WA T2/327/1.

43. Geoffrey Crabb to Robert Davidson, August 21, 1970, BBC WA T2/327/1.

44. Robert Davidson to Geoffrey Crabb, August 27, 1970, BBC WA T2/327/2.

45. Brian Young to Peter Orton, March 9, 1972, UM/HL/CTW/s12/ss3/b361/f3.

46. ITA, "Reactions to Sesame Street in Britain, 1971. Part 1," 8.

47. Ibid., 9.

48. Sims to Cooney, November 20, 1970, BBC WA T2/327/1. See also Peter Ridsdale Scott to Monica Sims, "Joan Ganz-Cooney's Press Reception," November 25, 1970, BBC WA T2/327/1.

49. Michale Irving to Dann, December 3, 1970, UM/HL/CTW/s12/ss3/b362/f2.

50. Sims to Attenborough (director of programs), explaining that her reason for writing the letter to the *Guardian* was that she was tired of replying to individual letters from the public, January 11, 1971, BBC WA T2/327/2.

51. Monica Sims, "Letter to the Editor," *The Guardian*, December 22, 1970.

52. For the use of child-centeredness in relation to program policy of the BBC's children's department in this period see Buckingham et al., *Children's Television in Britain*, 34.

53. Sims to Fox, July 29, 1969.

54. Jensen, *From Superman to Social Realism*.

55. Ibid.

56. Buckingham, *Children's Television in Britain*, 85.

57. Sims to Mrs. Groves, January 12, 1971, BBC WA T2/327/2.

58. ITA, "Reactions to Sesame Street in Britain, 1971. Part 1," 45–47.

59. Paradine to Pat Healy (CTW), October 25, 1971, UM/HL/CTW/s12/ss3/b361/f 17.

60. The regulations for scheduling were subsequently abolished when the government announced the deregulation of broadcasting hours in January 1972.

61. *Women's Guardian* (clipping), June 3, 1971, BBC WA T2/327/2.

62. ITA, "Reactions to Sesame Street in Britain, 1971. Part 1," 9.

63. Ibid.

64. Franck Blackwell, "Brief Notes to Field Observers on Some of the Educational Implications and Techniques of the Sesame Street Programmes," March 6, 1971, BBC WA T2/318/1. The CTW did not retain a copy of this study; someone gave a copy to the BBC.

65. ITA, "Reactions to Sesame Street in Britain, 1971. Part 1," 9.

66. Ibid.

67. Orton to Lesser, June 8, 1971.

68. Ibid. For more on *Sesame Street* in Canada, see Hayday, "Brought to You by the Letters C, R, T, and C."

69. Lesser, report to CTW, June 1, 1971, 6–7, UM/HL/CTW/s12/ss3/b365/f5.

70. Ibid., 6.

71. ITA, "Reactions to Sesame Street in Britain, 1971. Part 1," 10.

72. Ibid. 10.

73. *Sunday Times* (clipping), August, 1971, UM/HL/CTW/s12/ss3/b361/f16.

74. *A Marketing Proposal for Sesame Street Series II*, February 1971.

75. [Pa]Trish[a] Haynes to Michael Dann, September 1, 1971, UM/HL/CTW/s12/ss3/b361/f 2.

76. Ibid.

77. ITA, "Reactions to Sesame Street in Britain, 1971. Part 1," 11.

78. *The Guardian* (clippings), July 6, 1971, UM/HL/CTW/s12/ss3/b361/f 17.

79. As retold by Haynes in Haynes to Dann, September 1, 1971.

80. *Women's Guardian* (clipping), June 3, 1971, BBC WA T2/327/2. Clippings from the *Daily Express* (August 29, 1971) demonstrate the conclusion that the BBC made a monumental blunder in buying *Sesame Street*, as do those from the *Sunday Times* (August 29, 1971). But as *Sesame Street* was reviewed in the *Times* (March 31, 1971) and the *Telegraph* (March 30, 1971), both were in favor of the BBC's decision.

81. "B.B.C. Children's TV Stresses Respect for Intellect and Reality," *New York Times*, June 29, 1971, http://timesmachine.nytimes.com/timesmachine/1971/06/29/81953119.html?zoom=16.

82. Sims to managing director of television, September 6, 1971, BBC WA T2/327/2. What can be assumed to be her original seven-page *Sesame Street* paper is not preserved directly as an attachment to the letter but appears elsewhere in the same folder. Upon her return from the EBU meeting in Oslo, she sent a slightly longer eight-paged (dated) version to her bosses on September 14, 1971; see Sims to managing director, September 14, 1971, BBC WA T2/327/2. There are only two paragraphs added: one about children moving around when they watch television and whether the Workshop and the BBC believed this behavior should be encouraged; another about effects research from the Workshop. The version of her paper that the Workshop later objected to was nine pages and dated September 7, 1971, the day she departed for the EBU meeting in Oslo. This version is in its content identical to the one dated September 14, 1971, and also can also be found at BBC T2/372/2.

83. Assistant senior education officer to DPtel, April 26, 1971, BBC WA T47/113/1.

84. On Elaine Mee's report, see Steven Barclay, *BBC School Broadcasting: Progressivism in Education and Literacy, 1957–1979*, PhD thesis, June 2021, University of Westminster, 139.

85. Sims, paper on *Sesame Street*, no date, 7 pages, BBC WA T2/327/2. This argument is the same in the eight-page version dated September 14, 1971.

86. BBC, press release, September 3, 1971, BBC WA T2/327/2.

87. Ibid.

88. Ibid.

89. Ibid.

90. Thomas, *Education*, 77.

91. Searches in newspaper databases Newspapers.com and the British Newspapers Archive for September 7–10, 1971, show myriad newspaper articles that reported the conference—local, broadsheet, tabloid, and national papers in Britain and the States.

92. "B.B.C. Orders Ban on 'Sesame Street.'"

93. One example was from *Washington Post* (clipping), September 8, 1971, UM/HL/CTW/s12/ss3/b361/f13, but a search in newspaper databases Newspapers.com

and the British Newspapers Archive for September 7–10, 1971, show many more. A draft of the AP item exists in the CTW's archives, indicating that someone with a connection to the Workshop helped draft it (UM/HL/CTW/s12/ss3/b361/f2).

94. Parmar, *Foundations of an American Century*, 99.

95. This analysis of dislocation builds on Parmar's idea of how focus has been dislocated in debates about anti-Americanism; see his *Foundations of an American Century*, 100.

96. ITA, "Reactions to Sesame Street in Britain, 1971. Part 1," 51.

97. John Holt's criticism appeared in an article from the *Times Educational Supplement*, September 17, 1971. Not very favorable coverage about Sims also included John Crosby, *The Observer*, September 26, 1971 (UM/HL/CTW/s12/ss3/b361/f2), and Mary Waddington, "Case against Sesame Street," *The Guardian*, October 7, 1971 (BBC T2/327/2). An article in *New Society*, October 7, 1971, discussed educational policies in relation to *Sesame Street* (UM/HL/CTW/s12/ss3/b361/f18) and was critical of *Sesame Street*'s British detractors.

98. ITA, "Reactions to Sesame Street in Britain, 1971. Part 1," 51.

99. *The Guardian* (clipping), September 16, 1971, UM/HL/CTW/s12/ss3/b361/f16.

100. In the letter published on September 11, 1971, a BBC representative from its offices in New York explained that *Sesame Street* had not been banned, the BBC had merely decided not to buy it many months before; see https://nyti.ms/347f8SR.

101. Fred M. Hechinger, "Education," *New York Times*, September 12, 1971, https://www.nytimes.com/1971/09/12/archives/education-sesame-street-those-muppets-stir-up-a-storm-in-britain.html.

102. Sims to Ch.Pers.O.Tel, September 15, 1971, BBC WA T2/327/2.

103. Sims, draft of article for *New York Times Magazine*, September 30, 1971, BBC WA T2/298/1.

104. John Smith (head of personnel) to Monica Sims, September 20, 1971, BBC WA T2/327/2.

105. Robert Hatch to Joan Ganz Cooney et al., September 27, 1971 (UM/HL/CTW/s12/ss3/b361/f2) The version of Sims's paper attached to this letter, running nine pages, was dated September 7, 1971.

106. Ibid.

107. Doreen Stephens (head of family programmes, television) to director of television, "Proposed EBU Seminar for Producers and Directors of Children's Programmes," November 23, 1966 (notes on proposal for EBU seminar), BBC WA T10/57/8.

108. Ibid.

109. Ibid.

110. "Proposed EBU Seminar on Programmes for Youth," note 391, November 29, 1966, BBC WA T10/57/8.

111. Coleman to Palmer, September 28, 1971 (UM/HL/CTW/s12/ss3/b361/f2), says it was September 27; the ITA report says it was on September 20. The interest in the differences of opinions over *Sesame Street* in Britain led to another *Late Night Line Up* about *Sesame Street*. On September 20, 1971, Monica Sims had been invited

on the program together with Brian Groombridge from the ITA, Brian Jackson from the Advisory Centre for Education, and Dr. Mary Waddington from the University of London's Institute of Education to discuss Sesame Street. John Cain (assistant head of further education) to Monica Sims, September 29, 1971, BBC WA T2/327/2).

112. Sarah Frank to Michael Dann, October 4, 1971, UM/HL/CTW/s12/ss3/b361/f16.
113. Ibid.
114. Peter Orton and Edward Barnes (department head, children's television, BBC), undated notes from telephone call discussing the EBU meeting and an apology, BBC WA T2/327/2. On Orton's disappointment, see Frank to Dann, October 4, 1971.
115. Orton and Barnes, undated notes from telephone call.
116. Ibid.
117. Frank to Dann, October 4, 1971.
118. Sims to Attenborough (director of programs), October 7, 1971, BBC WA T2/327/2.
119. David Attenborough (director of programs) to chairman, October 20, 1971, BBC WA T47/113/1.
120. Sims to Attenborough (director of programs), October 7, 1971.
121. Michael Dann to Joan Cooney, October 8, 1971, UM/HL/CTW/b17/f51.
122. Attenborough to chairman, October 20, 1971.
123. Ibid.
124. Ibid.
125. Dann to Cooney et al., October 8, 1971, UM/HL/CTW/s12/ss3/b361/f13.
126. Dann to Cooney November 1, 1971, UM/HL/CTW/s12/ss3/b361/f13.
127. Dann to Wheldon, October 14, 1971, UM/HL/CTW/s12/ss3/b361/f13.
128. Hatch to Cooney et al., attachment to note: "Here is the revise of the possible Sims letter," November 3, 1971, UM/HL/CTW/s12/ss3/b361/f13. Multiple drafts of the letter appear in the collection's two folders named "Monica Sims."
129. "Dear Broadcasters." Date added in pencil, October 1971, BBC WA T47/113/1. This version has the full paragraph on point 15 compared to the drafts circulated within the Workshop on November 3, 1971 (previous note). However, the letter still looked like a draft when it reached the BBC and contained the same factual mistakes, like placing the meeting in Stockholm rather than Oslo.
130. Dann to Wheldon, November 12, 1971, UM/HL/CTW/s12/ss3/b361/f13.
131. Wording the same in Hatch to Cooney et al., November 3, 1971, UM/HL/CTW/s12/ss3/b361/f13 and "Dear Broadcasters." October 1971, BBC WA T47/113/1.
132. Wording the same in Hatch to Cooney et al., November 3, 1971, UM/HL/CTW/s12/ss3/b361/f13 and "Dear Broadcasters." October 1971, BBC WA T47/113/1.
133. Sims to DPtel, December 6, 1971, BBC WA T2/327/; but see also TV Guide, March 11, 1972, UM/HL/CTW/s12/ss3/b361/f18.
134. The person who told her to withdraw was David Webster from the BBC's New York office. Sims to Attenborough, February 26, 1973, BBC WA T2/327/2.
135. TV Guide, March 11, 1972; Sims to Attenborough, March 13, 1972, BBC WA T2/327/2.

136. Polk and Riktor, *Third EBU Workshop*. For accounts of the EBU workshop, see also Gert Müntefeing, "Der UER-Workshop über Kleinkinderprogramme vom 5. Bis 11. März 1972 in Marseille," *Fernsehen und Bildung* 6, no. 2 (1972): 102–5.

137. ITA, "Reactions to Sesame Street in Britain, 1971. Part 1," 52.

138. Ibid, 27.

139. Dann to Cooney, May 19, 1972, UM/HL/CTW/s12/ss3/b361/f3.

140. ITA, "Reactions to Sesame Street in Britain, 1971. Part 1," 28.

141. Ibid.

142. Sterling to Cooney, opening letter in sales report, July 31, 1972, UM/HL/CTW/s12/ss3/b362/f15.

143. TIE to CTW, sales report, July 31, 1972, 2, UM/HL/CTW/s12/ss3/b362/f15.

144. Ibid.

145. Peter Orton to Michael Dann, November 8, 1972, UM/HL/CTW/s12/ss3/b361/f3; Dann's letter to CTW internals, November 13, 1972.

146. Peter Orton to Michael Dann, November 8, 1972.

147. Ibid.

148. Ibid.

149. Orton to Sims, February 22, 1973, UM/HL/CTW/s12/ss3/b362/f4; Joan Ganz Cooney to Dann, handwritten note attached to letter, February 20, 1973, UM/HL/CTW/s12/ss3/b362/f4.

150. Sims to Orton, March 2, 1973, UM/HL/CTW/s12/ss3/b361/f15. See chapter 2 for details on this format.

151. Sims to Attenborough, February 26, 1973, BBC WA T2/327/2.

152. Connell to Orton, April 9, 1975, UM/HL/CTW/s12/ss3/b362/f1.

153. Sims to Kemble at the *Daily Express*, March 26, 1975, UM/HL/CTW/s12/ss3/b362/f1.

154. Sims to Connell, April 1, 1975, UM/HL/CTW/s12/ss3/b362/f1.

155. See also Thomson, *Lost Freedom*, chapter 4, for an argument about television as a new space children gained for children when the physical spaces of childhood became more restricted.

Chapter 4

1. Cooney and Lesser to Grossmann, September 9, 1972, UM/HL/CTW/s12/ss3/b365/f10.

2. On the centrality of World War II in the formulation of pedagogical policies in West Germany, see Carola Kuhlmann, "Antiautoritäre Pädagogik," in *Erziehung und Bildung: Einführung in die Geschichte und Aktualität pädagogischer Theorien*, ed. Carola Kuhlmann (Wiesbaden: Springer Fachmedien, 2013), 195–212, https://doi.org/10.1007/978-3-531-19387-8_11; Sonja Levsen, "Authority and Democracy in Postwar France and West Germany, 1945–1968," *Journal of Modern History* 89, no. 4 (December 1, 2017): 812–50, https://doi.org/10.1086/694614; Sonja Levsen, *Autorität und Demokratie: Eine Kulturgeschichte des Erziehungswandels in*

Westdeutschland und Frankreich, 1945–1975 (Göttingen: Wallstein Verlag, 2019), 441–556.

3. Till Kössler and Janosch Steuwer, "Kindheit und Soziale Ungleichheit in den langen 1970er Jahren," *Geschichte und Gesellschaft* 46, no. 2 (September 8, 2020): 183–99, https://doi.org/10.13109/gege.2020.46.2.183.

4. Michael Schmidbauer, *Die Geschichte des Kinderfernsehens in der Bundesrepublik Deutschland* (München: K. G. Saur, 1987), 62.

5. Andrea Scherell and Beate Jacobi, *10 Jahre Sesamstraße, was ist aus dieser Sendung geworden?* (Berlin: Spiess, 1980), 14.

6. For a comparative history of German preschool philosophy in English, see Amanda Taylor Allen, *The Transatlantic Kindergarten. Education and Women's Movements in Germany and the United States* (Oxford: Oxford University Press 2017), and on modern childhood in Germany, also Emilie Bruce, *Revolutions at Home: The Origin of Modern Childhood and the German Middle Class* (Amherst: University of Massachusetts Press, 2021).

7. On the West German approaches to education as a way to equality, see Kössler and Steuwer, "Kindheit Und Soziale Ungleichheit."

8. Götz, "Kinderfernsehen." ZDF, the second network, was established in 1963 and began providing programs for children and young people in 1967.

9. Marina Wladkowski, *Kinderfernsehen in Deutschland Zwischen Qualitätsansprüchen Und Ökonomie Unter Berücksichtigung Der Vorschulserie Sesamstraße*, Dissertation, Technischen Universität Carolo-Wilhelmina zu Braunschweig, 2003, 14, https://d-nb.info/968741541/34.

10. Ibid., 15.

11. The show was later broadcast under the title *Das Feuerrote Spielmobil* [The fiery-red play mobile].

12. Schmidbauer, *Die Geschichte des Kinderfernsehens*, 90.

13. Elke Schlote, "Bildungsfernsehen historisch," *Televizion* 28, no. 2 (2015): 17.

14. On ZDF and its considerations regarding BBC's *Play School*, see Schmidbauer, *Die Geschichte des Kinderfernsehens*, 90–91.

15. This title is hard to translate at it is slang; alternatives could be "Don't Bullshit Me" or "Stop Talking Now."

16. Later developed into *Die Sendung mit der Maus*.

17. Incidentally, the question of how *Sesamstraße* ended up on ARD became the question of a substantial lawsuit that involved not the Paris-based agents but an American company, United Film Enterprises, which sued Studio Hamburg/NDR for not recognizing (financially) that they had made the Workshop choose ARD. United Film Enterprises lost the case. See Staatsarchiv Hamburg 621-1-144/NDR/3953.

18. Schmidbauer, *Die Geschichte des Kinderfernsehens*, 91.

19. Ibid., 91 (my translation).

20. "Stellungnahme der ARD-Nachmittagsredaktre sum Vorschulprogramm: März 1971," as printed in Schmidbauer, *Die Geschichte des Kinderfernsehens*, 91–92 (my translation).

21. Program description in document dated June 1, 1971, Staatsarchiv Hamburg, Senatskanzlei 11, 131-1 II_6191; program description in document dated November 12, 1971.

22. "Stellungsnahme der ARD-Nachmittagsredakture sum Vorschulprogramm: März 1971," 91 (my translation).

23. Dann to Cooney et al., March 23, 1971, UM/HL/CTW/s12/ss3/b365/f4.

24. Ibid.

25. Ibid.

26. "Sesam Strasse," *Radiocorriere*, no. 34 (1972), 80, http://www.radiocorriere.teche.rai.it/Download.aspx?data=1972|34|80|I. Jimmy Stahr, "Børne-TV for reklame-skadede unger: Rædsel og inspiration," *Folkebladet for Randers*, March 23, 1972, 8; this long article reporting on the forthcoming trial runs was also published in *Demokraten Århus*. In Germany there was also an interest in how the British reception was going; see, for instance, "Vorm Schlafengehen kommt der Kommissar," *Der Spiegel*, January 16, 1972, https://www.spiegel.de/politik/vorm-schlafengehen-kommt-der-kommis sar-a-100ebf1a-0002-0001-0000-000043018812, and Klaus Schleicher, *Sesame Street für Deutschland: Die Notwendigkeit einer "vergleichenden Mediendidaktik"* (Düsseldorf: Schwann, 1972).

27. Klamroth to Dann, February 11, 1971, UM/HL/CTW/s12/ss3/b365/f4.

28. "Pappnasen aus USA," *Der Spiegel*, April 4, 1971, https://www.spiegel.de/kultur/pappnasen-aus-usa-a-5ecaeb28-0002-0001-0000-000043732485; "Vergebene Chance." *Der Spiegel*, May 2, 1971, https://www.spiegel.de/kultur/vergebene-chance-a-186a8e5c-0002-0001-0000-000043257745.

29. Schleicher, *Sesame Street für Deutschland*.

30. "Pappnasen aus USA," *Der Spiegel*; "Vergebene Chance," *Der Spiegel*; Heike Mundzeck, "Abschied von Märchentante und Bastelonkel," *Die Zeit*, April 30, 1971, https://www.zeit.de/1971/18/abschied-von-maerchentante-und-bastelonkel; Dieter E. Zimmer, "Sesame Street," *Die Zeit*, April 30, 1971, https://www.zeit.de/1971/18/sesame-street.

31. "Pappnasen aus USA," April 4, 1971.

32. Ibid.

33. Note dated May 6, 1971, for the agenda at the proposed conference in Baden-Baden, May 11–12, NDR/Sesamstraße/Binder 1971.

34. "Vergebene Chance."

35. Note dated May 6, 1971, for the agenda at the proposed conference in Baden-Baden (my translation).

36. Ibid.

37. "Vergebene Chance."

38. For more on Bayerische Rundfunk's refusal to air Sesamstraße, see Helmot Oeller, "Die Gründe, die der Bayerische Rundfunk 1973 gegen die Sesamstraße vortrug," *Fernsehen und Bildung* 10, no. 1–2 (1976): 108–9.

39. Note stamped June 1, 1971, NDR/Sesamstraße/Binder 1971. Five committed at this meeting, later three more, and in the end only three co-produced.

40. Schmidbauer, *Die Geschichte des Kinderfernsehens*, 96.

41. "Protokoll über die Programmkonferenz der verantwortlichen Redakteure des Nachmittagsprogramms der ADR 19–20 August 1971 in Colognie," as quoted in Schmidbauer, *Die Geschichte des Kinderfernsehens*, 96 (my translation).

42. This was called a co-production in all correspondence, but as this chapter shows, there was a substantial difference in the ways the Workshop collaborated with the Germans on Seasons I and II of *Sesamstraße* and the "full-blown" co-production of Season III.

43. Wright to Kennedy and Dann, April 29, 1971, UM/HL/CTW/s12/ss3/b365/f3.

44. On inspiration from France, see Rochat and Giroux, "Progress Report 1," with suggestions for local adaptations, March 1, 1971, UM/HL/CTW/s12/ss3/b365/f5.

45. Wright to Grossmann, June 11, 1971, UM/HL/CTW/s12/ss3/b365/f3 (note explaining the general guidelines).

46. Ibid.

47. Klamroth to Wright, July 1, 1971, UM/HL/CTW/s12/ss3/b365/f3.

48. Jérôme Bourdon, "From Discrete Adaptations to Hard Copies: The Rise of Formats in European Television," in *Global Television Formats: Understanding Television across Borders*, ed. Sharon Shahaf and Tasha Oren (London: Taylor & Francis, 2011), http://ebookcentral.proquest.com/lib/asb/detail.action?docID=957664.

49. Wright to Kennedy and Dann, April 29, 1971, UM/HL/CTW/s12/ss3/b365/f3.

50. Wright to Grossmann, June 11, 1971.

51. For an explanation of the CTW model as a concept, see Fisch, *G Is for Growing*.

52. Lesser to CTW, July 1, 1971, UM/HL/CTW/s12/ss3/b365/f6.

53. Ibid.

54. Ibid., 8.

55. Dwyer to Cooney et al., August 20, 1971, UM/HL/CTW/s12/ss3/b365/f7.

56. Wright to Klamroth, August 20, 1971, UM/HL/CTW/s12/ss3/b365/f7.

57. Ibid.

58. Grossmann, Bericht (report on meeting in New York), September 6, 1971, NDR, Binder 1971, Sesamstraße.

59. Ibid., point 9.

60. Klamroth to Cooney, October 18, 1971, UM/HL/CTW/s12/ss3/b365/f3 (letter in folder 3, report in folder 1).

61. Ibid.

62. Ibid.

63. Agreement made on January 1, 1972 (not signed; version signed on January 3 not in archive), NDR, binder 1971, *Sesamstraße*. The agreement covered 145 English-language programs to be aired between the summer of 1972 and 1974 and production of the German program. The undertaking of making a German version was very expensive. The three regional broadcasting corporations had to pay a license fee and also cover the expensive tape conversion and dubbing process, production of new German inserts, travel, and transport and materials. The three stations looked at costs between 6.4 million DM ($1.8 million in US dollars) for 145 shows plus another $0.2 million for 130 reruns, of which $0.85 million were license fees for the Workshop. Of this, the Federal Ministry for Education and Science would pay little

less than half and the three stations the rest. The ministry would also pay $140,000 for the research to be conducted in relation to the program. (Transcoding was to happen in Germany paid by the Postal Ministerium; see correspondence from September 17, 1971.) Grossmann to Interdant Schröder, von Hammerstein and Schwarzkopf, budget, September 17, 1971, NDR, Binder 1971, Sesamstraße.

64. Henderson to Kennedy et al., November 5, 1971, UM/HL/CTW/s12/ss3/b365/f8.
65. Ibid.
66. Wright to Klamroth, February 16, 1972, UM/HL/CTW/s12/ss3/b365/f6. This was one of several letters between the two on this day.
67. Ibid.
68. Vorschläge der Arbeitsgruppe Sesame-Strasse, Hamburg, February 17, 1972, UM/HL/CTW/s12/ss3/b365/f8.
69. Ibid. (my translation). Quote adjusted from one to two sentences for readability.
70. Wright to Grossmann, April 21, 1972 (Wright is referencing Lesser's opinions throughout the letter) UM/HL/CTW/s12/ss3/b365/f6.
71. Ibid.
72. Wright to Kennedy, August 17, 1972, UM/HL/CTW/s12/ss3/b365/f6.
73. Ibid.
74. Ibid.
75. Cooney and Lesser to Grossmann, September 9, 1972, UM/HL/CTW/s12/ss3/b365/f10.
76. Ibid.
77. Advisory board meeting minutes, September 29–30, 1972, translation by Bdo Fabian, October 5, 1972, UM/HL/CTW/s12/ss3/b365/f6.
78. Ibid.
79. NDR, status report in English, January 1973, UM/HL/CTW/s12/ss3/b365/f6.
80. Palmer and Brunner to Leuci, March 7, 1973, UM/HL/CTW/s12/ss3/b365/f8.
81. The booklets were titled Sesamstraße—Information für Eltern und Erzieher, Band 1–4 (Köln: Verlagsgesellschaft Schulfersehen, 1973). A summary of their content in English (albeit somewhat biased) can be found in Lisa Kuhmerker, "When Sesame Street Becomes Sesamstraße: Social Education for Preschoolers Comes to Television," Hunter College, 1974, UM/HL/CTW/s12/ss3/b365/f9.
82. "Kinder sind nämlich auch mal dran," Der Spiegel, March 4, 1973, https://www.spiegel.de/politik/kinder-sind-naemlich-auch-mal-dran-a-066e8a92-0002-0001-0000-000042645672.
83. Ibid.
84. Hans-Bredow-Institute, German report summary, July 5, 1973, included in Grossmann to Cooney, August 31, 1973, UM/HL/CTW/s12/ss3/b365/f9. For the full report, see Begleituntersuchungen Zur Fernsehserie 'Sesamstraße.' Ausgewählte Ergebnisse Des Gesamtprojekts (Hamburg: Hans-Bredow-Institut für Rundfunk und Fernsehen an der Universität Hamburg, 1975).
85. Begleituntersuchungen Zur Fernsehserie 'Sesamstraße, 4.

86. See, for instance, article from *Baltimore Sun* (clipping), January 18, 1973, UM/HL/CTW/s12/ss3/b365/f8.

87. Transcription from May 1, 1973, UM/HL/CTW/s12/ss3/b365/f6.

88. *Variety*, "'Sesamstraße' Rumpus and Rivalry" (clipping), October 24, 1972, UM/HL/CTW/s12/ss3/b365/f8.

89. Mrs. Werner H. (Janice) Müller to Workshop, attached to Wright to Dwyer et al., November 28, 1973, UM/HL/CTW/s12/ss3/b365/f4.

90. This was a longer correspondence in March and April 1973, but see specifically Dwyer to Wright, April 13, 1973; Grossmann to Wright, April 17, 1973; Wright to Grossmann, March 27, 1973, all UM/HL/CTW/s12/ss3/b365/f6.

91. It was not NDR but WDR that replied to some of the correspondence around this issue as the latter was also part of the broadcasting consortium behind *Sesamstraße*.

92. Horne to Vaughn, November 28, 1973, UM/HL/CTW/s12/ss3/b365/f4.

93. Wright to Dwyer et al., November 28, 1973, UM/HL/CTW/s12/ss3/b365/f4.

94. Horne to Vaughn, November 28, 1973.

95. A number of German critics had raised concerns about the representational side of *Sesame Street*. See Oeller, "Die Gründe, Die Der Bayerische Rundfunk 1973 Gegen Die Sesamstraße Vortrug." But also, for a wider criticism of representation on the American version of Sesame Street, see "Kinder sind nämlich auch mal dran"; Scherell and Jacobi, *10 Jahre Sesamstraße*; Klaus Schleicher, "Sesame Street als Sesamstraße," *Bildung und Erziehung* 25, no. 6 (December 1, 1972): 49–58, https://doi.org/10.7788/bue-1972-0604; Klaus Schleicher, "The Necessity of an Anthropo-Ecological Dimension in Education: Possibilities for Its Realisation," *International Review of Education* 21, no. 2 (1975): 231–60, https://doi.org/10.1007/BF00598126; Schleicher, *Sesame Street für Deutschland*.

96. Minutes from CTW/NDR conference, Hamburg, June 10, 1974, UM/HL/CTW/s12/ss3/b365/f14.

97. I cannot identify the original document in the CTW collection. The quotation is in Horne et al. to Cooney et al., September 6, 1974, UM/HL/CTW/s12/ss3/b365/f9 from a document that deals with NDR concerns and refers to the policy.

98. Irwin to Vaughn 27 August 1974, UM/HL/CTW/s12/ss3/b365/f14. See also Weitzel to Vaughn, telex, August 16, 1974, UM/HL/CTW/s12/ss3/b365/f9, and Vaughn to Weitzel, August 2, 1974, UM/HL/CTW/s12/ss3/b365/f14.

99. See note 97.

100. See note 97.

101. See note 97.

102. Schoenfeldt to Irwin, cable, attached to Irwin to Vaughn, November 6, 1974, UM/HL/CTW/s12/ss3/b365/f14.

103. License agreement, December 16, 1974, UM/HL/CTW/s12/ss3/b365/f14.

104. Horne to Connell, November 20, 1975, UM/HL/CTW/s12/ss3/b365/f18.

105. Ibid.

Chapter 5

1. "Politiske dyr i TV for børn," *Berlingske Tidende*, January 16, 1971; "De politiske mus er stoppet," *Berlingske Tidende*, January 18, 1971; "Katten Mogens, anmeldelse af Knud Holst," *Berlingske Tidende*, January 31, 1971.

2. Hanne Hastrup and Jannik Hastrup, "Cirkeline på ferie," aired January 17, 1971, https://www.larm.fm/Asset/aaddf456-0bf3-6391-b9fe-b4c1e500056a. See also Mogens Vemmer, *Fjernsyn for dig: 50 år med verdens værste seere* (København: Gyldendal, 2006). Both episodes—"Cirkeline på ferie" [Cirkeline on vacation] and "Flugten fra America" [The escape from America]—were released as part of a series on the DVD *Cirkeline. De go'e gamle* (Scanbox, 2008).

3. *Barn og kulur: Nordisk kulturkommisjons symposium, Hässelby slott 29.11–1.12.1969.* 1969. Unpublished symposium report, 24. From the archive of Norsk barnbokinstitutt, Olso.

4. Jensen, *From Superman to Social Realism*.

5. Sophie Heywood and Helle Strandgaard Jensen, "Exporting the Nordic Children's '68: The Global Publishing Scandal of the Little Red Schoolbook," *Barnboken*, November 15, 2018, https://doi.org/10.14811/clr.v41i0.332.

6. Jensen, "Scandinavian Children's Television in the 1970s," but for children's literature, see also Nina Christensen and Charlotte Appel, *Children's Literature in the Nordic World* (Aarhus: Aarhus University Press, 2021), chapter 5.

7. On Nordic childhoods from a historical perspective, see Reidar Aasgaard, Marcia Bunge, and Merethe Roos, *Nordic Childhoods, 1700–1960: From Folk Beliefs to Pippi Longstocking* (London: Routledge, 2017); Ning de Conink-Smith, Bengt Sandin, and Ellen Schrumpf, eds., *Industrious Children: Work and Childhood in the Nordic Countries, 1850–1990* (Odense: Odense University Press, 1997); Tora Korsvold, *Barn og barndom i velferdsstatens småbarnspolitikk* (Oslo: Universitetsforlaget, 2008).

8. Jensen, *From Superman to Social Realism*.

9. Ibid.; Christensen and Appel, *Children's Literature in the Nordic World*.

10. Minutes from Nordvision subcommittee meeting, Stockholm, October 1–4, 1974, RA/NRK, RA/S-48886/F/Fb/L0006.

11. Finnish broadcasting history diverges somewhat from the other Nordic countries, but that is of minor importance here as the national broadcaster, YLE, did not participate in the attempt to collaborate with the Workshop.

12. On the relationship between the concepts of Scandinavia and Norden, see Jani Marjanen, Johan Strang, and Mary Hilson, *Contesting Nordicness: From Scandinavianism to the Nordic Brand* (Berlin: De Gruyter Oldenbourg, 2021), https://www.degruyter.com/document/doi/10.1515/9783110730104/html.

13. On Nordic childhoods from a historical perspective, see Aasgaard, Bunge, and Roos. *Nordic Childhoods*; Johanna Einarsdottir and John A. Wagner, *Nordic Childhoods and Early Education: Philosophy, Research, Policy and Practice in Denmark, Finland, Iceland, Norway, and Sweden* (Charlotte, NC: Information Age, 2006); Korsvold, *Barn og barndom i velferdsstatens småbarnspolitikk*.

14. Ingmar Leijonborg to Henrik Dyfverman, June 26, 1970, Sveriges Radios Dokumentarkiv (SRD), TV2 Barn C90, series E1, folder "Ingrid Edström 1970–1974."

15. The program has many different titles in the material, but *Nordic Sesame* is the most frequent. I use it throughout for consistency and readability.

16. Rydin, *Barnens röster*, 137–41. Start date estimated from Rydin's text and searches in *Svensk Mediedatabas*.

17. Edström to Magold, June 15, 1970, SRD, TV2 Barn C90, series E1, folder "Ingrid Edström 1970–1974."

18. On the productions of the children's department at the time, see Christa Lykke Christensen, "Børne- og ungdoms-tv," in *Dansk tv's historie*, ed. Stig Hjarvad (Copenhagen: Forlaget Samfundsliteratur, 2006), 65–104.

19. Jimmy Stahr "Til Legestue's forfattere," April 1970, Rigsarkivet (RA(dk)), Danmarks Radio (DR), Børne og Ungdomsafdelingen (B&U), Småbørnsseksesionen, Diverse 1, identifier (id) 8017507571.

20. Indstilling, vedr. Ny TV-serie for mindre børn, May 5, 1969, RA(dk)/DR/B&U, Udsendelser 21, id 8017508871, folder "Legestue referater 1969–1970."

21. Programforslag, n.d., RA(dk)/DR/B&U, Udsendelser 21, id 8017508871, folder "Legestue referater 1969–1970."

22. Helle Strandgaard Jensen, *Tv til Børn*, unpublished master's thesis, Roskilde University, 2008.

23. Referat af forslag til Legestue's opbygning dated October 16, 1970 (Kursus for manuskriptforfatttere), RA(dk)/DR/B&U, Småbørnssektionen, Diverse 1, 1973–1979, identifier 8017507571; Referat af Legestuemøde, November 5, 1970, RA(dk)/DR/B&U, Udsendelser 21, folder "Legestue referater 1970," identifier 8017508871; Spørgsmål vedr. Sesame Street, November 12, 1970, RA(dk)/DR/B&U "Diverse," 1, 1973–1979, Småbørnssektionen, identifier 8017507571.

24. Jensen, "TV as Children's Spokesman."

25. Referat af Legestuemøde, November 5, 1970; RA(dk)/DR/B&U, Udsendelser 21, folder "Legestue referater 1970," identifier 8017508871; Referat af forslag til Legestue's opbygning dated October 16, 1970 (Kursus for manuskriptforfatttere); Spørgsmål vedr. Sesame Street, November 12, 1970.

26. Edström to Connell, November 20, 1970, SRD/TV2 Barn C90/sE1, folder "Ingrid Edström 1970–1974."

27. Edström to Hofsten, December 22, 1970, SRD/TV2 Barn C90/sE1, folder "Ingrid Edström 1970–1974."

28. "Referat af Nordvisionsmøte for børne- og ungdomsafdelingerne," Copenhagen 8–12 Februar 1971, Internal archive (IA) at Norsk Rikskringkasting (NRK), 3b, EBU, NET.

29. Ibid.

30. Indstilling, vedr. Ny TV-serie for mindre børn, May 5, 1969.

31. Report from the conference "International Television Exhibition of Programs for Young People" at New England Center for Continuing Education, University of New Hampshire, June 26–29, 1971, BBC WA T2/298/1.

32. Allegedly, the conference was so anticommercial that representatives from the three commercial networks were not even allowed to attend. Report from International

Television Exhibition of Programs for young people dated September 27, 1971, IA/ NRK, #2.4.0/7.

33. Ibid.

34. Jensen, *From Superman to Social Realism.*

35. Mogens Vemmer, "Some Remarks from a Little Country Far, Far Away," in report from the conference "International Television Exhibition of Programs for Young People" at New England Center for Continuing Education, University of New Hampshire, June 26–29, 1971, BBC WA T2/298/1 (emphasis in original).

36. Jensen, "Scandinavian Children's Television in the 1970s."

37. Vemmer, "Some Remarks from a Little Country," 6–7.

38. Ibid., 7 (emphasis in original).

39. NRK to Kjell Veirup (DR), Oslo, June 23, 1971, RA(n), NRK, Fjernsynsdirektøren, Nordvision, RA/S-4162/F/Ff/L0009/0001.

40. "Aims for Children's Programs. Swedish Broadcasting Corporation," in report from the conference "International Television Exhibition of Programs for Young People" at New England Center for Continuing Education, University of New Hampshire, June 26–29, 1971, BBC WA T2/298/1. For more information about this survey and how it was used in the children's department, see Rydin, *Barnens röster.*

41. Dann to Cooney et al., June 28, 1971, UM/HL/CTW/s12/ss3/b370-372/f "Sweden 20."

42. Edström to Orton, July 14, 1971, Stockholm SR/TV2 Barn C90/s E1, folder "TV2 Barn I Edström."

43. Report from trip to New York, July 1–3, 1971, IA/NRK.

44. Ibid.

45. Ibid.

46. Edström to Orton, July 14, 1971.

47. Report from trip to New York, July 1–3, 1971.

48. For an example of how the Workshop actively used its connections with Scandinavian journalists to pressure Nordvision, see its correspondence with journalist Hans Sidén from *Göteborgs-Posten* in February 1972: UM/HL/CTW/s12/ss3/b370-372/f "Scandinavia Sesame Street."

49. Report from trip to New York, July 1–3, 1971.

50. Hand-written notes, "Planning meeting, Scandinavia," October 12, 1971, four pages plus two attached, UM/HL/CTW/s1/ss12/b28/f71.

51. Ibid.

52. Ibid.

53. Summary of Nordvision meeting, Reykjavik, October 25–29, 1971, 1, RA(dk)/DR/ B&U, Internationalt, Nordvisionsmøder 1965–72, identifier, 8017503291.

54. Jensen, "Scandinavian Children's Television in the 1970s."

55. SVT to Orton, faxed schedule, October 21, 1971, UM/HL/CTW/s1/ss12/b28/f71.

56. The decision to initiate the work was made by Nordvision during its meeting in Stockholm, 9–11 1971, 1972, RA/NRK/Fjernsynsdirektøren/Nordvision, RA/S-4162/F/Ff/L0009/0001.

57. Telex with summary from Oslo meeting held May 31, 1972, telex sent June 2, 1972, SR/TV2 Barn 90c/s Handlingar rörande Nordisk Samarbete, 1969–72, F5A, 5, Sesame Street NV.

58. Minutes from meeting "manusmöte" in Gilleleje, June 8–15, 1972, SR/ST2 Barn C90, Handlingar rörande Nordisk Samarbete, 1969–72, F5A, 5, Sesame Street NV.

59. Ibid., 2.

60. Ibid.

61. Ibid.

62. Edström to Connell, July 14, 1972, SRD/TV2 Barn C90/s E1, Ingrid Edström.

63. Orton to Linné, August 1, 1972, SRD/TV 2 Barn C90/Handlingar rörande Nordisk Samarbete, 1969–72, F5A, 5, Sesame Street, Nordvisionsarbete, 1970–72.

64. Ibid.

65. Ibid.

66. Ibid.

67. "Tre tråd torsd. 10.8.72," SRD/TV 2 Barn C90/Handlingar rörande Nordisk Samarbete, 1969–72, F5A, 5, Sesame Street, Nordvisionsarbete, 1970–72.

68. Ibid. See also Linné to Connell, August 11, 1972, SRD/TV2 Barn C90/Handlingar rörande Nordisk Samarbete, 1969–72, F5A, 5, Sesame Street, Nordvisionsarbete, 1970–72.

69. On the Norwegian collaboration with the BBC: Norwegian producers would travel to the BBC and find manuscripts they thought could be adapted to the needs of Norwegian children. These were rewritten to an extent where there was "little left of the original English manuscript." In Norway, it was a simple studio production. R. Tangen, "Rapport ang. Nordisk Førskoleprogram fra NRK," September 19, 1974, SRD/TV 2 Barn C90, Handlingar rörande Nordisk Samarbete, F5A, 6.

70. Linné to Connell, August 11, 1972.

71. Wright to Kennedy, August 17, 1972 (cc to Bengt Linné) (internal CTW memorandum from SR archives) SRD/ TV2 Barn C90/Handlingar rörande Nordisk Samarbete, 1969–72, F5A, 5, Sesame Street, Nordvisionsarbete, 1970–72.

72. Report from Sesame pre-meeting in Oslo, October 23–25, 1972, included in a report from 1975, RA(dk)/DR/B&U, Udsendelser 27, id. 8017508931, folder Sesame Street 1975.

73. "Budget Børne- og Ungdomsafdelingen, 24. november 1970." RA(dk)/DR/B&U, Udsendelser 21, identifier 8017508871, folder "For de små TV 1971/1972"; Budget 1973, RA(n)/NRK/Fjernsynets barne- og ungdomsavdeling, RA/S-4888/D/L0002.

74. Mogens Vemmer, "Tanker indenfor murerne—om det, vi byder børn i radio og TV," Radio TV årbog 1970–71 (Danmarks Radio, 1971).

75. Report from Sesame pre-meeting in Oslo, October 23–25, 1972.

76. Ibid.

77. Report from official Nordvision meeting, Oslo, October 24–27, 1972, SRD/TV2 Barn C90/Handlingar rörande Nordisk Samarbete, 1969–72, F5A, 5, Sesame Street, Nordvisionsarbete, 1970–72.

78. Linné to Wright, April 6, 1973, UM/HL/CTW/s12/ss3/b370-372/f"Scandinavian SS Report."

79. Wright to Vaughn, April 10, 1973, UM/HL/CTW/s12/ss3/b370-372/f "Scandinavian SS Report."

80. "Nordiska förskolaprogram okt 1974" report, RA(dk)/DR/B&U "Internationalt," 1, Nordvisionsmøder 1974.

81. Ibid. (my translation).

82. Tangen, "Rapport ang. Nordisk Førskoleprogram fra NRK."

83. The Sámi are an Indigenous Finno-Ugric people inhabiting Sámpi, the northern parts of what is today Norway, Sweden, Finland, and Rusland.

84. Fem Myror, Program proposal, May 7, 1973, SRD/TV2 Barn C90/andlingar rörande skilda program, 1972–1974, F2, 33, Pedagogiskt Material.

85. Rydin, Barnens röster, 198.

86. Leni Filipson, "Sesame Street in Sweden," 164/72, report attached to Haynes to Palmer, November 9, 1973, UM/HL/CTW/s12/ss3/b370-372/f "Sweden 20."

87. Nordvision screening of preschool programs, Stockholm, February 27–28, 1974, Appendix, SRD/TV2 Barn C90/Handlingar rörande Nordisk Samarbete, F5A, 6.

88. Jimmy Stahr, report from visit in February 1972, May 18, 1972, part of document from 1975, RA(dk)/DR/B&U, Udsendelser 27, folder Sesame Street 1975, 8017508931.

89. "Legestue's Objectives" (official translation from DR; Danish version May 25, 1972), RA(dk)/DR/B&U, Udsendelser 21, id 8017508871, folder "Huskebog 1972."

90. Ibid.

91. Ibid.

92. Ibid.

93. Helle Strandgaard Jensen, "En Nordisk Sesame Street? Barnet Som Tvforbruger i Fællesnordisk Tv-Politik 1970–1975," in Butik, Forbruger, By: Forbrugets Kulturhistorie 1660 Til i Dag, ed. Mikkel Thelle, Kasper Andersen, and Kristoffer Jensen (Aarhus: Aarhus Universitetsforlag, 2017), 257–84.

94. Hagelund, "Open Sesame," October 14, 1974 (from the fall, but the visit took place in the spring) (my translation), SRD, TV 2 Barn C90, Handlingar rörande Nordisk Samarbete, 1969–72, F5A, 5, Sesame Street, Nordvisionsarbete, 1970–72 .

95. Ibid.

96. Minutes from meeting, Reykjavik, March 12–16, 1974, RA(n)/NRK, Nordvisjonen, RA/S-5874/A/L0011.

97. Horne to Vaugh, March 13, 1974, UM/HL/CTW/s12/ss3/b370-372/f "Scandinavian Sesame Street."

98. Official Nordvision meeting, Stockholm, October 1–4, 1974, RA(n)/NRK, Fjernsynets programredaksjon, RA/S/4886/F/Fb/L0006.

99. Hagelund, "Open Sesame."

100. Biondi to Frank, "Open Sesame I—Sweden," March 25, 1975, UM/HL/CTW/s12/ss3/b370-372/ "Scandinavian Sesame Street."

101. Press release, August 1975, UM/HL/CTW/s12/ss3/b370-372, Folder with promotional material titled "Sveriges Radio Channel 2, Information Kit."

102. Vemmer to Frank, June 18, 1975, UM/HL/CTW/s12/ss3/b370-372/f "Scandinavian Sesame Street."

103. Minutes from meeting, April 28, 1975, RA(dk)/DR/B&U, Udsendelser 21, folder 1975, 8017508871.

104. Jimmy Stahr om mulig pressemeddelelse, November 17, 1975, RA/DR/B&U/ Småbørnssektionen, Diverse 1, id. 8017507571.

105. Three papers by Jimmy Stahr, Kjeld Iversen, and Inger Tolstrup, all 1975, RA/DR/ B&U, Udsendelser 27, folder "Sesame Street 1972," Item A.

106. A viewer survey published August 19, 1971, showed that, on average, 275,000 adults watched *Legestue*, and twice as many children (the total population at the time was 4.9 million), RA/DR/B&U, Udsendelser, id. 8017508931 "Legestue referater 1970."

107. Orton to Riktor, September 17, 1975, UM/HL/CTW/s12/ss3/b370-372/f "Norway."

108. Riktor to Orton, November 25, 1975, UM/HL/CTW/s12/ss3/b370-372/f "Norway."

109. Haug to Orton, December 27, 1976, UM/HL/CTW/s12/ss3/b370-372/f "Norway."

110. Blackwell to Riktor, March 21, 1978, UM/HL/CTW/s12/ss3/b370-372/f "Norway."

111. Ibid.

112. Ibid. (emphasis in original).

113. Haug to Champtaloup, November 3, 1981, UM/HL/CTW/s12/ss3/b370-372/f "Norway."

114. Horne to Orton February 16, 1976, UM/HL/CTW/s12/ss3/b370-372/f "Sweden 1976."

115. Orton to Edström, 27 January 1976, UM/HL/CTW/s12/ss3/b370-372/f "Sweden 1976."

116. Frank to Edstöm, February 13, 1976, UM/HL/CTW/s12/ss3/b370-372/f "Sweden 1976."

117. Frank to Jellart-Lysander, November 3, 1976, UM/HL/CTW/s12/ss3/b370-372/f "Sweden 1976."

118. Edström to Frank, received September 16, 1976, UM/HL/CTW/s12/ss3/b370-372/f "Sweden 1976."

119. Ibid.

120. Rydin, *Barnens röster*.

121. Frank to Jellart-Lysander, November 3, 1976.

122. Press clippings from February 1976, UM/HL/CTW/s12/ss3/b370-372/f "Sweden 20."

123. Note, March 15, 1978, UM/HL/CTW/s12/ss3/b370-372/untitled folder.

124. Blackwell to Lysander, March 12, 1979, UM/HL/CTW/s12/ss3/b370-372/untitled folder; Horne to Conell, October 16, 1979, UM/HL/CTW/s12/ss3/b370-372/untitled folder (or Sweden 1979).

125. Horne to Conell, October 16, 1979.

126. Ibid.

127. Jimmy Stahr, talk, attached to letter for Dr. Cappel, May 6, 1974, RA(dk)/DR/B&U, Diverse 1, id. 8017507571, folder "Småbørnssektionen."

128. Ibid.

129. Ibid.

Chapter 6

1. Children's Television Workshop was renamed Sesame Workshop in 2000. Dunn, "Introduction," 10.

2. Ibid.

3. Preface by Joan Ganz Cooney in Cheryl Cole and June Lee, eds., *The Sesame Effect: The Global Impact of the Longest Street in the World* (New York: Routledge, 2016), https://doi.org/10.4324/9781315751399.

4. Joan Ganz Cooney as quoted in Francke, "The Games People Play on Sesame Street." See discussion of this quotation in chapter 2.

5. *Sesame Street 50 Years and Counting* (New York: Sesame Workshop, 2019), 21, https://www.sesameworkshop.org/who-we-are/our-history/sesame-street-history-50-years-impact.

6. Charlotte F. Cole and June H. Lee, "Acknowledgments," in *The Sesame Effect: The Global Impact of the Longest Street in the world*, ed. Charlotte F. Cole and June H. Lee (New York: Routledge, 2016).

7. *CTW Research Bibliography—Research Papers Relating to the Children's Television Workshop and Its Experimental Educational Series: "Sesame Street" and "The Electric Company,"* 1968–76 (New York: Children's Television Workshop Library, 1976), https://eric.ed.gov/?id=ED133079.

8. The Network Project, *Down Sesame Street* (New York: Columbia University, 1973).

9. Lesser, *Children and Television*, Preface.

10. *Fernsehen und Bildung, Sesame Street International* 10, no. 1–2 (1976)..

11. Herta Sturm, "Vorwort," *Fernsehen und Bildung, Sesame Street International* 10, no. 1–2 (1976): 9.

12. "Sésame ouvre-toi!," *Journal of communication* 26, no. 2 (Spring 1976): 108.

13. Edward Palmer, Milton Chen, and Gerald Lesser, "Sesame Street: Patterns of International Adaptation," *Journal of Communication* 26, no. 2 (Spring 1976): 109.

14. Ibid., 122.

15. Ibid., 112.

16. De Grazia, *Irresistible Empire*, 6; Parmar, *Foundations of the American Century*, 100.

17. Edward Will, report for the Center for Educational Research and Innovation of the Organisation for Economic Co-operation and Development, September 1974, UM/HL/CTW/s2/ss5/b42/f57.

18. Ibid., 16–17.

19. Ibid., 14.

20. Davis, *Street Gang*, 210–11.

21. Gettas's article is, for instance, cited in Silvia Bieger, "Sesam, Öffne Dich! Diskussion Zur Internationalen Sesamstraße Im Globalen Kontext Und Konzeption Einer Entsprechenden Themenausstellung," Technischen Universität Braunschweig, accessed November 14, 2021, https://opus.hbk-bs.de/files/17/MA_SesameStreet.pdf; Kristin C. Moran, "The Global Expansion of Children's Television: A Case Study of the Adaptation of Sesame Street in Spain," *Learning, Media and Technology* 31, no. 3 (September 1, 2006): 287–300, https://doi.org/10.1080/17439880600893333;

Geraldine Coertze. "Open Sesame! Learning Life Skills from Takalani Sesame: A Reception Study of Selected Grade One Learners in Pietermaritzburg, South Africa," University of KwaZulu-Natal, Durban, South Africa, 2011, https://ukzn-dspace. ukzn.ac.za/bitstream/handle/10413/6374/Coertze_Geraldine_2011.pdf?seque nce=1&isAllowed=y; Hayday, "Brought to You by the Letters C, R, T, and C"; Aaron Calbreath-Frasieur, "Localizing Sesame Street," in *Media across Borders: Localising TV, Film and Video Games*, ed. Andrea Esser, Miguel Á. Bernal-Merino, and Iain Robert Smith (New York: Routledge, 2016), 99–112.

22. Gettas, "The Globalization of Sesame Street."

23. Ibid., 57.

24. Shalom M. Fisch, *Children's Learning from Educational Television: Sesame Street and Beyond*, LEA's Communication Series (New York: Taylor and Francis, Routledge, 2014), 19, https://doi.org/10.4324/9781410610553.

25. Ibid., 26.

26. Ibid., 19.

27. Ibid., 30. The criticism was raised in Hendershot, "Sesame Street."

28. Moland, *Can Big Bird Fight Terrorism?*, 24.

29. Ibid., 29.

30. Ibid., 217.

31. Feyal Awan, "Occupied Childhoods: Discourses and Politics of Childhood and Their Place in Palestinian and Pan-Arab Screen Content for Children," PhD thesis, University of Westminster, 2016, 122–27, https://westminsterresearch.westminster. ac.uk/download/79d58ddf59c864051871ca9460e3336a3ee0c1971e586527ee843 2e9c618428c/16288975/Awan_Feryal_thesis.pdf.

32. Rosemary Truglio, interview with Sophie Brickman, in Brickman, *Baby, Unplugged*, 201–5.

33. Ibid., 204.

34. On the lack of testing in this area, see Dafna Lemish, *Children and Television: A Global Perspective* (Malden, MA: Blackwell, 2007), 176.

35. In recent publications highlighted on the Workshop's website—e.g., J. A. Kotler, T. Z. Haider, and M. H. Levine, *Identity Matters: Parents' and Educators' Perception of Children's Social Identity Development* (New York: Sesame Workshop, 2019), https:// www.sesameworkshop.org/what-we-do/research-and-innovation/sesame-works hop-identity-matters-study, and C. B. Wong Chin, J. N. Baran, G. M. Maurar, and C. Jhee, *Coming Together: Family Reflections on Racism* (New York: Sesame Workshop 2021), https://www.sesameworkshop.org/what-we-do/research-and-innovation/ coming-together-family-reflections-racism-study—references are heavily biased toward psychological research. Both publications also use quantitative methods as the main methodological approach.

36. On American-*cum*-neutral views of childhood in an international space, see Cook, *The Moral Project of Childhood*, 166–67, and Balagopalan, "Childhood, Culture, History."

37. Recording of Prix Jeunesse ceremony 2014, Bayerisches Rundfunk, internal archives of the Prix Jeunesse International, 2014, 02:04:05.

Bibliography

50 Jahre IZI, no. 28. Munich: Internationalesentralinstitut für das Jugend-und Bildungsfernschen, 2015.

Aasgaard, Reidar, Marcia Bunge, and Merethe Roos, eds. *Nordic Childhoods 1700–1960: From Folk Beliefs to Pippi Longstocking*. London: Routledge, 2017.

Ackerman, Colin. "Public or Private Interest? The History and Impacts of Children's Television Public Policy in the United States, 1934 to Present." *Journal of the History of Childhood and Youth* 12, no. 2 (2019): 285–304. https://doi.org/10.1353/hcy.2019.0024.

Adamou, Christina, Isabelle Gaillard, and Dana Mustata. "Institutionalising European Television: The Shaping of European Television Institutions and Infrastructures." In *A European Television History*, edited by Jonathan Bignell and Andreas Fickers, 79–100. Hoboken, NJ: Wiley, 2008.

Akerman, Anna J., Alison Bryant, and Mariana Diaz-Wionczek. "Educational Preschool Programming in the US: An Ecological and Evolutionary Story." *Journal of Children and Media* 5, no. 2 (2011): 204–20. https://doi.org/10.1080/17482798.2011.558284.

Alexander, Leslie, and Michelle Alexander. "Fear." In *The 1619 Project: A New American Origin Story*, edited by Nikole Hannah-Jones, Caitlin Roper, Ilena Silverman, and Jake Silverstein, 97–128. London: W. H. Allen, 2021.

Alexander, Stephan, ed. *The Americanization of Europe: Culture, Diplomacy, and Anti-Americanism after 1945*. New York: Berghahn Books, 2005.

Allan, Ann Taylor. *The Transatlantic Kindergarten: Education and Women's Movements in Germany and the United States*. Oxford: Oxford University Press, 2017.

Aronsson, Karin, and Bengt Sandin. "The Sun Match Boy and Plant Metaphors: A Swedish Image of a 20th-Century Childhood." In *Images of childhood*, edited by Philip Hwang, Michael Lamb, and Irving Sigel, 185–202. New York: Psychology Press, 1996.

Ash, Michell. "Psychology." In *The Cambridge History of Science*, edited by Roy Porter and Dorothy Ross, 251–74. Cambridge: Cambridge University Press, 2003. doi:10.1017/CHOL9780521594424.016.

Awan, Feryal. "Occupied Childhoods: Discourses and Politics of Childhood and Their Place in Palestinian and Pan-Arab Screen Content for Children." PhD thesis, University of Westminster, 2016. https://westminsterresearch.westminster.ac.uk/download/79d58ddf59c864051871ca9460e3336a3ee0c1971e586527ee8432e9c618428c/16288975/Awan_Feryal_thesis.pdf.

Bak, Meredith A. *Playful Visions. Optical Toys and the Emergence of Children's Media Culture*. Cambridge: MIT Press, 2020.

Balagopalan, Sarada. "Childhood, Culture, History: Redeploying 'Multiple Childhoods.'" In *Reimagining Childhood Studies*, edited by Spyros Spyrou, Rachel Rosen, and Daniel Thomas Cook, 23–39. London: Bloomsbury, 2019.

Banet-Weiser, Sarah. *Kids Rule!: Nickelodeon and Consumer Citizenship*. Durham, NC: Duke University Press, 2007.

Barclay, Steven. *BBC School Broadcasting: Progressivism in Education and Literacy 1957–1979.* PhD thesis, June 2021, University of Westminster. https://westminsterresearch. westminster.ac.uk/item/vw731/bbc-school-broadcasting-progressivism-in-educat ion-and-literacy-1957-1979.

Baxter, Jorge. "Building Relevance and Impact: Lessons of Sustainability from Plaza Sésamo in Mexico and Beyond." In *The Sesame Effect: The Global Impact of the Longest Street in the World,* edited by Charlotte F. Cole and June H. Lee, 206–23. New York: Routledge, 2016.

"B.B.C. Children's TV Stresses Respect for Intellect and Reality." *New York Times,* June 29, 1971. http://timesmachine.nytimes.com/timesmachine/1971/06/29/81953119.html? zoom=16.

"B.B.C. Orders Ban on 'Sesame Street.'" *New York Times,* September 8, 1971. https://www. nytimes.com/1971/09/08/archives/bbc-orders-ban-on-sesame-street-sesame-street- barred-by-bbc.html.

Bereiter, Carl, and Siegfried Engelmann. *Teaching Disadvantaged Children in the Preschool.* Englewood Cliffs, NJ: Prentice Hall, 1966.

Bieger, Silvia. *Sesam, öffne dich! Diskussion zur internationalen Sesamstraße im globalen Kontext und Konzeption einer entsprechenden Themenausstellung.* Master's thesis, 2005, Technischen Universität Braunschweig. Accessed November 14, 2021. https://opus. hbk-bs.de/files/17/MA_SesameStreet.pdf.

Bielby, Denise D., and C. Lee Harrington. *Global TV: Exporting Television and Culture in the World Market.* New York: NYU Press, 2008.

Bondebjerg, Ib, Helle Strandgaard Jensen, Michele Hilmes, Isabelle Veyrat-Masson, Susanne Vollberg, and Tomasz Goban-Klas. "American Television: Point of Reference or European Nightmare?" In *A European Television History,* edited by Jonathan Bignell and Andreas Fickers, 154–83. Malden. MA: Wiley-Blackwell, 2009.

Bourdon, Jérôme. "From Discrete Adaptations to Hard Copies: The Rise of Formats in European Television." In *Global Television Formats: Understanding Television across Borders* edited by Sharon Shahaf and Tasha Oren, 111–27. London: Taylor & Francis, 2011.

Brickman, Sophie. *Baby, Unplugged: One Mother's Search for Balance, Reason, and Sanity in the Digital Age.* New York: HarperOne, 2021.

Briggs, Asa, and Peter Burke. *A Social History of the Media: From Gutenberg to the Internet.* Cambridge: Polity, 2009.

Brink, Berit. "Between Imagination and Reality: Tracing the Legacy of Childhood as a Utopian Space in the Free Schooling and Unschooling Movements." *Strenæ. Recherches Sur Les Livres et Objets Culturels de l'enfance,* no. 13 (May 15, 2018). https://doi.org/ 10.4000/strenae.1795.

Brown, Laura Cade. "Building Vila Sésamo: Children's Television and the Race across the Nation." Presentation at "Brazilian Regionalism in a Global Context" conference, Alice Campbell Alumni Center, University of Illinois, Urbana, April 26–27, 2019.

Bruce, Emilie. *Revolutions at Home: The Origin of Modern Childhood and the German Middle Class.* Amherst: University of Massachusetts Press, 2021.

Buckingham, David. *After the Death of Childhood: Growing Up in the Age of Electronic Media.* Cambridge: Polity Press, 2000.

Buckingham, David. "Bridging the Gaps? Sesame Street, 'Race' and Educational Disadvantage." *Growing Up Modern* (blog). Accessed March 15, 2021. https://ddbuc kingham.files.wordpress.com/2019/12/sesame-street.pdf.

Buckingham, David. "Watching with (and without) Mother: Education and Entertainment in Television for Pre-school Children." *Growing Up Modern* (blog), accessed November 23, 2022. https://davidbuckingham.net/growing-up-modern/watching-with-and-without-mother-education-and-entertainment-in-television-for-pre-school-child ren/watch-wit.h-mother/

Buckingham, David, Hannah Davies, Ken Jones, and Peter Kelley. *Children's Television in Britain: History, Discourse, and Policy*. London: British Film Institute, 1999.

Buckingham, David, and Helle Strandgaard Jensen. "Beyond 'Media Panics.'" *Journal of Children and Media* 6, no. 4 (2012): 413–29. DOI: 10.1080/17482798.2012.740415.

Buckingham, David, and Margaret Scanlon. *Education, Entertainment, and Learning in the Home*. Buckingham: Open University Press, 2003.

Buckingham, David, and Margaret Scanlon. "Selling Learning: Towards a Political Economy of Edutainment Media." *Media, Culture & Society* 27, no. 1 (2016): 41–58. https://doi.org/10.1177/0163443705049057.

Calbreath-Frasieur, Aaron. "Localizing Sesame Street." In *Media across Borders: Localising TV, Film and Video Games*, edited by Andrea Esser, Miguel Á. Bernal-Merino, and Iain Robert Smith, 99–112. New York: Routledge, 2016.

Chiarenza, Franco. *Il cavallo morente. Storia della Rai*. Vol. 2. Milan: FrancoAngeli, 2002.

Christensen, Christa Lykke. "Børne- og ungdoms-tv." In *Dansk tv's historie*, edited by Stig Hjarvad, 65–105. Copenhagen: Forlaget Samfundslitteratur, 2006.

Christensen, Nina, and Charlotte Appel. *Children's Literature in the Nordic World*. Aarhus: Aarhus University Press, 2021.

Coertze, Geraldine. "Open Sesame! Learning Life Skills from Takalani Sesame: A Reception Study of Selected Grade One Learners in Pietermaritzburg, South Africa." University of KwaZulu-Natal, Durban, South Africa, 2011. https://researchspace.ukzn. ac.za/xmlui/handle/10413/6374.

Cole, Charlotte, and June H. Lee. "Acknowledgements." In *The Sesame Effect: The Global Impact of the Longest Street in the World*, edited by Charlotte F Cole and June H. Lee, xix–xx. New York: Routledge, 2016.

Cole, Charlotte F., and June H. Lee, editors. *The Sesame Effect: The Global Impact of the Longest Street in the World*. New York: Routledge, 2016. https://doi.org/10.4324/ 9781315751399.

Cole, Charlotte, Beth Richman, and Susan Brown. "The World of Sesame Street Research." In *G Stands for Growing: Thirty Years of Research on Children and Sesame Street*, edited by Shalom Fisch and Rosemarie Tuglio, 147–80. New York: Routledge, 2001.

Coleman, James S., *Equality of Educational Opportunity*. Inter-University Consortium for Political and Social Research, 1966. https://doi.org/10.3886/ICPSR06389.v3.

Coninck-Smith, Ning de. *Skolen, Lærerne, Eleverne Og Forældrene: 10 Kapitler Af Den Danske Skoles Historie*. Århus: Klim, 2002.

Coninck-Smith, Ning de, Bengt Sandin, and Ellen Schrumpf, eds. *Industrious Children: Work and Childhood in the Nordic Countries, 1850–1990*. Odense: Odense University Press, 1997.

Connell, David. "The Iddy Bitty Nitty-Gritty Farm and City Little Kiddies Show and How It Grew." Printed speech. Cincinnati: University of Cincinnati, 1970.

Conrad, Sebastian. *What Is Global History?* Princeton, NJ: Princeton University Press, 2016. https://doi.org/10.1515/9781400880966.

Cook, Daniel Thomas. *The Moral Project of Childhood: Motherhood, Material Life, and Early Children's Consumer Culture*. New York: NYU Press, 2020.

Cook, Thomas, Hilary Appelton, Ross Conner, Ann Shaffer, Gary Tamkin, and Stephen Weber. *Sesame Street Revisited.* New York: Russell Sage Foundation, 1975.

Cooney, Joan Ganz. "Der Children's Television Workshop." *Fernsehen und Bildung,* 3, no. 3/4 (1968): 156–58.

Cooney, Joan Ganz. *The First Year of Sesame Street: A History and Overview.* Final report, Volume 1. New York: Children's Television Workshop, December 1970.

Cooney, Joan Ganz. "Preface." In *The Sesame Effect: The Global Impact of the Longest Street in the World,* edited by Charlotte F. Cole and June H. Lee, xxi–xxiv. New York: Routledge, 2016.

Couldry, Nick, and Andreas Hepp. "Comparing Media Cultures." In *The Handbook of Comparative Communication Research,* edited by Frank Esser and Thomas Hanitzsch, 271–83. New York: Routledge, 2012.

Cronqvist, Marie, and Christoph Hilgert. "Entangled Media Histories: The Value of Transnational and Transmedial Approaches in Media Historiography." *Media History* 23, no. 1 (January 2, 2017): 130–41. https://doi.org/10.1080/13688804.2016.1270745.

Cross, Gary S. *Kids' Stuff: Toys and the Changing World of American Childhood.* Cambridge, MA: Harvard University Press, 2009.

CTW Research Bibliography. Research Papers Relating to the Children's Television Workshop and Its Experimental Educational Series: "Sesame Street" and "The Electric Company," 1968–76. New York: Children's Television Workshop Library, 1976. https://eric.ed.gov/?id=ED133079.

D'amato, Marina. *La TV Dei Ragazzi: Storie, Miti, Eroi.* Roma: Rai Libri, 2002.

Dann, Michael. "Television." *New York Times,* August 6, 1972.

Davies, Máire Messenger. "Production Studies." *Critical Studies in Television* 1, no. 1 (2012): 21–30. https://doi.org/10.7227/cst.1.1.5.

Davis, Michael. *Street Gang: The Complete History of Sesame Street.* New York: Viking, 2008.

De Block, Liesbeth, and David Buckingham. *Global Children, Global Media: Migration, Media and Childhood.* New York: Palgrave Macmillan, 2010.

De Grazia, Victoria. *Irresistible Empire: America's Advance through Twentieth-Century Europe.* Cambridge, MA: Harvard University Press, 2009.

"De politiske mus er stoppet." *Berlingske Tidende,* January 18, 1971.

Deutsch, Martin. *The Disadvantaged Child.* New York: Basic Books, 1967.

Dizard, Wilson P. *Television: A World View.* Syracuse, NY: Syracuse University Press. 1966.

Downs, Laura Lee. *Childhood in the Promised Land.* Durham, NC: Duke University Press, 2002.

Dunn, Jeffery. "Introduction." In *Sesame Street: 50 Years and Counting,* Sesame Workshop, 10–11. New York: Sesame Workshop, 2019. https://www.sesameworkshop.org/who-we-are/our-history/sesame-street-history-50-years-impact.

EBU Workshop for Producers and Directors of Television Programmes for Young People, Doreen Stephens and European Broadcasting Union, eds. *Report of Second EBU Workshop for Producers and Directors of Television Programmes for Young People, Stockholm, 22nd–27th February 1970.* Geneva: European Broadcasting Union, 1970.

Einarsdottir, Johanna, and John A. Wagner, eds. *Nordic Childhoods and Early Education: Philosophy, Research, Policy and Practice in Denmark, Finland, Iceland, Norway, and Sweden.* Charlotte, NC: Information Age, 2006.

Erdbrink, Thomas, and Martin Selsoe Sorensen. "A Danish Children's TV Show Has This Message: 'Normal Bodies Look Like This.'" *New York Times,* September 18, 2020.

https://www.nytimes.com/2020/09/18/world/europe/denmark-children-nudity-sex-education.html.

Fass, Paula S. *The End of American Childhood: A History of Parenting from Life on the Frontier to the Managed Child*. Princeton, NJ: Princeton University Press, 2017.

Feldman, Bob. "Entertaining Australians to Be Americans," *The Bulletin* (Sydney), September 26, 1970, 41–44.

Fernsehen und Bildung. Sesame Street International. Special issue. 10, no. 1–2 (1976).

Fickers, Andreas, and Catherine Johnson, eds. *Transnational Television History: A Comparative Approach*. London: Routledge, 2013.

Fisch, Shalom M. *Children's Learning from Educational Television: Sesame Street and Beyond*. New York: Routledge, 2014. https://doi.org/10.4324/9781410610553.

Fisch, Shalom M., and Rosemarie T. Truglio, eds. *G Is for Growing: Thirty Years of Research on Children and Sesame Street*. New York: Routledge, 2001.

Francke, Linda. "The Games People Play on Sesame Street." *New York*, April 5, 1971.

García, Marilisa Jiménez. *Side by Side: US Empire, Puerto Rico, and the Roots of American Youth Literature and Culture*. Jackson: University Press of Mississippi, 2021.

Gettas, Gregory J. "The Globalization of Sesame Street: A Producer's Perspective." *Educational Technology Research and Development* 38, no. 4 (December 1, 1990): 55–63. https://doi.org/10.1007/BF02314645.

Gjerløff, Anne Katrine, Anette Faye Jacobsen, Ellen Nørgaard, and Christian Ydesen. *Da skolen blev sin egen. 1920–1970*, vol. 6, *Dansk skolehistorie*, edited by Charlotte Appel and Ning de Coninck-Smith. Aarhus: Aarhus Universitetsforlag, 2014.

Goldsen, Rose K., and Azriel Bibliowicz. "Plaza Sesamo: 'Neutral' Language or 'Cultural Assault?'" *Journal of Communication* 26, no. 2 (June 1976): 124–25.

Götz, Maya. "Kinderfernsehen." In *Handbuch Kinder- und Jugendliteratur*, edited by Tobias Kurwinkel and Philipp Schmerheim, 251–57. Stuttgart: J. B. Metzler, 2020.

Hans-Bredow-Institut für Rundfunk und Fernsehen. *Begleituntersuchung zur Fernsehserie "Sesamstraße." Ausgewählte Ergebnisse des Gesamtprojekts*. Hamburg: Hans Bredow Institut für Rundfunk und Fernsehen an der Universität Hamburg, 1975.

Hayday, Matthew. "Brought to You by the Letters C, R, T, and C: Sesame Street and Canadian Nationalism." *Journal of the Canadian Historical Association / Revue de La Société Historique Du Canada* 27, no. 1 (2016): 95–137.

Hechinger, Fred M. "Education." *New York Times*, September 12, 1971. https://www.nytimes.com/1971/09/12/archives/education-sesame-street-those-muppets-stir-up-a-storm-in-britain.html.

Hendershot, Heather. "Sesame Street: Cognition and Communications Imperialism." In *Kid's Media Culture*, edited by Marsha Kinder, 139–76. Durham, NC: Duke University Press, 1999.

Hendershot, Heather. *Saturday Morning Censors: Television Regulation before the V-Chip*. Durham, NC: Duke University Press, 1998. https://hdl-handle-net.ez.statsbiblioteket.dk:12048/2027/heb.08296.

Hendy, David. *The BBC: A People's History*. London: Profile Books, 2022.

Heywood, Sophie. "Adapting Jules Verne for the Baby-Boom Generation: Hachette and the Bibliothèque Verte, c. 1956–1966." *Modern & Contemporary France* 21, no. 1 (February 1, 2013): 55–71. https://doi.org/10.1080/09639489.2012.722613.

Heywood, Sophie. "Children's 68: Introduction," *Strenæ. Recherches Sur Les Livres et Objets Culturels de l'enfance*, no. 13 (May 15, 2018). https://doi.org/10.4000/strenae.1998.

Heywood, Sophie. "Pippi Longstocking, Juvenile Delinquent? Hachette, Self-Censorship and the Moral Reconstruction of Postwar France," *Itinéraires. Littérature, Textes, Cultures*, no. 2015-2 (January 19, 2016). https://doi.org/10.4000/itineraires.2903.

Heywood, Sophie, and Helle Strandgaard Jensen. "Exporting the Nordic Children's '68: The Global Publishing Scandal of The Little Red Schoolbook." *Barnboken*, November 15, 2018. https://doi.org/10.14811/clr.v41i0.332.

Hilmes, Michele. *Network Nations: A Transnational History of British and American Broadcasting*. London: Routledge, 2012.

Hohlmeier, Monika. *A Market of Good Ideas: 40 Years of Prix Jeunesse International*. Munich: Prix Jeunesse International, 2004.

Holiday, Steven. "How They Got to Sesame Street: Children's Television Workshop's Appropriation of Advertising Tactics for Effective Childhood Literacy Education." *Journal of Early Childhood Literacy* (April 1, 2021). https://doi.org/10.1177/146879 84211003245.

Holmes, Su. "Revisiting Play School: A Historical Case Study of the BBC's Address to the Pre-School Audience." *Journal of Popular Television* 4, no. 1 (January 1, 2016): 29–47. https://doi.org/10.1386/jptv.4.1.29_1.

Holt, John. "Big Bird, Meet Dick and Jane." *The Atlantic*, May 1, 1971. https://www.thea tlantic.com/magazine/archive/1971/05/big-bird-meet-dick-and-jane/305125/.

Home, Anna. *Into the Box of Delights: History of Children's Television*. London: BBC Books, 1993.

Hulbert, Ann. *Raising America: Experts, Parents, and a Century of Advice about Children*. New York: Vintage, 2011.

Hunt, Lynn. *Writing History in the Global Era*. New York: W. W. Norton & Company, 2015.

Jellinek, Roger. "Is Sesame Street One Way to Reading?" *New York Times*, September 20, 1970. https://www.nytimes.com/1970/09/20/archives/is-sesame-street-one-way-to-reading.html.

Jensen, Helle Strandgaard. "En Nordisk Sesame Street? Barnet Som Tv-forbruger i Fællesnordisk Tv-Politik 1970–1975." In *Butik, Forbruger, By: Forbrugets Kulturhistorie 1660 Til i Dag*, edited by Mikkel Thelle, Kasper Andersen, and Kristoffer Jensen, 257–84. Aarhus: Aarhus Universitetsforlag, 2017.

Jensen, Helle Strandgaard. *From Superman to Social Realism*. Amsterdam: John Benjamins, 2017.

Jensen, Helle Strandgaard. "Prix Jeunesse and the Negotiation of Citizenship in Children's Television." *Journal of the History of Childhood and Youth* 11, no. 1 (2018): 101–7.

Jensen, Helle Strandgaard. "Scandinavian Children's Television in the 1970s: An Institutionalisation of '68'?" *Strenae*, no. 13 (2018). https://doi.org/10.4000/stre nae.1998.

Jensen, Helle Strandgaard. "TV as Children's Spokesman: Conflicting Notions of Children and Childhood in Danish Children's Television around 1968." *Journal of the History of Childhood and Youth* 6, no. 1 (2013): 105–28. https://doi.org/10.1353/hcy.2013.0010.

Jensen, Helle Strandgaard. *Tv til Børn*. Master's thesis. Roskilde University, Department of History and Department of Danish, 2008.

Jensen, Helle S., and Katalin Lustyik. "Negotiating 'Non-Profit': The Survival Strategies of the Sesame Workshop." *Media International Australia Incorporating Culture & Policy* 163, no. 1 (2017): 97–106. https://doi.org/10.1177/1329878X17693930.

Jørgensen, Steen Bille, and Hans-Jürgen Lüsebrink. "Introduction: Reframing the Cultural Transfer Approach." In *Cultural Transfer Reconsidered*, edited by Steen Bille Jøregense and Hans-Jürgen Lüsebrink, 1–20. Leiden: Brill, 2021.

Kamp, David. *Sunny Days: The Children's Television Revolution That Changed America.* New York: Simon & Schuster, 2020.

"Katten Mogens." *Berlingske Tidende*, January 31, 1971.

Keslassy, Elsa. "Danish Broadcaster Defends Kids Show about Man with Superhuman Penis: 'It's as Desexualized as It Can Possibly Get.'" *Variety* (blog), January 8, 2021. https://variety.com/2021/tv/global/denmark-children-john-dillermand-dr-123 4881201/.

"Kinder sind nämlich auch mal dran." *Der Spiegel*, March 4, 1973. https://www.spiegel. de/politik/kinder-sind-naemlich-auch-mal-dran-a-066e8a92-0002-0001-0000-00004 2645672.

Kleeman, David. "Prix Jeunesse as a Force for Cultural Diversity." In *Handbook of Children and the Media*, edited by Dorothy G. Singer and Jerome L. Singer, 521–32. Thousand Oaks, CA: Sage, 2001.

Kocka, Jurgen, and Heinz-Gerhard Haupt. *Comparative Transnational History: Central European Approaches and New Perspectives.* New York: Berghahn Books, 2009.

Korsvold, Tora. *Barn og Barndom i Velferdsstatens Småbarnspolitikk: En Sammenlignende Studie Av Norge, Sverige Og Tyskland 1945–2000.* Oslo: Universitetsforlaget, 2008.

Kössler, Till, and Janosch Steuwer. "Kindheit und Soziale Ungleichheit in den langen 1970er Jahren." *Geschichte Und Gesellschaft* 46, no. 2 (September 8, 2020): 183–99. https://doi.org/10.13109/gege.2020.46.2.183.

Kuhlmann, Carola. "Antiautoritäre Pädagogik." In *Erziehung und Bildung: Einführung in die Geschichte und Aktualität pädagogischer Theorien*, edited by Carola Kuhlmann, 195–212. Wiesbaden: Springer Fachmedien, 2013. https://doi.org/10.1007/978-3-531-19387-8_11.

Lagemann, Ellen Condliffe. *An Elusive Science: The Troubling History of Education Research.* Chicago: University of Chicago Press, 2002.

Lagemann, Ellen Condliffe. *Politics of Knowledge: Carnegie Corporation, Philanthropy and Public Policy.* Chicago: University of Chicago Press, 1992.

Lasker, Harry. "Sesame Street among the Mountains of Jamaica." *Harvard Graduate School of Education Bulletin* 17 (Spring 1973): 18–22.

LastWeekTonight. "John Dillermand: Last Week Tonight with John Oliver (Web Exclusive)." YouTube, 2021. https://www.youtube.com/watch?v=A51mJjFyG_w.

Lemish, Dafna. *Children and Television: A Global Perspective.* Malden, MA: Blackwell, 2007.

Lepore, Jill. "How We Got to Sesame Street." *New Yorker*, May 11, 2020.

Levsen, Sonja. "Authority and Democracy in Postwar France and West Germany, 1945–1968." *Journal of Modern History* 89, no. 4 (December 1, 2017): 812–50. https://doi.org/10.1086/694614.

Levsen, Sonja. *Autorität und Demokratie: Eine Kulturgeschichte des Erziehungswandels in Westdeutschland und Frankreich, 1945–1975.* Göttingen: Wallstein Verlag, 2019.

Lesser, Gerald S. *Children and Television: Lessons from Sesame Street.* New York: Random House, 1974.

Lindgren, Anne Li. *Från små människor till la"rande individer. Föreställningar om barn och barndom i förskoleprogram 1970–2000.* Stockholm: Stiftenseln Etermedierna i Sverige, 2006.

Looker, Benjamin. *A Nation of Neighborhoods: Imagining Cities, Communities and Democracy in Postwar America.* Chicago: University of Chicago Press, 2015.

Maricato de Souza, Adriana. "Programas Educativos de Televisão para Crianças Brasileiras: Critérios de Planejamento Proposto a partir das Análises de Vila Sésamo e Rá Tim Bum." PhD dissertation, Universidade de São Paulo, 2000. https://www.teses. usp.br/teses/disponiveis/27/27149/tde-24062005-181909/pt-br.php.

Marjanen, Jani, Johan Strang, and Mary Hilson. *Contesting Nordicness: From Scandinavianism to the Nordic Brand.* Berlin: De Gruyter Oldenbourg, 2021. https:// doi/10.1515/9783110730104.

Mayo, John, Joao Batista Araujo e Oloveira, Everett Rogers, Sonia Dantus, Pinto Guimarães, and Gerdinando Morett. "The Transfer of Sesame Street to Latin America." *Communication Research* 11, no. 2 (1984): 259–80.

McCulloch, Gary. "Learners and Learning." In *A Cultural History of Education in the Modern Age,* edited by Judith Harford and Tom O'Donoghue, 99–118. London: Bloomsbury Academic, 2020.

Menand, Louis. *The Free World: Art and Thought in the Cold War.* New York: Farrar, Straus and Giroux, 2021.

Milland, Jeffrey. "Courting Malvolio: The Background to the Pilkington Committee on Broadcasting, 1960–62." *Contemporary British History* 18, no. 2 (June 1, 2004): 76–102. https://doi.org/10.1080/1361946042000227742.

Minow, Newton. "Television and the Public Interest" speech delivered by Newton N Minow, May 9, 1961. National Association of Broadcasters, Washington, DC. Transcript and audio recording retrieved from *American Rhetoric Online Speech Bank,* accessed January 3, 2023. https://www.americanrhetoric.com/speeches/newtonmi now.htm.

Mintz, Steven. *Huck's Raft: A History of American Childhood.* Cambridge, MA: Belknap Press of Harvard University Press, 2006.

Moland, Naomi A. *Can Big Bird Fight Terrorism?: Children's Television and Globalized Multicultural Education.* New York: Oxford University Press, 2019.

Moran, Kristin C. "The Global Expansion of Children's Television: A Case Study of the Adaptation of Sesame Street in Spain." *Learning, Media and Technology* 31, no. 3 (September 1, 2006): 287–300. https://doi.org/10.1080/17439880600893333.

Morrow, Robert. *Sesame Street and the Reform of Children's Television.* Baltimore: Johns Hopkins University Press, 2006.

Mosco, Vincent. *The Political Economy of Communication.* 2nd edition. London: Sage, 2009.

Moynihan, Daniel Patrick. *The Negro Family: The Case for National Action.* The US Department of Labor, 1965. https://www.dol.gov/general/aboutdol/history/webid-moynihan.

Mundzeck, Heike. "Abschied von Märchentante und Bastelonkel." *Die Zeit,* April 30, 1971. https://www.zeit.de/1971/18/abschied-von-maerchentante-und-bastelonkel.

Müntefeing, Gert. "Der UER-Workshop über Kleinkinderprogramme vom 5. Bis 11. März 1972 in Marseille." *Fernsehen und Bildung* 6, no. 2 (1972): 102–5.

Network Project, The. *Down Sesame Street.* New York: Columbia University, 1973.

Newell, David, Mark Collins, and Margret Kimmel, eds. *Mister Rogers' Neighborhood: Children, Television, and Fred Rogers.* 2nd edition. Pittsburgh: University of Pittsburgh Press, 2019.

Oeller, Helmut. "Die Gründe, die der Bayerische Rundfunk 1973 gegen die Sesamstraße vortrug." *Fernsehen und Bildung* 10, no. 1–2 (1976): 108–10.

O'Malley, Tom. "The BBC Adapts to Competition." In *The Television History Book,* edited by Michele Hilmes and Jason Jacobs, 86–87. London: BFI, 2003.

Osgood, Alan. *Total Cold War: Eisenhower's Secret Propaganda Battle at Home and Abroad.* Lawrence: University of Kansas, 2006.

Palmer, Edward. "Begleitunterschungen zu der Sendreihe Sesame Street." *Fernsehen und Bildung* 3, no. 3-4 (1970): 258–62.

Palmer, Edward L., Milton Chen, and Gerald S. Lesser. "Sesame Street: Patterns of International Adaptation." *Journal of Communication* 26, no. 2 (June 1, 1976): 108–23. https://doi.org/10.1111/j.1460-2466.1976.tb01389.x.

"Pappnasen aus USA." *Der Spiegel,* April 4, 1971. https://www.spiegel.de/kultur/pappna sen-aus-usa-a-5ecaeb28-0002-0001-0000-000043732485.

Paris, Leslie. "'Send It to ZOOM!': American Children's Television and Intergenerational Cultural Creation in the 1970s." In *Literary Cultures and Twentieth-Century Childhoods,* edited by Rachel Conrad and L. Brown Kennedy, 237–54. Literary Cultures and Childhoods. Cham: Springer International, 2020. https://doi.org/10.1007/978-3-030-35392-6_14.

Parmar, Inderjeet. *Foundations of the American century.* New York: Columbia University Press, 2014.

Parmar, Inderjeet. "The US-Led Liberal Order: Imperialism by Another Name?" *International Affairs* 94, no. 1 (January 1, 2018): 151–72. https://doi.org/10.1093/ia/ iix240.

"Politiske dyr i TV for børn." *Berlingske Tidende,* January 12, 1971.

Polk, Lee, and Rolf Riktor, eds. *Third EBU Workshop for Producers and Directors of Television Programmes for Children. Marseilles, 20–25 February 1972.* English ed. Geneva: European Broadcasting Union, 1973.

Polsky, Richard. *Getting to Sesame Street: Origins of the Children's Television Workshop.* New York: Praeger, 1974.

Potter, Jeremy. *Independent Television in Britain,* volume 3, *Politics and Control, 1968–80.* Basingstroke, UK: Macmillan, 1989.

Qvistgaard, Magnus. "Cultural Transfers in the Shadow of Methodological Nationalism." In *Cultural Transfer Reconsidered,* edited by Steen Bille Jørgensen and Hans-Jürgen Lüsebrink, 44–63. Leiden: Brill, 2021.

Rose, Elizabeth. *The Promise of Preschool: From Head Start to Universal Pre-Kindergarten.* Oxford: Oxford University Press, 2010.

Rose, Nikolas. *Governing the Soul: The Shaping of the Private Self.* London: Routledge, 1990.

Rotskoff, Lori, and Laura L. Lovett, eds. *When We Were Free to Be: Looking Back at a Children's Classic and the Difference It Made.* Chapel Hill: University of North Carolina Press, 2012.

Rydin, Ingegerd. *Barnens röster: program för barn i Sveriges radio och television 1925– 1999.* Stockholm: Prisma, 2000.

Sakr, Naomi. "Smarter, Stronger, Kinder." *Middle East Journal of Culture and Communication* 11, no. 1 (March 19, 2018): 9–28. https://doi.org/10.1163/18739865-01101002.

Scherell, Andrea, and Beate Jacobi. *10 Jahre Sesamstraße, was ist aus dieser Sendung geworden?* Berlin: Spiess, 1980.

Schleicher, Klaus. "The Necessity of an Anthropo-Ecological Dimension in Education: Possibilities for Its Realisation." *International Review of Education* 21, no. 2 (1975): 231–60. https://doi.org/10.1007/BF00598126.

Schleicher, Klaus. "Sesame Street als Sesamstraße." *Bildung und Erziehung* 25, no. 6 (December 1, 1972): 49–58. https://doi.org/10.7788/bue-1972-0604.

Schleicher, Klaus. *Sesame Street für Deutschland: die Notwendigkeit einer vergleichenden Mediendidaktik.* Düsseldorf: Schwann, 1972.

Schlote, Elke. "Bildungsfernsehen historisch." *Televizion* 28, no. 2 (2015): 17.

Schmidbauer, Michael. *Die Geschichte des Kinderfernsehens in der Bundesrepublik Deutschland.* München: K. G. Saur, 1987.

Selznick, Barbara. *Global Television: Co-producing Culture.* Philadelphia: Temple University Press, 2008.

"Sésame Ouvre-toi!" *Journal of Communication* 26, no. 2 (Spring 1976): 108.

Sesame Street: 50 Years and Counting. New York: Sesame Workshop, 2019. https://www.sesameworkshop.org/who-we-are/our-history/sesame-street-history-50-years-impact.

"Sesame Street Responds." *New Yorker,* May 25, 2020.

"Sesam Strasse." *Radiocorriere,* no. 34 (1972): 80.

Sims, Monica. "Letter to the Editor." *The Guardian,* December 22, 1970.

Stahr, Jimmy. "Børne-TV for reklame-skadede unger: Rædsel og inspiration." *Folkebladet for Randers,* March 23, 1972, 8.

Steemers, Jeanette. *Creating Preschool Television: A Story of Commerce, Creativity and Curriculum.* Houndmills: Palgrave Macmillan, 2010.

Sturm, Herta. "Preface." *Fernsehen und Bildung* 10, no. 1–2 (1976): 9–11.

Third EBU Workshop for Producers and Directors of Television Programmes for Children. Marseilles, 20–25 February 1972. English ed. Geneva: European Broadcasting Union, 1973.

Thomas, Gary. *Education: A Very Short Introduction.* Oxford: Oxford University Press, 2013.

Thomson, Mathew. *Lost Freedom: The Landscape of the Child and the British Post-War Settlement.* Oxford: Oxford University Press, 2013.

Tisdall, Laura. *A Progressive Education?: How Childhood Changed in Mid-Twentieth-Century English and Welsh Schools.* Manchester: Manchester University Press, 2019.

Tröhler, Daniel. "Knowledge, Media and Communication." In *À Cultural History of Education in the Modern Age,* edited by Judith Harford and Tom O'Donoghue, 35–56. London: Bloomsbury Academic, 2020.

Tröhler, Daniel. "The Technocratic Momentum after 1945, the Development of Teaching Machines, and Sobering Results." *Journal of Educational Media, Memory, and Society* 5, no. 2 (2013): 1–19.

Vemmer, Mogens. *Fjernsyn for dig: 50 år med verdens værste seere.* København: Gyldendal, 2006.

Vemmer, Mogens. "Tanker indenfor murerne—om det, vi byder børn i radio og TV." *i Radio TV årbog* 1970–71 (Danmarks Radios årbog), 99–102. Copenhagen: Danmarks Radio, 1971.

"Vergebene Chance." *Der Spiegel,* May 2, 1971. https://www.spiegel.de/kultur/vergebene-chance-a-186a8e5c-0002-0001-0000-000043257745.

"Vorm Schlafengehen kommt der Kommissar." *Der Spiegel,* January 16, 1972. https://www.spiegel.de/politik/vorm-schlafengehen-kommt-der-kommissar-a-100ebf1a-0002-0001-0000-000043018812.

Wasko, Janet, Mark Phillips, and Eileen R. Meehan. *Dazzled by Disney?: The Global Disney Audiences Project.* London: Continuum, 2005.

Werner, Michael, and Bénédicte Zimmermann. "Beyond Comparison: Historie Crosée and the Challenge of Reflexivity." *History and Theory* 45, no. 1 (2006): 30–50. https://doi.org/10.1111/j.1468-2303.2006.00347.x.

Wladkowski, Marina. *Kinderfernsehen in Deutschland Zwischen Qualitätsansprüchen Und Ökonomie Unter Berücksichtigung Der Vorschuleserie Sesamstraße.* Dissertation, Technischen Universität Carolo-Wilhelmina zu Braunschweig, 2003. https://d-nb.info/968741541/34.

Wojcik, Pamela Robertson. *Fantasies of Neglect: Imagining the Urban Child in American Film and Fiction.* New Brunswick, NJ: Rutgers University Press, 2016.

Yamamoto, Toru. "The Japanese Experience." *Journal of Communication* 26, no. 2 (June 1976): 136–37. https://doi.org/10.1111/j.1460-2466.1976.tb01392.x.

Zeus, Leonardo. *Race, Whiteness, and Education.* New York: Routledge, 2009.

Zimmer, Dieter E. "Sesame Street." *Die Zeit*, April 30, 1971. https://www.zeit.de/1971/18/sesame-street.

Index

Fernsehen und Bildung, 49, 54–55,
  62, 132, 133, 199–200,
  201–2
Finland, 170, 175, 178–79, 181
Fisch, Shalom, 207
Ford Foundation, 30, 112
foreign versions
  gaining revenue from, 73
    national versions as opposed to
      language versions, 75, 80
  streamlining the approach to, 139–41
formative research. *See* research
France, 1, 3–4, 6–7, 8–9, 12–13, 16–17,
  53, 71–77, 134. *See also* French
  version
French version, 72–73, 75–81. *See also*
  France
funding. *See also* revenue
  of broadcasting in Europe, 14–15, 43
  for the Children's Television
    Workshop in the US, 22, 40, 43–44,
    172–73
  via international sales, 52, 70–71, 72–
    73, 206–7

German version, 75–77, 206–7. *See also*
  Sesamstraße; West Germany
Germany. *See* West Germany
Gettas, Gregory, 206–7
Giroux, Claude. *See* Eric Rochat
global history, as an approach, 5–6
Grampian, 105
Great Society. 19–20. *See also* Head Start
Groombridge, Brian, 107
Grossmann, Karl-Heinz, 143–44

Halloran, James, 59–60, 61–62
Hamburg. *See* Norddeutscher
  Rundfunk
Hans-Bredow-Institut, 150–51, 153–54,
  200–1
Harlech, Lord, 114, 117, 118
Harlech Television, 102–3, 114, 117
Haug, Ada, 118; 192–93
Hausman, Louis, 40
Haynes, Patrisha, 107
Head Start, 28. *See also* Great Society
Hendershot, Heather, 207

Henson, Jim, ix, 2
Hill, Lord, 114, 117, 118
historiography, of *Sesame Street* and the
  Children's Television Workshop,
  4–5, 15–16, 17, 22, 199–207
Holt, John, 48–49, 109–10
Horne, Lutrelle, 1, 159, 194–95
Hours of broadcasting for children. *See*
  broadcasting landscape
Howdy Dowdy, 20
Husmusa og Skogsmusa, 55

Independent Television Authority, 58–59,
  91–92, 102–3, 104–6, 107–8,
  120–24
Independent Television (ITV), 89, 91–92,
  99, 102–8, 113, 120–24, 125–26
India, 51
Individualization, 26–27
International Central Institute for Youth
  and Educational Television (IZI),
  54–55, 56–57
International Market for Content
  Development and Distribution
  (MIP), 78–79, 193
Ireland, 69
Italian version, 75–77
Italy, 3–4, 84–85, 134, 139
  Open Sesame in, 1, 79–80
Izard, Christoff, 80–82, 85–86

Japan, 68
Johnson, Lyndon, 10, 19, 28
Journal of Communication, 201, 202–4

Kaj (puppet), ix, 188
Kemble, Bruce, 113
Kennedy, Thomas, 79, 84–85
Kermit the Frog (Muppet), ix, 188
Kernig, Wendla, 104–5
Klamroth, Ursula, 134, 135, 143–46
Kli-Kla-Klawitter, 183–84
Kwatschnich, 131–32

*Lach- und Sachgeschichten für
  Fernsehanfänger*, 131–32
language versions vs national
  versions, 75–76

in Europe, 59–60
funded by the Prix Jeunesse, 55, 61 (*see
also* International Central Institute
for Youth and Educational
Television; Halloran, James)
in Germany, 150–51, 153–54 (*see also*
Hans-Bredow-Institut)
historical on *Sesame Street* (*see*
historiography)
used in the promotion of *Sesame Street*,
42, 60–61, 125–26, 135
in Scandinavia, 166–67
revenue. *See also* funding; merchandise
from foreign sales, 43–44, 90
from merchandising. 43–44, 46–47 (*see
also* merchandise)
Riktor, Rolf, 191, 192–93
Rochat, Eric, 72–86. *See also* Compagnie
Française de Co-production
Romper Room, 36–37, 42, 69–70, 94–95,
175

sales agents, 16–17, 53, 65–66. *See
also* Compagnie Française de
Co-production International;
Television International
Enterprise
Samson (Muppet), 160
Scandinavia, 12–13, 17, 165–66, 180–81.
See also Nordvision
broadcasting landscape in, 170
children's media culture in, 164–67,
195–96
Schedule approach, 14–15, 94
Sesam, 190–91, 193–94
Sesame Square, 208
Sesam Stasjon, 193
Sesame Street. *See also* Children's
Television Workshop
branding of, 70
ideas behind (*see* philosophy)
difference from European preschool
productions, 56–57, 59–60, 88,
144, 149–50
learning areas and goals, 41
solution to an American problem, 49,
174–75
style and use of Muppets, 34–35

Sesame Street Revisited, 200
Sesame Workshop, x, 198–99. *See also*
Children's Television Workshop
Sesamgade, 193.
Sesamstraße. See also Norddeutscher
Rundfunk; West Germany
American perspectives on, 154–56
Children's Television Workshop's dislike
of elements in, 146–47, 149, 150,
159–60
setting up production of, 128, 142–47
social learning on, 147–51
Shara'a SimSim, 208–9
Sims, Monica, 88, 97–98, 99–102, 106–7,
108–14, 124, 176–77, 205–6. *See
also* British Broadcasting Service
skills. *See also* education
opposition to school-type skills, 20–21,
89, 169
school-type, 10, 20, 22–23, 24–25, 27–
28, 34, 41, 208, 209–10
soft-power, 44, 208. *See also* liberal
internationalism
Spanish version for Latin America. *See*
Latin America
Spain, 79–80, 95, 164
spokesperson, television as children's 3–4,
166–67, 171, 173
Springle, Herbert, 200
Stahr, Jimmy, 188, 196
summer seminars 1968, 30–33. *See also*
Lesser, Gerald
Sveriges Radio, 170–71. *See also* Sveriges
Television
Sveriges Television
Channel 1 (SVT1), 170, 190
Channel 2 (SVT2), 170–71, 177–78,
190, 191–92
Sweden, 3–4, 170
Open Sesame in, 1, 79–80

Taff, Paul, 228n.12
target audience. *See* underprivileged
children
teaching. *See* education
Televisa, 71–72
television. *See* broadcasting
Télévision Française 1(TF1), 85–86

About the Author

Photo by Wilfred Gachau.

Helle Strandgaard Jensen is an Associate Professor of contemporary cultural history at the Department of History and Classical Studies, Aarhus University, Denmark. She received her PhD from the European University Institute in Florence, Italy, in 2013 and has since been a visiting fellow at several universities in the United Kingdom, the United States, Norway, and Sweden. She is the author of *From Superman to Social Realism: Children's Media and Scandinavian Childhood* (John Benjamins Publishing Press, 2017), and her work has appeared in *Media History; Journal of Children and Media; Media, Culture & Society; Journal for the History of Childhood and Youth; The Programming Historian;* and elsewhere. She lives in Åbyhøj, Denmark, and her favorite time is spent cooking, reading, and playing video games with her family.